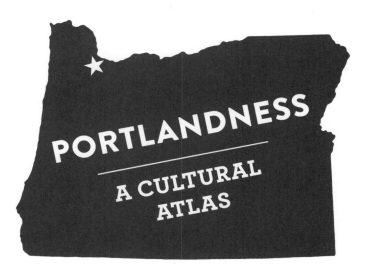

PORTLANDNESS

A CULTURAL ATLAS

PORTLANDNESS

A CULTURAL ATLAS

David Banis and Hunter Shobe

LEAD CARTOGRAPHERS
Corinna Kimball-Brown
Randy Morris
Jon Franczyk
Dan Coe
Kirk McEwen

GRAPHIC DESIGN
Joan Lundell

SASQUATCH BOOKS
SEATTLE

CONTENTS

PREFACE

Maps have a strong hold on people's imaginations. When presented with a map, most people take it as authority—this is what's in this place. But all cartographers make decisions about what to include and what not to include and how best to represent the world. Maps tell stories, and the mapmaker chooses how to tell that story. So many of the maps that people encounter are similar and use the same sets of conventions to symbolize the places that make up the world. To break free of these conventions, this book offers a large variety of map styles in an effort to provide a new look at Portland and a new look at cartography.

This atlas is an effort to use cartography to facilitate social understanding among different groups of people. A cultural atlas provides people with a new cartography, a new way of understanding places. A cultural atlas reveals previously hidden constellations of social relations. It challenges and develops people's geographic imaginations. It allows different stories about places to be told, largely by maps, at scales from the personal to the city limits to the global.

This project emerged from Portland State University's Department of Geography. In 2007, a graduate student in the department, Wayne Coffey, came up with the idea of making a cultural atlas for

Portland, although nobody in the department seemed to have any idea how to go about making such a thing. That summer, David Banis taught a seminar where students designed pages that could go into a cultural atlas. The following year, we collaborated on a teaching and research project called Portlandness, which involved mapping surrogate measures for things that students associated with Portland. That project, completed in 2009, was the earliest version of the Portlandness section of this book.

In Fall of 2011 and then again in Fall of 2012, we cotaught a class called Maps and Society, a course that largely consisted of analyzing dozens of maps each class period. As one of their projects, students created a two-page spread that might appear in a cultural atlas. Several ideas generated in those classes became part of this book. In Summer of 2012, we taught a course called Cultural Atlas Production. The students in that class conducted fieldwork for the book—these are the people who, for example, helped us count all those surveillance cameras for the Mission Invisible pages.

In 2012, an atlas working group composed of PSU alumni, students, and friends formed and met every few months at the Lucky Labrador Brew Pub on Southeast Hawthorne Boulevard to develop maps and atlas-spread ideas. We all shared a vision that became this book. Our team made the *Atlas* to provide people with a wide variety of views and perspectives of Portland to consider. In approaches both serious and humorous, the *Atlas* challenges accepted narratives of the city. It seeks to reveal the geographies of Portland that often go unnoticed. This atlas is intended to be more than an assortment of good-looking maps. We wanted a book that stood together as a collection, and we also wanted each map to stand on its own and tell a story about Portland.

This atlas is not intended to be comprehensive in any way. Rather, it is a collection of stories. Like any other place, Portland means many different things to different people. Some of those views of Portland are well known and have become stereotypes connected to the city. For example, in the 2000s Portland developed a reputation in some circles as a hipster, foodie, locavore paradise. This is the *New York Times*' Portland. This is *Portlandia*'s Portland. But for Portlanders, that's just a small part of the city. We examine some of the trendy ideas about Portland but try to show a much broader expanse of how the city is viewed and experienced.

As authors of the *Atlas*, we each have our own relationship with Portland. For David, living in Seattle while it was the "it" city in the '90s, Portland was a great weekend getaway as a tourist, a surprising change of pace. Portland still seemed to be connected to another era of the Pacific Northwest. A charming, walkable downtown with an odd collection of stump-like high-rises, nice views of Mount Hood, lots of trees, beautiful Washington Park, and just a touch of trendy. But Portland was also a working person's stronghold—worn, grungy (not necessarily the music), and edgier than Seattle. The river city in a land of coastline. The Pearl District was a wonderfully funky place with art galleries scattered amid the warehouses, the Henry Weinhard factory still existed right next to Powell's, and BridgePort Brewery was an outpost in the North Pearl. The Hawthorne neighborhood, one of the only eastside

neighborhoods to appear in tourist guides, still had a hippie vibe and felt way out of town to the east; little did David know that Hawthorne, the neighborhood where he would later live, is much closer to downtown than the eastern edge of Portland.

Flash forward to the present, and Portland has changed in many ways, becoming a full-fledged big city, something like Seattle of twenty-five years ago but without all the money. David has lived in Portland for thirteen years, first arriving to attend graduate school in geography and then getting a job in that very same geography department. In the process the city has become for him much more than that tourist destination, even if the initial impressions are never forgotten. Cartographers, by the very nature of their craft, must be interested in a wide variety of subjects. Making and analyzing maps for a living, combined with a predilection for nontraditional cartographic subject matter such as cultural values and human perceptions of places, has provided David with the opportunity to study the city from many perspectives ranging from the bird's eye to personal experiences. On top of that, factor in David's fascination with so-called dystopian landscapes, such as the industrial and polluted zones, the "bad neighborhoods," urban decay, and the many uncomfortable intersections of nature and society, and the cartographic inquiries reach into the most obscure corners of town. Working on this atlas project was a logical extension of these explorations already in progress.

For Hunter Shobe, moving to Portland followed years of graduate school in Eugene, Oregon (which to him often felt like living in the Shire), and was a welcome return to a place that felt like a city. Having lived previously in San Francisco and Washington, DC, Hunter still sees Portland as a little small sometimes, but it has one of the things he likes most about cities: living among so many people with so many connections to other places in the world. When he moved to take a job at PSU in 2006, Portland was already undergoing an urban and social transformation. Much has changed in the city since even then, giving him a small hint of what lifelong residents must often feel about change and how quickly it's occurring. Several things that helped him form a special connection to the city when he first arrived are still here—Powell's Books, the Timbers, and the Burnside Bridge—but each exists in a slightly different form (Powell's and the bridge were renovated, as in a sense were the Timbers, who began competing as a Major League Soccer team in 2011).

What allowed Hunter to develop a deeper connection to the city and gave him the confidence to teach an Urban Geography course after just two months of living here was the act of walking almost everywhere he went. Walking around different parts of the city allowed him to experience each place intimately in the way that a car, bus, or even bicycle often inhibits. By walking from neighborhood to neighborhood and exploring the places in between, he developed an appreciation for how one neighborhood transitioned into the others near it—an appreciation for how places were connected and linked and how, in many cases, they weren't. This walking-based way of initially exploring the city is now a fundamental part of his teaching approach, particularly in urban-focused courses. An interest in how different people experience, understand, and view places and how those views can be represented with a combination of maps, other graphics, and text is what motivated him to work on this atlas.

Some of our own perspectives found their way into this book, but we wanted to facilitate the creation of something that represented a broader and fuller investigation of the city with views and ideas different from our own. Therefore, the book came about as a collaborative project. Dozens of PSU students, colleagues, and alumni contributed to the *Atlas*, which also includes the work of several Portland Community College students and a faculty member there. What we tried to make was a book that would get people thinking differently about Portland. We hoped that every reader, whether a lifelong resident or someone who has only visited recently, would learn something new about it and be challenged to see the city from other perspectives. It seems to us that there is inherent value in trying to see the city from new points of view.

In making this book, we entertained ideas for hundreds of topics. We found that some topics, although typically Portland in nature, just didn't lend themselves to a good story about the city that could be told with maps. Coming up with ideas for the *Atlas* was easy; coming up with ideas that could be turned into a compelling suite of maps, graphics, and text that also told an interesting story was the hard part.

This is not meant to be the last word on Portland. Maps are representations of how people see places; they're not the places themselves. A map represents a point of view, so many people will disagree with many of the maps. We expect to hear "That map is wrong" in reference to every map in the book. That's exactly the point—to engage people in discussing Portland and what the city means to each of us as individuals. It was that discussion that drove us to collaborate with an extraordinary extended community of students, alumni, and friends.

This book represents countless hours of mapping, researching, and writing about this place. It is our tribute to Portland. We hope that in reading the *Atlas* and examining the maps and graphics, you enjoy learning about Portland as much as our team did in putting this book together.

It's widely known that Pioneer Courthouse Square is "Portland's Living Room" because the public square is often lauded as the city's center of social interaction.

This begs bigger questions: Why does Portland only have a living room? What about all the other rooms? What kind of a house only has a living room?

The obvious issue then becomes: Where's everything else? Where's Portland's kitchen? The master bedroom? The balcony? How about the in-law suite? This map presents an effort to further sketch out the vision of Portland as a house.

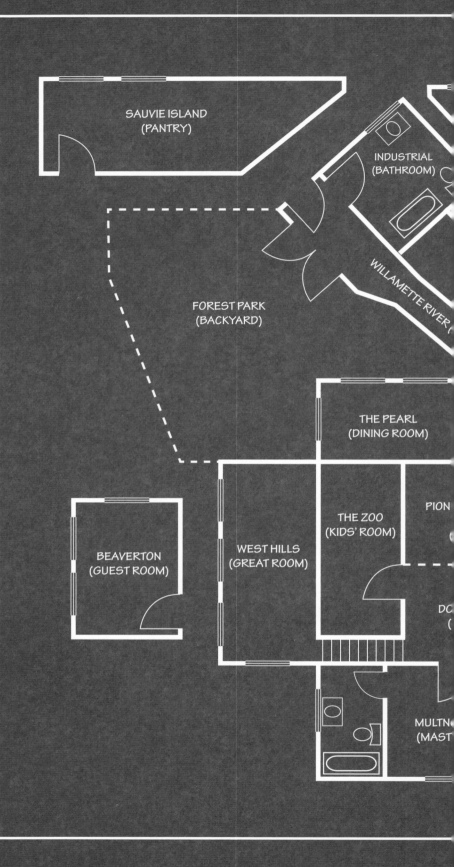

SAUVIE ISLAND
(PANTRY)

INDUSTRIAL
(BATHROOM)

WILLAMETTE RIVER (

FOREST PARK
(BACKYARD)

THE PEARL
(DINING ROOM)

THE ZOO
(KIDS' ROOM)

PION

BEAVERTON
(GUEST ROOM)

WEST HILLS
(GREAT ROOM)

DC
(

MULTN
(MAST

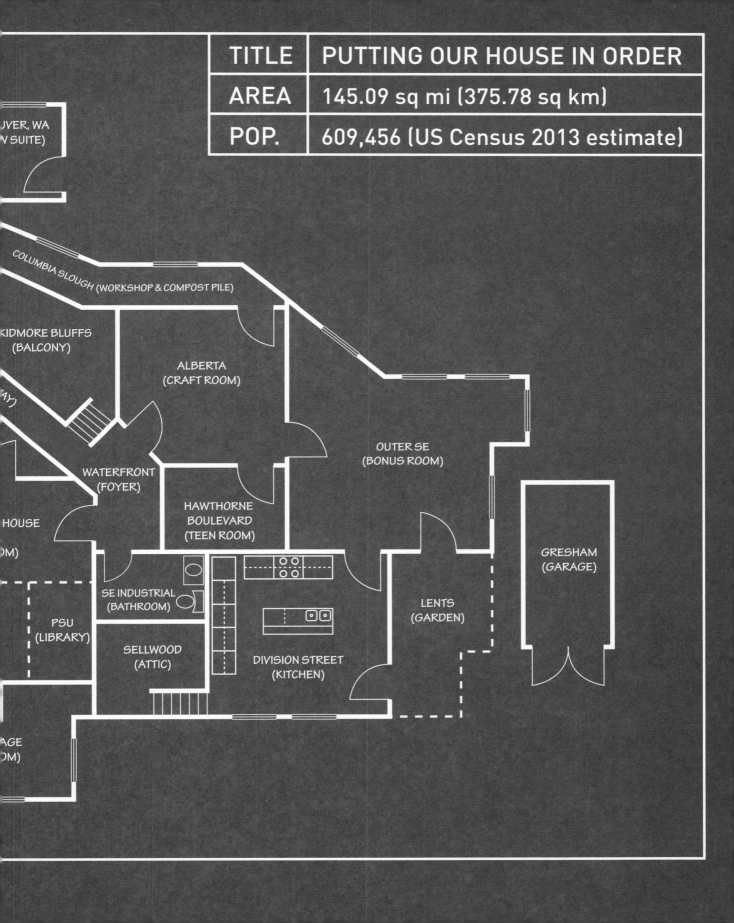

TITLE	PUTTING OUR HOUSE IN ORDER
AREA	145.09 sq mi (375.78 sq km)
POP.	609,456 (US Census 2013 estimate)

VANCOUVER, WA
(___ SUITE)

COLUMBIA SLOUGH (WORKSHOP & COMPOST PILE)

KIDMORE BLUFFS
(BALCONY)

___AY)

ALBERTA
(CRAFT ROOM)

OUTER SE
(BONUS ROOM)

WATERFRONT
(FOYER)

HAWTHORNE
BOULEVARD
(TEEN ROOM)

___ HOUSE

___M)

GRESHAM
(GARAGE)

SE INDUSTRIAL
(BATHROOM)

LENTS
(GARDEN)

PSU
(LIBRARY)

SELLWOOD
(ATTIC)

DIVISION STREET
(KITCHEN)

___AGE

___M)

NEIGHBORHOOD COLOR PALETTES

While the colors represented here might at first appear to be random, a more detailed viewing reveals patterns that speak to the varied personalities of Portland's streets and neighborhoods. Buildings in commercial districts tend to be bold, bright, and varied. Colors in residential zones are more subdued but still reflect neighborhood characteristics: the blandness of suburban-style development; the trendy colors of gentrification; or the size, style, and age of the housing stock. And even if the meaning of the colors remains a mystery, there's a story in the patterns. To make these maps, buildings' colors from selected streets in a variety of neighborhoods were sampled from Google Maps Street View.

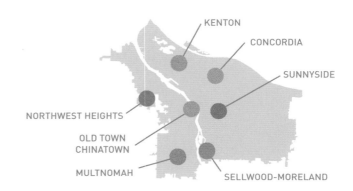

MULTNOMAH NEIGHBORHOOD • SW PORTLAND

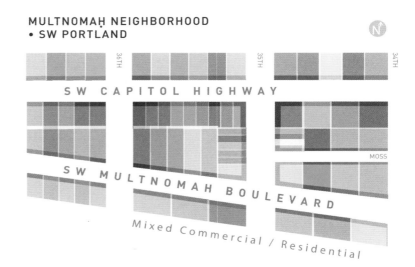

SUNNYSIDE NEIGHBORHOOD • SE PORTLAND

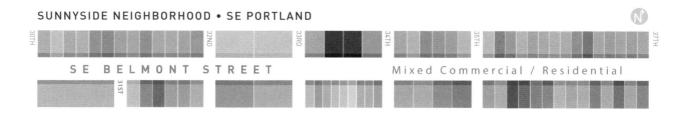

CONCORDIA NEIGHBORHOOD • NE PORTLAND

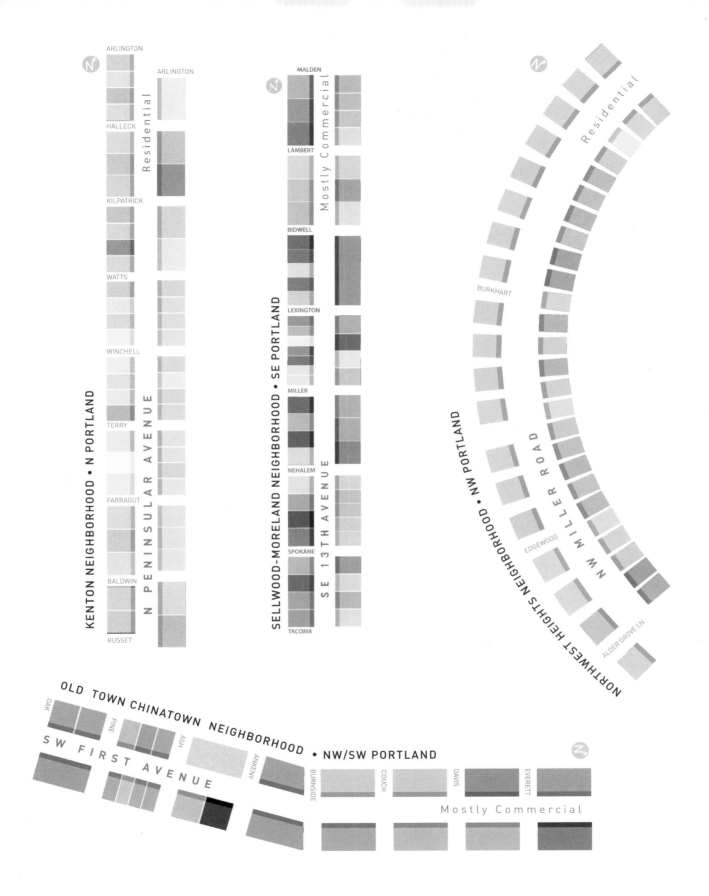

KENTON NEIGHBORHOOD • N PORTLAND

N PENINSULAR AVENUE

ARLINGTON
HALLECK
KILPATRICK
WATTS
WINCHELL
TERRY
FARRAGUT
BALDWIN
RUSSET

ARLINGTON

Residential

SELLWOOD-MORELAND NEIGHBORHOOD • SE PORTLAND

SE 13TH AVENUE

MALDEN
LAMBERT
BIDWELL
LEXINGTON
MILLER
NEHALEM
SPOKANE
TACOMA

Mostly Commercial

NORTHWEST HEIGHTS NEIGHBORHOOD • NW PORTLAND

NW MILLER ROAD

BURKHART
EDGEWOOD
ALDER GROVE LN

Residential

OLD TOWN CHINATOWN NEIGHBORHOOD • NW/SW PORTLAND

SW FIRST AVENUE

OAK
PINE
ASH
ANKENY

BURNSIDE
COUCH
DAVIS
EVERETT

Mostly Commercial

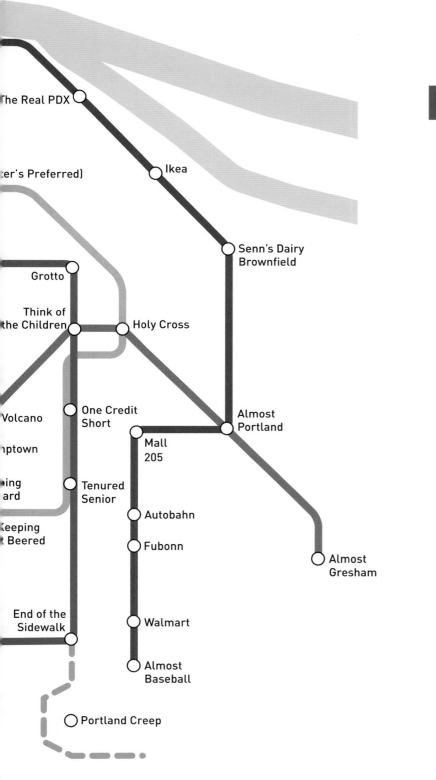

The Real PDX

er's Preferred)

Ikea

Grotto

Senn's Dairy
Brownfield

Think of
the Children

Holy Cross

Volcano

One Credit
Short

Almost
Portland

ptown

Mall
205

ing
ard

Tenured
Senior

Keeping
Beered

Autobahn

Fubonn

Almost
Gresham

End of the
Sidewalk

Walmart

Almost
Baseball

Portland Creep

PDX TUBE

- - - - - - - - -
Vancouver Line
(Est. Completion = Never)

- - - - - - - - -
Too Boring Line

- - - - - - - - -
To Jobs Line

○ Station

HIPSTER LINE

BLEEDING HEART LINE

ONE PERCENT LINE

TREE HUGGER LINE

ALMA MATER LINE

ANYTOWN LINE

INTRODUCTION
PORTLAND: A CASCADIAN CITY

Portland is a city in Oregon. Portland is a city in the Pacific Northwest. Portland is a city in the United States. Portland is a city in Cascadia. All are possible ways to begin this atlas. If we introduce Portland as part of Oregon, we reinforce a very common understanding of Portland as Oregon, and everything that people think that they know about Oregon becomes the basis of their understanding of Portland. If we introduce Portland as part of the Northwest or the West Coast, then we encourage people to think about what defines the Northwest or the West Coast and then fit Portland into that framework. Introducing Portland in a way that emphasizes Portland as a city in the United States supports the idea that Portland is best understood by drawing attention to its location within the United States.

These are all standard ways of framing Portland as a place, and there's nothing wrong with any of them. But they're also very common ways of placing Portland and, as such, tend to promote conventional and often stereotypical views about Oregon, the Northwest, the West Coast, and the United States that feed our understanding of Portland. This atlas aims to examine places (specifically Portland) from many different perspectives. In that vein, we opt to introduce Portland in a different context, as part of Cascadia. For some, Cascadia already carries great meaning, positive or negative. For many more, it's a bit of a mystery, an unknown.

There's no universally agreed upon set of borders that demarcate Cascadia, and people have many different ideas about how to draw them. Borders give cohesion to a region. The acts of choosing and drawing boundaries are so important because they help to structure how a place should be understood. A cartographer decides which characteristics should define a place and then draws boundaries accordingly.

Each map not only tells us where Cascadia is but suggests ideas about how to think about Cascadia. This is important because each view of Cascadia suggests different contexts and different starting points for understanding Portland as a place. Every map emphasizes and includes certain features at the expense of others.

The power to represent something on a map is the power to help structure how people see places, and ultimately it is through our understanding of places that we make sense of the world.

CASCADIA AS BIOREGION

This map depicts one of the most popular representations of Cascadia—David McCloskey's Cascadia. McCloskey drew these borders and coined the term Cascadia in the 1970s when he was a professor of sociology at Seattle University. McCloskey's vision of Cascadia is rooted in an ideology of bioregionalism, the notion that places should be organized in accordance with ecological realities rather than sociopolitical ones. In the case of Cascadia, McCloskey argued that the distinctive and emblematic role that water plays in the area makes it a discrete region. In that vein, these boundaries are drawn with respect to watersheds. This version of Cascadia breaks from state and provincial borders and uses the Pacific Ocean and the Cascade Range as the primary western and eastern borders of the region, which stretches from Cape Mendocino to the Alaskan Panhandle.

McCloskey's emphasis on the Cascades ties him to an important figure in the history of European settlement in the area—David Douglas. Douglas famously gave the Cascade Mountains their name because of the stunning waterfalls he saw throughout the range. Oddly, neither Lewis and Clark nor Vancouver gave the mountain range a name. McCloskey echoes Douglas's focus on water in emphasizing that the region should be understood foremost as a land of cascading waters.

The McCloskey map is used by several organizations that promote increased bioregional autonomy for Cascadia. A key precept of bioregionalism is the eschewing of global systems in favor of more regionally and locally based approaches to how we live and consume. Bioregionalism calls for an intense reengagement with and commitment to the place where we live.

One group using the McCloskey map is The Cascadian Independence Project/Cascadia Now (CIP), a "grass roots social movement dedicated to building awareness and support for local democracy, global community, and the freedom and eventual independence of Washington, Oregon and British Columbia." They champion "land rights, individual rights, environmental sustainability, social justice and freedom" throughout the region. Increased autonomy from Washington, DC, and Ottawa seems to be the initial focus. Their stated goals are to draw attention to the sociocultural characteristics of the region, increase "bioregional independence," and advance a platform of social justice.

This version of Cascadia is also used by the Sightline Institute, a Seattle-based think tank that promotes environmentalism and social justice. The organization seeks to help the region's inhabitants "succeed at reconciling themselves with the natural heritage of this place—the greenest part of history's richest civilization." Every year since 1994, the Sightline Institute releases a sustainability report card they call The Cascadia Scorecard. The annual report investigates environmental and social well-being throughout the region by researching health care, population trends, energy use and creation, urban and suburban sprawl, wildlife, and pollution.

CASCADIA AS SUBDUCTION ZONE

However, it's not from the mountain range that McCloskey coins the region's name. Geology seems to have given us the name Cascadia. McCloskey's use of the term Cascadia is drawn from Bates McKee's 1972 *Cascadia: The Geologic Evolution of the Pacific Northwest*, a detailed examination of the geology of the region. In McKee's work, the term Cascadia is used sparingly and only refers to a hypothetical "offshore landmass." McKee describes the Cascadia Basin as "located between an actively eroding continent and an oceanic mountain belt" beyond the continental shelf.

The area McKee refers to is now commonly called the Cascadian Subduction Zone. Subduction is the convergence of tectonic plates—one plate is forced into the earth's mantle as the other plate grinds over it. This phenomenon accounts for the presence of volcanoes throughout the region. With the irony that some might expect from the region, Cascadia Day is celebrated on May 18, the anniversary of Mount Saint Helens' eruption in 1980. As a geologist, McKee didn't examine the biogeography of the terrestrial region that is so often evoked in descriptions of Cascadia. This subductive view of Cascadia is not well known; however, it was this geologic place's name that McCloskey appropriated, repurposed, and popularized for the bioregion.

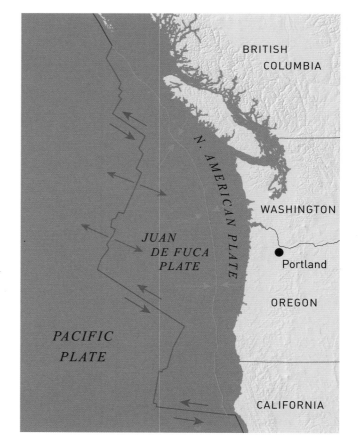

CASCADIA AS COLUMBIA RIVER BASIN

Whereas McCloskey's Cascadia is drawn to include a much larger system of watersheds, this view of Cascadia focuses exclusively on the Columbia River Basin. The Columbia River is central to the experiences of many native people in the region and also proved vital to the Europeans who largely displaced them in the region. This isn't a widely adopted version of Cascadia because this region doesn't include Seattle and Vancouver. Thus, this is the version of Cascadia in which Portland is the biggest city. There are some who consider this area to be a bioregion unto itself and have referred to it as "Columbiana."

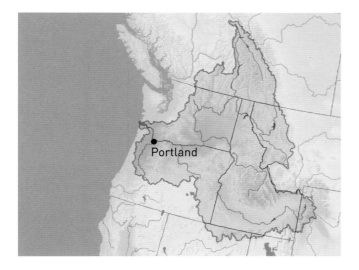

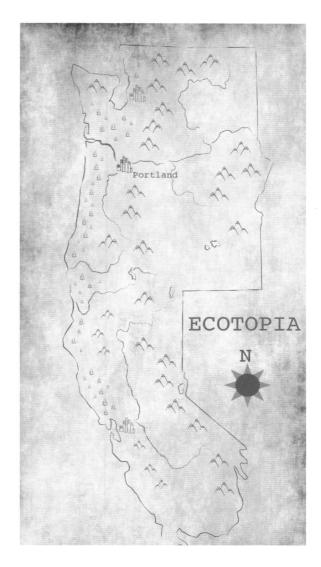

CASCADIA AS CALLENBACH'S ECOTOPIA

Ecological . . . Utopia . . . Ecotopia! Such a self-evident term, yet someone had to introduce it into the popular lexicon. Two books in particular played key roles in promoting the idea that an environmental Shangri-La is emerging along the West Coast of North America. Through these books, Ecotopia became fixed to a particular place.

Ernest Callenbach's 1975 novel *Ecotopia: The Notebooks and Reports of William Weston* emerged from the environmental movement of the 1970s. Recounted within is the narrative of the first American reporter in twenty years to visit the breakaway republic of Ecotopia. Callenbach largely follows existing political boundaries including all of Oregon, Washington, and part of Northern California on the book's original cover to designate Ecotopia. San Francisco is

the capital of Callenbach's region. In fact, his book focuses almost exclusively on Northern California, which he considers an apt representation of the entire area.

Callenbach's Ecotopia is a land of carless cities, organic fertilizers, pollution-free energy sources, high-quality picture phones, anarchically decentralized media outlets, and a twenty-hour work week. Marijuana is legal; however, microwave ovens are outlawed. Divisive team-based spectator sports have been replaced with outdoorsy participatory activities. The citizens are "unnervingly relaxed," "horribly over-emotional," and prone to taking a childish delight in windmills. So utopian is this region that citizens no longer hold petty jealousies, and laws are not so much enforced as they are universally followed by a populace who seem hardwired to simply do the right thing. And yet quite disturbingly, Callenbach's vision is one where most black residents have been relegated to city-states within the region—a redlining scheme on a massive scale.

Ecotopia received little critical acclaim, but the cult classic's importance to Cascadia lies in Callenbach's decision to place the environmental promised land in the Pacific Northwest. Although fiction, *Ecotopia* reinforces the notion that an ecological paradise is emerging in this area and promotes the idea that there is a distinct, almost national identity already in place.

CASCADIA AS GARREAU'S ECOTOPIA

The second book key to promoting Cascadia as Ecotopia is Joel Garreau's *Nine Nations of North America* (1981). Garreau challenges the conventional way of looking at North America by creating nine regions that he suggests better reflect the lived realities of the continent. Garreau cites Callenbach's work as the inspiration for his own nation of Ecotopia. Garreau's Ecotopia extends farther north than Callenbach's, but not as far east. His region stretches from the Kenai Peninsula in Alaska to Point Conception on the California Coast, between San Luis Obispo and Santa Barbara. The eastern border of the region is the Coast Range in Canada and the Cascades in the United States. The key environmental characteristic of Garreau's region is the climate. The region mimics quite closely the zone of high rainfall that's found on North American precipitation maps.

Although published in 1981, Garreau's descriptions of the region ring true for many today. Garreau describes Ecotopia as a social and environmental paradise, a place where countercultural movements and alternative lifestyles not only flourish but predominate. Garreau observes that Ecotopians place a premium on quality of life over material possessions and social status. Garreau claims that for Ecotopians, less (money, production, cars, factories) is more (better quality of life).

But it isn't easy being Utopia. For Garreau, life in the Pacific Northwest is not so far off from Callenbach's fantasy, although he does reserve some sharp criticism for the area and its inhabitants. Garreau derides Ecotopia as smug, elitist, and a bastion of white privilege. He also suggests that Ecotopians are obsessed with the "Californication" of the region's wilderness and tends to see the rest of the continent as "screwed up." Garreau's suggested motto for the region is "Leave. Me. Alone."

CASCADIA AS BRITISH COLUMBIA, OREGON, AND WASHINGTON

This map depicts Cascadia as British Columbia, Washington, and Oregon. Several other configurations of Cascadia drawn upon state and provincial boundaries do exist. Another version includes only Oregon, Washington, and Idaho—others add Montana too. These are popular ways of representing the region because the provincial/state boundaries already exist. This makes Cascadia less threatening, in a way, because of the default to some familiar demarcation of space. The British Columbia, Oregon, and Washington version of Cascadia is prominently represented on bottles of Portland-based Hopworks Urban Brewery's seasonal beer, Organic Secession Cascadian Dark Ale.

Boundaries drawn from existing political borders also make coming up with demographic and economic statistics for Cascadia pretty straightforward, as the data already exists for the province and states. This allows Cascadia supporters, particularly the pro–free trade regionalists, to boast impressive numbers about gross national product and future growth potential.

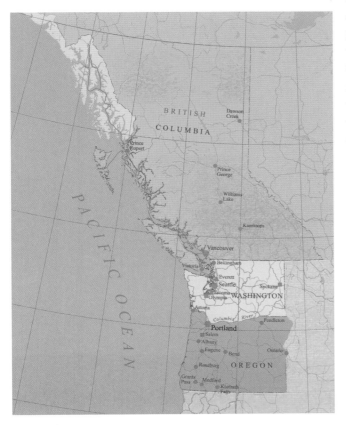

CASCADIA AS GLOBALLY COMPETITIVE FREE-TRADE REGION

"Cascadia is the ultimate in the environment experience coupled with shopping." —Paul Schell

Since the passage of the Canada–United States Free Trade Agreement (CUFTA) in 1989, a new brand of cross-border regional boosterism has emerged among free-trade advocates, business owners, and politicians. From this perspective, Cascadia is understood as an ideal vehicle for becoming a successful part of the highly competitive global economy. Paul Schell, mayor of Seattle from 1999 to 2002, advanced this idea through advocacy of the Main Street Cascadia transportation corridor. This map represents

that narrative and depicts the Cascade line, which free-trade Cascadians hope will eventually be a high-speed rail network from Vancouver to Eugene.

Free-trade advocates argue that Cascadia is ideally situated to connect Asia, North America, and Europe. In this narrative, promoting Cascadia becomes inseparable from celebrating globalization. A key organization is the Seattle-based Discovery Institute, whose projects seek "to examine a balanced, seamless and expanded transportation system between Washington, Oregon, and British Columbia with the belief the system is needed to keep the region globally competitive." Regional cooperation is said to be developing through mechanisms such as the Cascadia Corridor Commission, the Cascadia Mayors Council, and the Pacific Corridor Enterprise Council (PACE).

Curiously, Schell was mayor of Seattle during the 1999 World Trade Organization protests that descended into riots. Although generally seen in the context of contesting globalization, the "Battle of Seattle" can also be read as a clash of the two main competing visions of Cascadia—bioregional Ecotopia vs. the high-tech, global free-trade zone. Critics are concerned that free-trade boosterism is co-opting Cascadia from the Ecotopians.

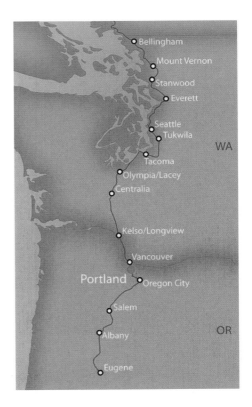

CASCADIA RISING?

It might be best to resist constructing too idyllic an image of Cascadia. Philip Resnick warns against constructing utopic views of Cascadia in pointing out that many tensions—US/Canada, coastal/high desert, liberal/conservative, organized religion/nonaffiliated—characterize the region as much as the similarities for which Cascadia is sometimes known. In many ways, Seattle, Vancouver, and Portland are in competition with one another more than they are in cooperation.

Resnick cautions that "we will need to do better than simply invoking Cascadia as a mantra for an alternative west-coast lifestyle. We may become more sensitive ecologically . . . learn to live with less . . . develop deeper cultural and spiritual formulations for the kind of existence we seek to map out for ourselves in this particular corner of the continent and of the planet. But we also need to cultivate modesty, rather than hubris, in our endeavor. . . . Let us attempt to imagine new beginnings, knowing at the same time that BC and the Pacific Northwest may not be the harbingers of . . . utopias here on earth."

In a similar spirit, we caution against relying too heavily on default interpretations about Portland—whether they be popular assessments of the city represented in media or the individual views that each local carries subconsciously every day. This atlas is a guidebook for understanding Portland from new and wide-ranging perspectives. It's a primer for encountering unexpected geographies of Portland, and it's a cartographic tribute to the city that inspires our curiosities.

THE DOUG

Although Cascadians have created several flags to represent the region, the most widely adopted is the Doug. For many, the Doug has become the most recognizable symbol of Cascadia. The Doug references the Douglas fir, named for David Douglas, who figures prominently in Cascadian lore.

The flag's designer, native Portlander Alexander Baretich, explains the symbolic significance of the flag elements: "The blue represents the moisture rich sky above, the Pacific Ocean, along with the Salish Sea, lakes, rivers, and other inland waters. . . . The white is for the snow and clouds which are the catalyst of water changing from one state of matter to another. The green is the forests and fields which also carry life giving water through our biodiverse land. The lone standing Douglas Fir symbolizes endurance, defiance."

Baretich's vision of Cascadia is rooted in a bioregionalism that emphasizes the notion that taking care of the region is taking care of oneself—and that damage inflicted on the region is damage inflicted on oneself.

Martin Patail of *Portland Monthly* magazine made an intriguing comment about Cascadian nationalism and the Doug: "Political nonexistence might be Cascadia's greatest asset. This phantom country gives Northwesterners a rare chance to belong to a 'nation' that doesn't demand taxes or wage wars, and isn't run by insufferable politicians. And, should you feel the urge to pledge allegiance, you can still salute a flag."

PORTLANDNESS

As a classroom exercise in a Sense of Place course in 2008, we asked students to list characteristics that made Portland unique—not just their personal impressions, but traits that people from outside the area might use to describe Portland. This group of forty students listed more than eighty different characteristics. However, a number were repeatedly mentioned.

The top twelve were:
1. Environmentally conscious
2. Liberal
3. Microbreweries
4. Coffee
5. Rainy/cloudy
6. Innovative
7. Art/music/culture
8. Rose City
9. Public transit
10. Cycling-friendly
11. Outdoorsy
12. Diversity/tolerance

Well, what to make of this? Do these characteristics represent Portland as a whole, or do they describe a cultural subset? Is Portland confined by its city boundaries, or does it extend into parts of suburban communities (see map below)? Those of us who live in the area can imagine places that we might describe as quintessential Portland and other places that don't fit that image. So are there different levels of Portlandness? This is where geographic information systems, or GIS, enter the picture; the maps shown here are the result of using GIS analysis to visualize some of these cultural characteristics. To create these spatial representations, we needed surrogate measures for the listed cultural traits. These would have to be attributes that could be placed on a map with sufficient spatial resolution to show variation throughout the metro area. This representation of Portlandness is not static; we've replaced one trendy cultural phenomenon from the original list (coffee) with a newer one: food carts.

FOOD CARTS

LESS ▬▬▬ MORE

Food Cart Density

Food carts were not on the original list of Portland characteristics in 2008. Since then, there's been a food cart explosion, and they've become one of the signature representations of the burgeoning Portland food scene. Unlike food carts in most cities, Portland's carts can be stationary, allowing for a unique street-food experience. Food cart locations were extracted from online listings (there are more than 600 food carts in the area) and used to calculate food cart density.

BREWERIES

LESS ▬▬▬ MORE

Brewery Density

Portland has a well-established reputation for having more breweries than any other city in the world. We geocoded brewpubs and other beer-centric establishments from business listings and calculated point density. Certainly population and employment density play a role in the number of brewpubs in a given area, so these characteristics are conflated with the beer density calculation.

LIBERAL

NO ▮▮▮▮▮▮ YES
>70 >60-70 >50-60 >50-60 >60-70 >70
Voter Percentage

Election results are often used to describe spatial distributions of liberals and conservatives, such as the ubiquitous red state/blue state maps. We took the 2012 vote for Measure 80, an attempt to legalize marijuana in Oregon, as a good representation of liberal/conservative tendencies. Many other ballot measures don't break along such clear lines. Election results are available by precinct, of which there are over 600 in the metro area. Measure 80 lost statewide by a 54 percent to 46 percent tally.

ENVIRONMENTALISTS

NO ▮▮▮▮▮▮ YES
>70 60-70 50-60 50-60 60-70 >70
Voter Percentage

Election results also seemed a good place to look for signs of environmental consciousness. We took Measure 76 from the 2010 election—an initiative to continue lottery funding for parks, beaches, wildlife habitats, and wastershed protection—as an example of whether residents prioritize environmental measures over other considerations. Measure 76 won statewide with a 69 percent to 31 percent vote.

GREEN ENERGY USE

LESS ▬▬▬▬▬ MORE

Green Living Density

Through Portland General Electric (PGE), which serves the greater metro area, residents can choose to pay a premium for green energy. One can choose to have 100 percent of one's energy offset with renewable energy (low-impact hydro, new wind, and new biomass energy), purchase units of wind energy equal to 200 kWh per unit, or support stream habitats for salmon and other fish by paying an additional $2.50 per month. The data shown is collected by zip code of either residents or businesses who purchase a green energy option.

CARLESS COMMUTING

LESS ▬▬▬▬▬ MORE

Green Communting Density

Portland is noted for its public transit system, so one would expect Portlanders to be big public transit users. Portland is also regularly voted one of the nation's most bicycle-friendly cities, so one might expect to see high bicycle use. The Census Bureau collects statistics on commuting, so we used data from the 2007–2012 American Community Survey five-year estimates. Here we combine public transit use with bicycle use.

PORTLANDNESS

LESS ▬▬▬▬▬▬▬▬ MORE

Portlandness Density

The map shown here combines the characteristics of the environmentally conscious, liberal, public transit/bicycle commuting, green-energy buying, food cart–patronizing and beer-drinking Portlander on a common scale to create a measure of Portlandness. Certain characteristics, such as brewery and food cart density, liberal voting, and green energy use, are concentrated in the central core of the city. The patterns for environmental voting and carless commuting are much more diffuse. The heart of Portlandness can be found in the Pearl and Northwest Districts downtown, and the inner eastside out to Mount Tabor. Pockets of Portlandness are found in other neighborhoods, from Sellwood in the south to Mississippi Avenue and Alberta Street in the northeast to the West Hills and Multnomah Village in the west and southwest. In irregular concentric rings, Portlandness generally decreases from the inner core. However, Portland manages to creep its way into the suburbs, including small parts of Beaverton and Hillsboro, as well as Lake Oswego. The anti-Portland is in the east and south suburbs, including many communities within the Portland city boundary east of Interstate 205—those most recently annexed by the city. The map suggests that the real city borders may be not be the official ones.

Of course, this is only one possible way to visualize some of the cultural traits of Portland, and it suggests as many questions as it answers.

- Are the high Portlandness areas truly the Portland of the popular imagination or just what the *New York Times* thinks Portland is?

- Are those outlying areas of the Portland metro area really so culturally different?

- Would Seattle or San Francisco look similar if one mapped the same kinds of measures?

- If we changed the characteristics that were included in this calculation, would the spatial distribution of Portlandness look much different?

- How does this representation of Portland match with any given individual's personal Portland? Where would you draw the boundaries?

PORTLAND VS. PORTLAND

It's a story told countless times about how Asa Lovejoy of Boston, Massachusetts, and Francis Pettygrove of Portland, Maine, flipped a coin in 1845 to see who would name this new city on the bank of the Willamette River after his hometown on the East Coast. Pettygrove won and Portland, Oregon, was born.

It seems silly to leave such a decision to a coin toss. How would Portland, Oregon, have turned out if it had been Boston, Oregon, for the last 160-odd years? Would the city be different if it was named Chinook or Multnomah after Native Americans of the area? Or what if Francis Pettygrove took a more arrogant turn and named this new town Francispolis or Pettyville? What kind of place is our namesake? And how different is Portland, Maine, from Portland, Oregon, anyways?

Portland, Maine, was named for the Isle of Portland located on the southernmost tip of Dorset County in England, which juts out into the English Channel. It is a workingman's place, mostly a large quarry of the beautiful limestone of which the Isle is made. The fruit of generations of laborers' work was used to adorn St. Paul's Cathedral and Buckingham Palace in London many miles and many more social classes away. The settlers from the Isle of Portland ended up in Portland, Maine, and may have seen similarities in their new home, where clearing lumber and fishing brought back memories of the hard-working nature of quarry labor. However, as time passes and the Isle of Portland remains a working-class area, Portland, Maine, has shifted from working class to boutique. There are very few similarities left.

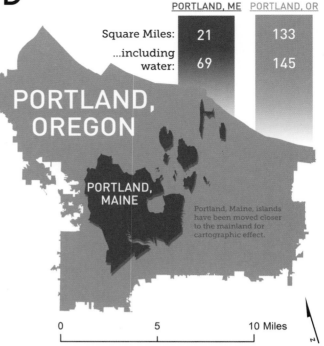

	PORTLAND, ME	PORTLAND, OR
Square Miles:	21	133
...including water:	69	145

Portland, Maine, islands have been moved closer to the mainland for cartographic effect.

0   5   10 Miles

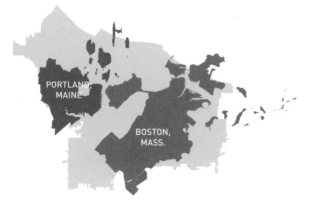

The contenders in the coin toss relative to Portland, Oregon, today

Portland, Maine, and Portland, Oregon, however, share many cultural characteristics. Both Portlands come from working-class backgrounds, where logging industries made up the bulk of the economy, but each has shifted from the plaid-shirted men of the timber industry to the plaid-shirted men and women of the hipster era.

Beer holds a central cultural role in both cities as beer snobs run rampant and unchecked. Order a Heineken in either city and witness how people start moving away from you at the bar. In either city an off-hand comment about the smooth flavor of a beer's finish evokes sincere discussions about the caramel notes and yeasty nose of that same beer. In these cities, prepare to pay five dollars for a beer that might be served in a mason jar.

Both cities contain a large contingent of all-season bicycle enthusiasts. In Maine, people ride their bikes in the heart of bitter winter snowfall; all it requires is a change in tire tread. In Portland, Oregon, where there is little snow but a lot of rain, cyclists will not only ride through the occasional heavy downpour but also endure eight months of wet streets and neoprene gear. In both places, dealing with the elements is the price one pays for the honor of being part of the bike culture.

Both cities are also acutely pro-dog. Canines are welcome at many restaurants, galleries, museums, and other events. If not, people bring them anyway. In both Portlands, this is the norm and dogs are accepted in all levels of society. People in both these cities rally around animals and being dog-friendly is a source of pride. Even banks, not known for handouts, leave bowls of water out for the pups.

Farmers' markets are everywhere in both Portlands. Monument Square hosts the largest of the farmers' markets in Portland, Maine but is still is not as large as the Saturday Farmers Market held on the South Park Blocks by Portland State University in Portland, Oregon.

Both Portlands have a vibrant LGBTQ community, and people are relatively free and safe to express their sexuality. Both are liberal cities located in somewhat conservative states, but the population disparity makes it so the city holds the most voting power. Both places laud their diversity and acceptance of others, but both are extremely white. In particular, the city center of both Portlands seem mostly comprised of young whites who possess (or are pursing) a college degree.

Hanging out in Monument Square in Portland, Maine, is a lot like hanging out in Pioneer Courthouse Square in Portland, Oregon.

The only difference is that Monument Square is in the heart of the Arts District, so the coffee is made from a locally owned shop or stand because the city council has banned all nonlocally owned businesses from the Arts and Old Port Districts. In Pioneer Courthouse Square in Oregon, there is a Starbucks in the square itself for immediate caffeine fixes.

However, there are multiple arts districts within the city limits of Portland, Oregon, where locally owned businesses and cafés are the norm. The Last Thursday festival held every month in the Arts District of Alberta in Portland, Oregon, is similar in some ways to the First Friday Art Walk every month in Portland, Maine, where galleries are open extended hours and are free to the public. There are street performers and people selling handmade artsy items at each of these events. Only in Maine, First Friday takes up the entirety of the downtown area.

Both Portlands are, as one would expect, partially surrounded by water; Portland, Maine, by Casco Bay and Portland, Oregon, by the Willamette and Columbia Rivers. However, it is the drinking water of the each city that is cause for boasting. There is an abundance of clean, fresh water in both cities and drinking bottled water is discouraged. Of course good local water is the most important ingredient for beer, which is the topic to which conversations in both cities (and essays about them) seem to invariably return.

BEAUTY VS. YOUTH?

1700 to 1850	1851 to 1913	1914 to 1945	1946 to 1980	1981 to 2015

Comparing Downtown Building Eras

I. URBAN LANDSCAPES

For many people, the word *landscape* is only associated with natural settings. This makes sense, because for thousands of years most people worldwide lived in rural places. People would read landscapes—analyzing the space before the horizon for places that might provide water, food, and shelter, as well as for places that might bring danger.

In today's world, most people live in urban settings, so increasingly, people read and navigate urban landscapes. Although seemingly different, pastoral and urban landscapes have many things in common. For those who look carefully, landscapes reveal stories that are otherwise hidden. Landscapes are quite often more complicated than they first appear, and, as with other texts, hold new meanings for those who learn to read between the lines.

Portland has a reputation for forward-thinking planning and innovative urbanism. Many elements of the urban landscape are part of that reputation. Many popular images of Portland highlight alternative forms of transportation, including bicycles, light rail, and streetcars. Other obvious representations of this include city parks, food carts, and rose gardens. Yet there is more to Portland's urban landscapes than the lifestyle magazines write about. Historically, for example, Portland's urban landscape had a strong industrial presence, particularly along the Willamette River, and there are efforts to preserve some of the industrial past in the contemporary landscape.

Portland is also a city of distinct neighborhoods with discrete characteristics. This is evident and expressed in the landscapes of each part of the city. The pages in this chapter invite us to examine the urban landscapes of Portland and its neighborhoods from many unconventional perspectives.

BRIDGETOWN

PORTLAND AND THE WILLAMETTE RIVER

Bascule, cantilever, deck truss, tied arch, suspension, vertical lift: Portland has a wide variety of both fixed and movable bridge types. Some are classic and dramatic, such as the St. Johns and Fremont Bridges. Others are downright ugly: Does anyone like the glorified freeway ramp that is the Marquam Bridge? The Burnside Bridge hides notable urban landscapes beneath it, the Saturday Market on one side and the skate park on the other. The Steel Bridge is uniquely functional, allowing for all the different transportation modes in the city, while the new Tilikum Crossing will be a car-free bridge when it opens.

But then again, most cities in the country are river settlements and logically have notable bridges. Manhattan and San Francisco have famous bridges. Pittsburgh, of Three Rivers fame, is known as the City of Bridges. So how did Portland get to be Bridgetown? This city nickname was the brainchild of Bridgetown Realty in the 1980s, and it has stuck. Portland actually has almost 500 bridges, but most of them are of unremarkable design and span concrete; we seem to count bridges only as those over bodies of water.

In most cities, rivers form a peripheral boundary, much as the Columbia River divides Portland (and Oregon) from Washington. More bridges cross the Willamette River within the Portland city limits than cross the Columbia River over its entire 300-plus miles as the Washington-Oregon border. And from the southern fringes

1

2

1. ST. JOHNS BRIDGE (1931)

7. MORRISON BRIDGE
(1887 / 1905 / 1958)

3. FREMONT BRIDGE (1913)

4. BROADWAY BRIDGE (1913)

2. BURLINGTON NORTHERN
RAILROAD BRIDGE
(1908 / 1989)

of town down the Willamette Valley to Salem, there are still only four automobile bridges across the Willamette River. However, there are two working ferries, and street names in Portland such as Taylors Ferry Road and Boones Ferry Road remind us that the time before bridges was not so long ago.

Having a river divide a city, as the Willamette River does in Portland, means the bridges over the river are connections that most residents know and use often. The city is integrated with the Willamette River in a way it never will be with the Columbia, yet the east-west divide carved by the Willamette River is still an important boundary, both physical and cultural; wealth on the west side and most of the population on the east side, but perhaps less so than in the past.

5. STEEL BRIDGE (1888 / 1914)

6. BURNSIDE BRIDGE (1894 / 1926)

11. ROSS ISLAND BRIDGE (1926)

8. HAWTHORNE BRIDGE (1891 / 1900 / 1910)

10. TILIKUM CROSSING LIGHT RAIL BRIDGE (2015)

12. SELLWOOD BRIDGE (1925 / 2015)

9. MARQUAM BRIDGE (1966)

3
4
5
6
7
8
9
10
11
12

UNDER THE BRIDGES

A look underneath Portland's iconic bridges reveals a whole different world than that on the topside. Photos on this map reveal glimpses from under each bridge in the city. Each horizontal strip of photos corresponds with a bridge beginning at the top of the page with the St. Johns Bridge.

Many of the bridges span as much land as water. A wide variety of urban life exists under the bridges of the city—homeless encampments, businesses, passing trains, urban trails such as the Springwater Corridor, and various activities that occur at the water's edge. The phrase "under the bridge" connotes different things—a place of danger, a place of misfortune, a place of refuge. In Portland, spaces under bridges are quite varied but collectively they are surprisingly active places.

The Burnside Bridge, for example, has a skate park under its east side and the Saturday Market under its west side. The gothic-style buttresses of the St. Johns Bridge frame the aptly named Cathedral Park below. The bottom level of the Steel Bridge supports pedestrian, bike, and freight train traffic. Longtime late night comfort food establishment Le Bistro Montage is nestled under the Morrison Bridge. Somewhere under the Marquam Bridge sits the Oregon Museum of Science and Industry. Different from the rest is the soaring Fremont Bridge, whose elevation creates an underbelly of large and open amorphous spaces.

ST. JOHNS **1**

BURLINGTON NORTHERN **2**

FREMONT **3**

BROADWAY **4**

STEEL BRIDGE **5**

BURNSIDE **6**

MORRISON **7**

HAWTHORNE **8**

MARQUAM **9**

TILIKUM **10**

ROSS ISLAND **11**

SELLWOOD **12**

WHERE THE SIDEWALK ENDS

REVITALIZED WALK SCORE FOR THE PEARL

The Pearl District is the apple of every progressive city's eye. It's an urban-renewal gem replete with converted warehouse-to-loft residences interspersed with green, mixed-use, high-rise condos and the high-end retail shops and restaurants that accompany them. Artfully designed public spaces such as Jamison Square Park, Tanner Springs, and The Fields offer places to linger. Rounding out the picture of an idyllic neighborhood is the Portland Streetcar, part of the vanity transit that brands this neighborhood as accessible. Added to all of these livability indicators is a high walk score from the popular web tool walkscore.com, which is often referred to in real estate advertisements.

Walkscore.com features a well-known internet measure of walkability based on the distance a location is from amenities such as grocery store, nightlife, parks, shopping, and restaurants. An algorithm that includes intersection density per square mile, block length, and distances to the above-mentioned amenities generates a walkability score. In other words, the walk score is largely based on how easy it is to walk someplace where you can buy something. Although a convenient way of computing walkability on paper, this approach is often unhelpful to on-the-ground pedestrians. In fact, the Pearl is full of dead-end walking paths, sidewalks reclaimed by vegetative growth, and entire blocks with no sidewalks at all. It turns out that it matters how a walkability score is computed.

The accompanying map offers a more personal snapshot of a neighborhood. Instead of basing the indices on consumptive destinations, this rating system seeks to provide a functional walking map. Equity, presence of trees, condition of sidewalks, presence of barriers, and general traffic conditions were factors used in this coding scheme. PSU students collected the data by walking each street of the Pearl for a firsthand, on-the-ground look at walkability.

The core area of renewal at the south end of the neighborhood is the most consistently connected. Areas developed around the neighborhood's main parks, Jamison Square and Tanner Springs, are also well paved. Between the amenities of shopping and repose are the mediocre paths that create difficult connections to the more walkable areas. Much of Thirteenth Street is, in fact, devoid of sidewalks altogether.

Best

Good

Okay

Bad

Worst

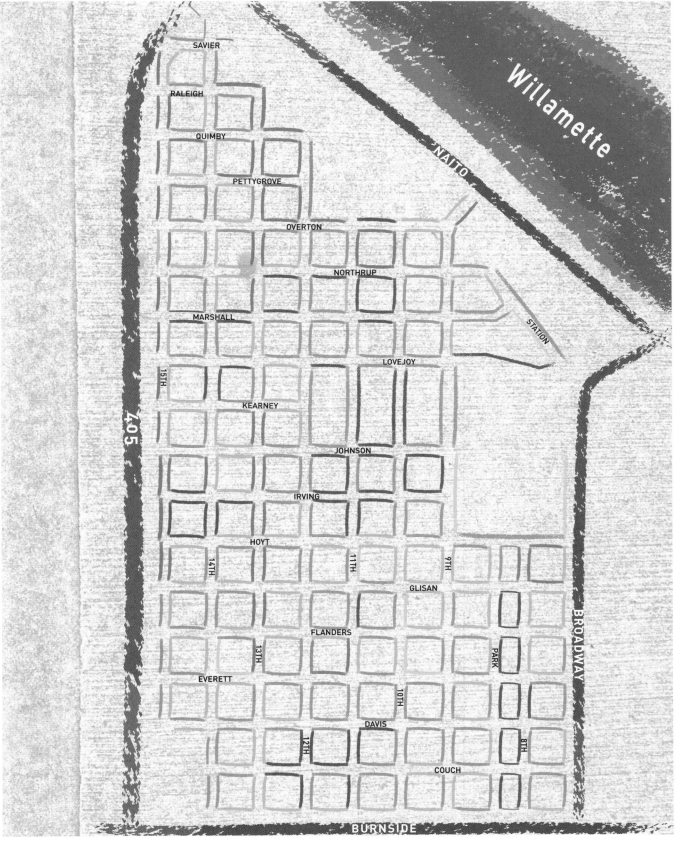

PORTLAND CEMENT

Portland lauds its walkability. However, many parts of the city lack sidewalks altogether. There's a striking difference between inner Portland and the periphery when it comes to presence of sidewalks. While historic inner eastside neighborhoods like Alameda, Irvington, Sunnyside, and Richmond have sidewalks on nearly all of their streets, some parts of outer Portland lack them almost entirely. The neighborhoods with few sidewalks fall on both ends of the socioeconomic spectrum. The affluent West Hills leads the city in sidewalklessness. Several outer Southwest neighborhoods and Brentwood-Darlington in Southeast have some of the lowest

poverty rates in the city and some of the lowest rates of streets with sidewalks. At the same time, several of the eastside neighborhoods with the highest rates of poverty also tend to lack sidewalks.

Our city shares the name of the most commonly used cement in the world, yet we have a stunningly large percentage of unpaved streets. According to our bureau of transportation, fifty-nine miles of street remain unpaved—nearly 3 percent of the total. Cascadian neighbors such as San Francisco and Sacramento have none, and even the frontier outpost of Seattle has just four miles of unpaved

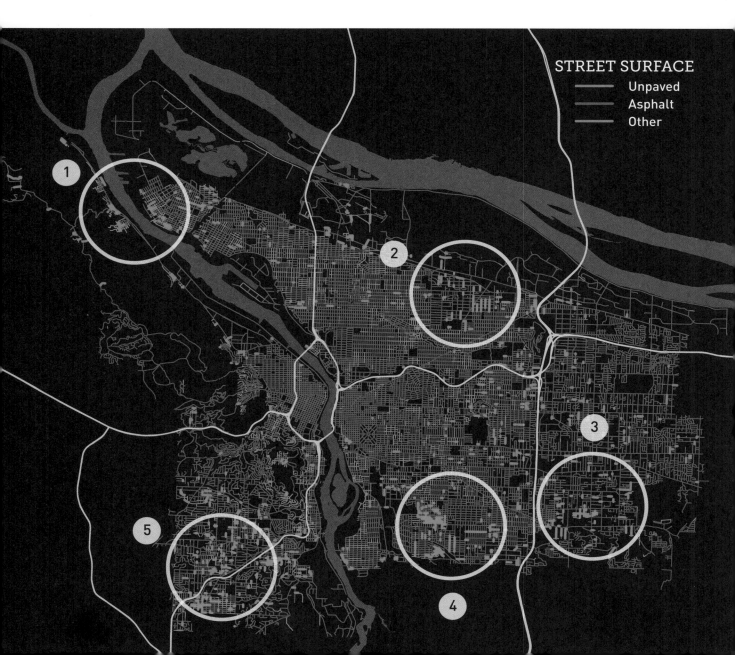

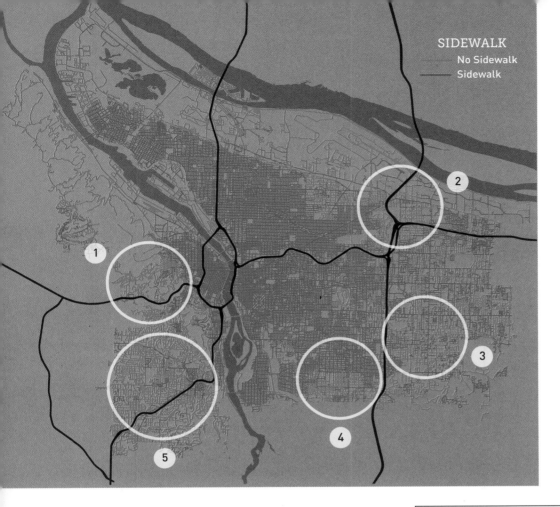

SIDEWALK
— No Sidewalk
— Sidewalk

streets remaining. Many of these dirt and gravel roads are in more recently annexed parts of the city, such as the outer Southeast, but other areas, such as the St. Johns neighborhood, have been part of the city for more than one hundred years. The Southwest Hills may have topography and drainage issues that affect street paving, but a number of residents also seem to enjoy the "charming" nature of these residential country lanes. Even the heavily unpaved Woodstock neighborhood in the Southeast Portland grid seems to be evenly split on the evils and benefits of those modern paved streets. Of course, when 44 percent of Portland's maintained streets are rated in poor or very poor condition (no, unpaved streets are not maintained since they are not up to city standards), maybe paving is overrated. So go for a ride: kick up some dust, rattle your bones, knock your teeth, and hope that muddy puddle is not too deep. No wonder so many locals own an all-wheel-drive vehicle . . . or a bike.

TOP UNPAVED NEIGHBORHOODS

1. Linnton & Cathedral Park: 10% unpaved

2. Cully & Sumner: 8% unpaved

3. Lents & Powellhurst-Gilbert: 8% unpaved

4. Woodstock, Brentwood-Darlington & Ardenwald-Johnson Creek: 7 to 14% unpaved

5. Outer Southwest: 7 to 26% unpaved

NEIGHBORHOODS WITHOUT SIDEWALKS

1. The West Hills: 89% without sidewalks

2. Parkrose-Sumner: 78% without sidewalks

3. Lents & Powellhurst-Gilbert: 70% without sidewalks

4. Brentwood-Darlington: 75% without sidewalks

5. Outer Southwest: 85 to 99% without sidewalks

YOUR ATTENTION PLEASE

BILLBOARDS AND OTHER VISUAL NOISE

As a rule, Portland is fixated on the appearance of its urban land-scape. Known for planning and design, green spaces, and an urban growth boundary, the city prides itself on the attractive aesthetics of the urban landscape. Portland even tries to limit the size of business signs. However, a tour through the city reveals that the urban landscape, at times, isn't the gentle retreat of planner design charrettes, but rather a cacophony of visual distraction. This is most common, but not entirely limited, to major arterials.

Here we examine the flow of visual noise recorded on four arterial streets: North Interstate Avenue, Southeast Powell Boulevard, East Eighty-Second Avenue, and Woodstock Boulevard.

Not all visual noise is the same. On some streets, such as Eighty-Second, billboards make up a great deal of the visual onslaught—but so do the endless brightly colored flags and red, white, and blue streamers of used car lots, the tangled webs of

BILLBOARD DENSITY

High

Low

BILLBOARD SUBJECTS
Sized by number of occurrences

NONPROFIT
FOOD
TRAVEL
AUTO
ALCOHOL
GOODS
HEALTH CARE
OTHER SERVICES
CASINO
FINANCIAL
ENTERTAINMENT
TELECOMMUNICATIONS

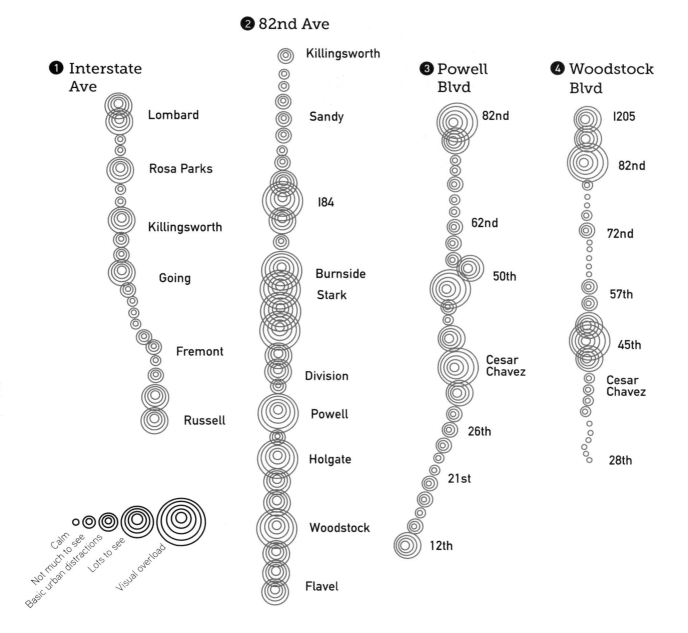

❶ Interstate Ave

Lombard

Rosa Parks

Killingsworth

Going

Fremont

Russell

❷ 82nd Ave

Killingsworth

Sandy

I84

Burnside

Stark

Division

Powell

Holgate

Woodstock

Flavel

❸ Powell Blvd

82nd

62nd

50th

Cesar Chavez

26th

21st

12th

❹ Woodstock Blvd

I205

82nd

72nd

57th

45th

Cesar Chavez

28th

Calm

Not much to see

Basic urban distractions

Lots to see

Visual overload

telephone and cable wires, and the barbed and razor wire fencing that secures so many businesses and parking lots. Then there are the twenty-foot undulating inflatable air-blown stick figures, officially called air dancers or air puppets, that wobble, buckle, and surge beside car washes and RV lots. Giant signs meant to be read by people driving forty miles per hour are a major reason optical noise can be so jarring on parts of Powell and Eighty-Second.

And yet there are contours, texture, and a rhythm to visual noise. A street like Woodstock has a great deal to look at, but the experience is softened by tree-lined streets, slower traffic, and signage intended to be read by pedestrians on the sidewalk. Compared to the general chaos of Eighty-Second, the scene on Woodstock seems managed and placid by comparison. Interstate and Powell vary more widely because of the residential stretches they contain, which tend to mitigate the impact of commercial strips. Interstate has a web of light-rail tracks, overhead power cables, and large street lights running down the middle of it—visually noisy, perhaps, but more quaint than grating. Even a street like Eighty-Second, which many people only think of as a complete eyesore, has areas with parks and trees that relay a calmer and more soothing visual signal.

STOP! WRITING ON STOP SIGNS

Stop signs can be easily commandeered to advance quick and pointed statements. By simply writing or placing a sticker below the word "STOP," the traffic sign becomes a message board. The stop signs in inner Southeast and Northeast Portland sometimes reflect the liberal political views often associated with the city.

During the time this data was collected, signs such as "STOP using your bank," "STOP beating protesters," and "STOP the 1%" alluded to the Occupy Wall Street protests. "STOP the drug war," "STOP homophobia," and "STOP Eating Animals" also reflect left-of-center political opinions.

Cities sometimes encourage citizens to clean up graffiti in their neighborhoods but forbid residents from touching graffiti on stop signs. Most paint or paint removers applied to a stop sign would compromise the sign's reflective attributes. Thus, a buffed stop sign could be difficult to see and lead to an accident for which the city could be held liable. This is why graffiti on stop signs sometimes lasts a long time. The city of Portland is looking into a substance that, once applied to a sign, would allow paint to be wiped off rather easily with no damage to the reflectivity of the sign. If that happens, then perhaps this very common form of graffiti will become very uncommon.

STOP Exorcism	1
STOP Wanting	2
STOP The Drug War	3
STOP You Are Under Surveillance	4
STOP Driving	5
STOP Shaving	6
STOP Glamour	7
STOP Rewarding Failure	8
STOP Giving In	9
STOP KFC Cruelty	10
STOP Oppose Chris Dudley	11
STOP The Electoral College	12
STOP The 1%	13
STOP NAFTA	14
STOP Peddling	15
STOP Weird	16
STOP Entropy	17
STOP Using Your Bank	18
STOP Believing Your Vote Counts	19
STOP You Are Alone In This	20
STOP War	21
Peace STOPs War	22
Don't STOP Beating Protesters	23
STOP Homophobia	24
STOP Or My Mom Will Shoot	25
STOP Hammertime	26
STOP Collaborate & Listen	27
STOP Religion	28
STOP HMOs	29
STOP People	30
STOP Animals	31
STOP Now Is All You Have	32
STOP Eating Animals	33
STOP Profit	34
STOP Obey	35
STOP Voldemort	36
STOP Make Portland Normal	37
STOP Global Warming	38
STOP Hipsters	39
STOP Kanye	40
STOP Wearing Fur	41

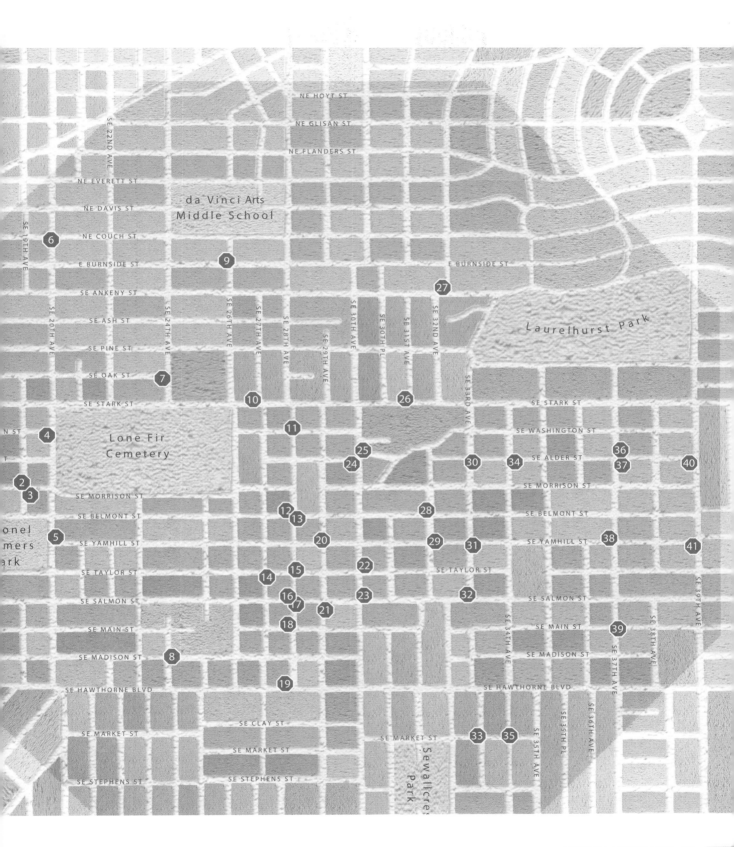

MANUFACTURED SPACES

Everyone knows that as service industry jobs have increased, manufacturing jobs have been declining for decades. In Portland, the manufacturing footprints are small and tend to focus on transportation and distribution. For these reasons, industrial sections of the city are outside the consciousness of most Portland residents. Yet Portland's industrial areas still supply 30 percent of jobs citywide, and 30 percent of those jobs are in manufacturing. More than half of all industrial jobs are associated with the Columbia Harbor.

It's unlikely that most people could name many companies that have manufacturing facilities in Portland, especially when the region's largest employer and manufacturer, Intel, is located in the suburbs, along with another even more well-known fellow Fortune 500 company, Nike. Flying under the radar is the metro area's other Fortune 500 company, Precision Castparts, with a manufacturing facility located in a dispersed industrial area in outer Southeast, one of its many worldwide locations.

Manufacturing and industrial work does not fit the new urbanism dream of Portland. In this city, land use categories formerly called industrial are ironically reclassified as employment zones, a zoning arrangement that allows a mix of commercial uses. Former industrial areas have become incubator districts, including the Central Eastside and Lower Albina. Curiously named industrial sanctuaries are created to protect these endangered spaces.

Perhaps another reason for turning a blind eye to the industrial areas of Portland is the havoc that's been wreaked upon the Willamette River, Columbia Slough, and surrounding lands by over a century of industrial production. In the Portland Harbor Superfund Site many hazardous substances are present, including heavy metals, polychlorinated biphenyls (PCBs), polynuclear aromatic hydrocarbons (PAH), dioxins, and pesticides. While this six-mile stretch of the Willamette River is in the long-term process of cleanup, other superfund sites are also in various stages of repair, and still others have now been mitigated. We can rightfully blame our collective past ignorance of the deleterious long-term effects of these chemicals for this mess, a problem that exists elsewhere too and seems to be part of the price we pay for building our society.

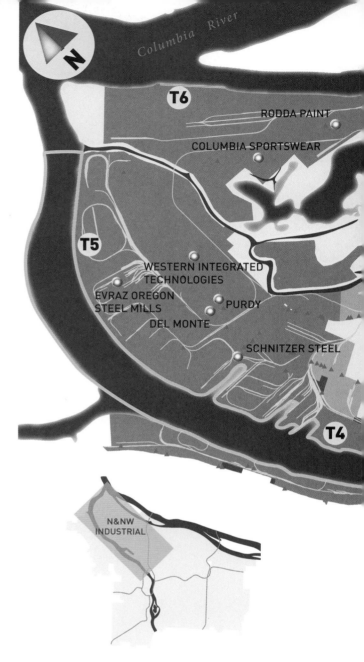

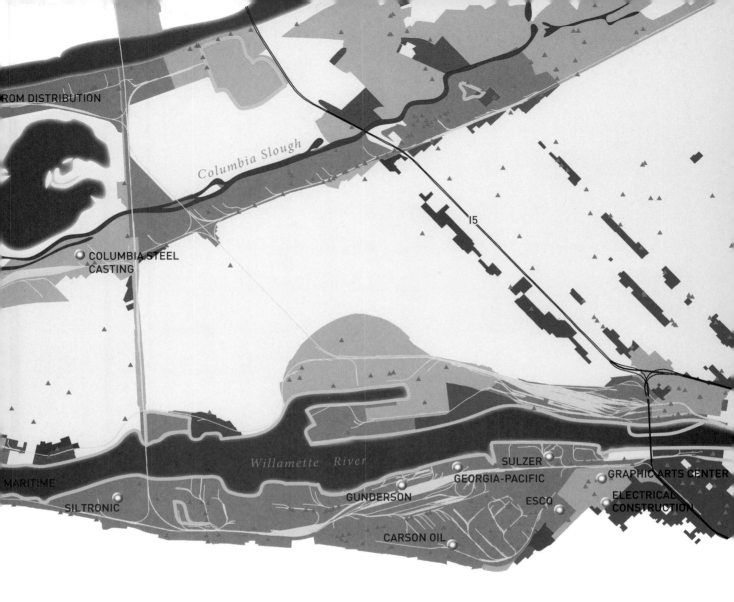

ROM DISTRIBUTION

Columbia Slough

COLUMBIA STEEL
CASTING

I5

Willamette River

SULZER

GEORGIA-PACIFIC

MARITIME

SILTRONIC

GUNDERSON

ESCO

GRAPHIC ARTS CENTER

ELECTRICAL
CONSTRUCTION

CARSON OIL

ZONING

GENERAL EMPLOYMENT

CENTRAL EMPLOYMENT

GENERAL INDUSTRIAL

HEAVY INDUSTRIAL

▲ Spill Site

◉ Major Employers

Rail Lines

T Port Terminal

Past Or Current
Superfund Site

COLUMBIA HARBOR INDUSTRIAL ZONE

JOBS BY SECTOR

Transportation and Warehousing
Manufacturing
Services
Retail
Construction
Information and Design
Public
Education and Health

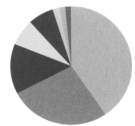

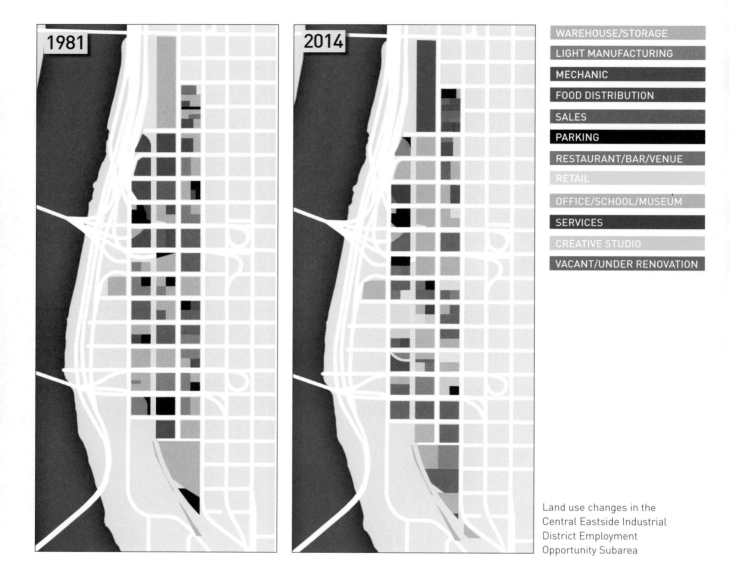

1981

2014

Land use changes in the
Central Eastside Industrial
District Employment
Opportunity Subarea

The Central Eastside Industrial District is one of Portland's oldest industrial areas, although it's not clear there will be industry there much longer. Back in 1869, the first railroad linking Portland and California was built there. By the late 1890s the area contained diverse businesses, including brickmaking plants, hardware stores, and farm stands. After World War II, the district expanded as industrial warehouses replaced some of the Victorian lined blocks. Light industry, distribution and warehousing, and transportation were identified as key components of the district, and it became an industrial reserve in 1981. But much like we create reserves to protect endangered wildlife, this designation was the first indication that someone else had designs on this area of "blight and disinvestment," in the words of the Portland Development Commission (PDC). The PDC declared the area an urban renewal district in

1986, which further accelerated the decline of industrial work performed there.

The area has been further rezoned, now as an "Innovation District" with former warehouses now filled with creative spaces, personal services, and expensive food. The Streetcar arrived a few years ago, and as those who planned it admit, it serves more as an urban development tool than it does as an effective means of getting around. The MAX Orange Line, having already displaced many a business, will skirt the southern part of the district. The "new urban economy" seems to be taking hold, as the maps of the Employment Opportunity Subarea on this page illustrate. Back in 1981, 63 percent of the core of the Central Eastside Industrial District had industrial uses, with parking, vacant land, and

Graffiti covers the burned-out shell of the Taylor Electric Supply warehouse

a small amount of retail making up the balance. Now industrial uses comprise only 35 percent of the area. The old employment types are being replaced with service sector jobs. It has become apparent that the self-aggrandizing creators of the hip, creative Portland prefer an industrial area without much industry. Better to hide those eyesores up north. But the shells of old warehouses are cool as long as what is actually in them changes. At the east end of both the Burnside and Morrison Bridges, art installations of weathered steel and iron were erected in 2012 in order "to evoke the neighborhood's industrial past." Strangely, celebrating the industrial past of neighborhood necessitates driving the remaining industry away.

THE RUINS OF TAYLOR ELECTRIC

The abandoned ruins of the Taylor Electric Supply warehouse are a unique Portland landmark and a sanctuary for artists, rebels, and outcasts. Over the years, this burned-out factory has been reinvented by the people of the city. Unbeknownst to many, it has functioned as a richly occupied public space. Left to stand outside the political economy of development and not subjected to the exclusionary controls of commercialization, Taylor Electric is a

crack in the urban environment that offers free space and refuge to diverse communities who would otherwise not have space in the city. Because of this state of uncertainty, Taylor Electric has become a vibrant cultural space bursting with possibilities.

In 2006, a massive fire engulfed the wooden frame of Taylor Electric in inner Southeast Portland. This was one of Portland's largest fires, burning into the night and causing power outages and an oil spill into the Willamette River. The following day, the smoldering building collapsed, leaving a hollow, charred skeleton.

This decaying shell now serves as a refuge for marginal urban communities and a temporary home for freight hobos, houseless populations, and graffiti artists. It's in the heart of the city, near mass transit and railroad tracks. At night, the space is dark and difficult to see from the road. These characteristics make it a relatively easy, safe, and private space. During the day the building comes alive with photographers, film crews, performance artists, and urban *flâneurs* who explore and use its aesthetics as a gritty backdrop for projects and antics.

Future plans for the Taylor Electric site

This space is unique because it might be Portland's only "unofficial free wall." The city of Portland doesn't provide any sanctioned free walls as other Cascadian cities do, like Eugene, Tacoma, Olympia, and Seattle. What often results in Portland is an abundance of quick tags all over the city, which most people dislike, instead of more elaborate pieces painted on designated walls or districts. Portland's strict zero-tolerance graffiti policy has been playing out on the walls of Taylor Electric for years. The entire building has been buffed (painted out) every few months to remove the graffiti even though it's an unsalvageable building with no residential neighbors.

In Portland it's illegal to paint imagery on an outdoor wall even if you have permission from a property owner. You must have a mural or advertisement permit from the city. If unpermitted "art" is not removed within ten days of being reported, property owners run the risk of being issued substantial fines from the city. The premise behind this continued abatement effort is that it "reduces social deterioration within the city and promotes public safety and health." The assumption is that consistently covered-up graffiti will deter more from occurring. However, some research suggests

that buffing doesn't make any difference. If anything, the solid paint provides a fresh canvas to work on and motivation to fight back in an endless cycle of creation and destruction.

Urban governments and property developers envision streets purged clean of marginalized populations, unsolicited interventions, and trash. These uncomfortable reminders of neglect counter a narrative of a city made safe for endless, effortless consumption and full of programmed activities. Officials often present redevelopment as economic salvation or as social and cultural stimulation—restoring *their* version of a quality of life. Compared to fixing other urban "problems," graffiti is an easy scapegoat. Graffiti is often negatively stereotyped as promoting blight, urban decay, and a deteriorating quality of life. But a thriving street and graffiti art scene can also be a sign of a vibrant, innovative, and creative city with democratic public spaces.

Under use and decay of built environments is not caused by the presence of graffiti; it can be a byproduct of an area that's already in disrepair. Artists are drawn to these spaces because of their accessibility, gritty aesthetics, and anonymity. Cities such as Berlin,

London, Melbourne, and Miami have realized that fostering creative activities in public (both planned and unplanned) can be beneficial to the city, financially and culturally. In many cities like these, graffiti removal is mostly targeted to the central downtown core. The extent of graffiti abatement outside the city is left to individual neighborhoods to decide and manage. Some neighborhoods are mostly free of graffiti and other areas burst with color. For many urban residents, colorful and accessible public spaces are essential for their quality of life. They choose to live in the city for its energy, unexpectedness, and grit.

From an economic development perspective, there's potential in the Taylor Electric site. With panoramic views of the city, Taylor Electric sits on the east bank of the Willamette River, just minutes away from the Oregon Museum of Science and Industry, the new Tilikum Crossing only for public transit and pedestrians, the new streetcar line, and the Eastbank Esplanade. Distillery Row, the heart of Portland's craft distilling movement, is just down the road, along with several of Portland's famous food cart pods and a hub of trendy bars and restaurants.

Unsurprisingly, in 2013 it was announced that the Taylor Electric property had been sold to developers who plan to transform it into a 60,000-square-foot industrial-chic office space called 240 Clay, complete with green roofs, bioswales, and electric-car charging spaces. This development will surely change the urban landscape, its uses, and its demographics significantly. According to the development schematics, at least some of the existing building remnants will be repurposed and used to frame the outside of

the parking lot. This redevelopment was inevitable, as Portland's urban growth boundary ensures that most urban space is put to use. Portland is also one of the fastest-growing metro regions in the United States. This influx of population and density makes finding hidden, underused spaces that allow for alternative uses increasingly difficult.

Places like Taylor Electric serve as a reminder that there *is* value in not having *all* urban space in continuous official use. These spaces in between are useful voids that allow for unscripted and emergent activities. Although many people might see these spaces as uninviting, boring, and even dangerous, other people see great potential in these derelict wastelands. These spaces offer respite from the city's watchful eyes. These are zones of uncertainty, in limbo between uses, and therefore open to endless possibilities.

Graffiti in the remains of the
Taylor Electric Supply warehouse

NAKED CITY

STRIP CLUB CAPITAL OF THE COUNTRY?

A 1993 *Willamette Week* article based on an anecdotal police report first identified Portland's status as the city with the most strip clubs per capita, a factoid cited repeatedly in weekly alternative tabloids nationwide and the *Oregonian*, and by any savvy strip club bouncer. It turns out the claim is largely meaningless—what Portland has is a preponderance of small venues. Nevertheless, it has engaged in a self-fulfilling prophecy where the region's quirky identity is in some small measure connected to this status.

The story of Portland's strip club phenomenon speaks to geography, history, and especially to identity. Historic court cases that reinterpret the Oregon Constitution's definition of free expression are often cited as catalysts for the rapid growth of all adult entertainment; the continued growth of strip clubs in the Portland region appears to be more like a cottage industry. The war over public decency breaks down into battles over what's "obscene," where obscenity is acceptable, and whether soy burgers make explicit nudity more politically correct.

Portland certainly ranks high, but city standing depends on how one slices up the numbers and sets the geographical scale. It's not a mystery why it *should* rank so high: most other cities and metropolitan regions simply cannot compete because they lack Portland's—and Oregon's—combination of free expression protections and the right to serve alcohol (or not) with nudity. Also, many residents have taken pride in this reputation (whether accurate or not) as part of the "keep Portland weird" identity. Perhaps this has bred some tolerance absent in other places. At the same time, something often overlooked in the popular imagination of the region is the presence of strip clubs with male performers, including at least one that's primarily geared toward gay patrons. Most national and local strip club databases don't even bother to list these types of strip clubs.

Portland alone, with a population around 600,000 circa 2014, has about forty-eight full-nudity strip clubs inside the city, or around

Carnaval
Kit Kat Club
Golden Dragon
Acropolis
Ark Angels Gentlemen's Club   **The Pallas**
Hawthorne   **Riverside Corral**   Front Avenue Strip Club
Strip
Peek a Boo   **PlayPen**   Diamonds/Mynt Gentlemen's Club
Black
Cauldron   **Silverado**   JAG's Clubhouse   **Devils Point**
Magic   **Shimmers Gentlemen's Club**
Garden   Spearmint Rhino   Seductions   **Glimmers**
Spyce Gentlemen's Club   **Exotica International**   Pitiful Princess
Pirate's Cove   **Blush** **Lucky Devil Lounge**
PORTLAND   **Mary's Club**   **Sassy's Bar & Grill**   Club Rouge
STRIP CLUBS   **Nicolai Street**   Safari Showclub   **DV8**
Clubhouse   **King's Wild**   **Dream On Saloon**
Mystic Gentlemen's Club   Foxy Girls   **Union Jacks**
Dancin' Bare   Casa Diablo   **Tommy's Too**   Heat
Jody's Bar & Grill
Boom Boom Room   **Rose City Strip**   Club Fantasy
Club 205   Soobie's   **Club Skinn**

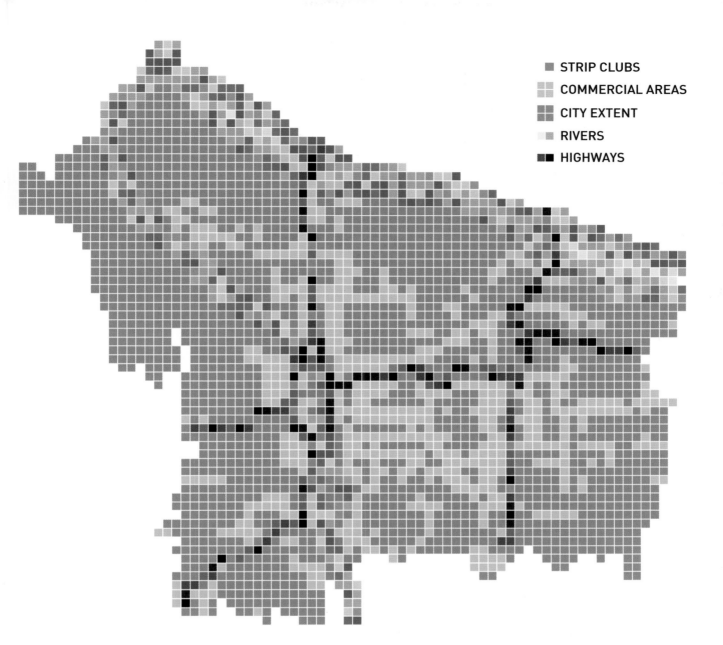

eight clubs per 100,000 residents. This rate places Portland somewhere between the fourth and eighth spots among the one hundred largest cities in the United States for strip clubs per capita. But counting strip clubs is not as easy as it would seem.

What constitutes a strip club? How do you count them? A quick internet search of club listings nationwide will illustrate that many are not conventional full-nudity strip clubs. (The quick search will also likely put a virus on your computer.) For those working in the industry, lingerie modeling, peep shows, massage parlors, and video arcades do not quite fit into the same category; not

to mention that the laws in many states strictly regulate a club's activity depending on the type of alcohol served (if it's served). To the casual viewer, there may not be much difference between dancing fully nude and wearing a bikini, but ask most patrons and they will tell you it matters. Consider also that venues in cities like Las Vegas are more likely to be large-scale gentlemen's clubs with significantly more stages, dancers, and patrons.

Those who defend free speech rarely intend to embolden the fringe, but adult entertainment has served historically as the focal point to test that right. In *State of Oregon v. Brooks, 1976*, nudity

Mary's Club, downtown, oldest strip club in Portland sized by age of establishment.

of any kind was allowed as long as it was confined to a controlled setting that prevented free entry and excluded minors. The Brooks trial opened the door for free expression protections to be applied to nudity in Oregon, which may have jump-started the rise in strip club openings in the region from four to six and in stage counts from four to ten by the end of 1977. The *Henry v. State*, 1987, decision protected obscenity as free speech in Oregon. Soon thereafter, *Tidyman v. Portland*, 1988, banned targeting zoning (against obscenity) as an infringement on free speech.

It was *Sekne v. Portland*, 1986, that challenged the restriction of nudity in bars with support from the Oregon State Court of Appeals. This case expanded free expression protections for nudity from controlled settings (like theaters) to bars and clubs more generally. The Graffic Tavern, located outside Portland's 1981 corporate limits, found itself engulfed in the city's aggressive annexation

practices of the 1980s. The owner, Sekne, argued that his club was illegally annexed and that the nudity ordinance was unconstitutional as other forms of nudity were permitted. While the annexation case went nowhere, the ban on nudity was overturned. The court cases led to a rise in legitimately recognized clubs along with repeated legislative battles, voter initiatives, community conflict, and eventually more court cases—all of which helped to confirm more *naked* free expression protections.

Even the best attempts at limiting and regulating strip clubs in the Portland area have been frustrated. From 1994 to 2000, three voter initiatives (Ballot Measures 19, 31, and 87) attempted to override free expression protections for all forms of "obscenity" (including nudity) in the state of Oregon beyond what is allowed by the US Constitution, but all were defeated. Since then, open strip club and stage numbers in the region have continued to rise steadily at

Standard Portland-style club. Safari Club, Powell Avenue

a rate of more than one club per year with nearly two stages per club. Given the state's tradition of providing nudity and obscenity with free expression protections, efforts to limit these types of activities have gone nowhere except to call out Oregon's divergent cultural and political uniqueness to anyone paying attention. The voting patterns in relation to the ballot measures also helped reveal a widening cultural gap between Portland and the rest of the state, except Eugene and Corvallis, the state's primary college towns.

What makes Portland's strip club scene so significant? (It was featured in a 2011 *Economist* article, after all.) Is it the homey where-everybody-knows-your-name quality epitomized at the Magic Garden club by self-made diva and stripper Viva Las Vegas? The rowdy roadhouse feel of The Acropolis and Dancin' Bare south and north of town? The supreme tattooed hipness at Devils Point, the vegan do-gooder vibe at Casa Diablo, and the iconic crustiness of Mary's Club? All add to the special Portlandness of the region's strip clubs. While these clubs are practically landmarks, these images fail to consider the sometimes unsavory, sometimes pitiful, and mostly unnoticed scattering of clubs across east Portland and Columbia Boulevard. Perhaps what makes the strip club phenomenon in Portland unique and noticeable is the fact that they're found scattered throughout many different neighborhoods across the city rather than concentrated in a few areas, as is common in most other cities.

The internet has certainly swept pornography from its storefront edifice. Massage parlors were outlawed in the 1990s. Lingerie modeling huts enjoy modest success but seem to self-marginalize to the seediest segments of town and suffer the ubiquitous designation as "jack shacks." Strip clubs, however, continue to prosper and likely will for some time as a peculiar social venue which often serves to either express antiquated versions of masculinity or remake new ones. For some, this may seem a smudge in the ascendancy of Portland; for others, it's a muffled affirmation of our freedoms over government intrusion. And whether or not it's actually true, Portland's reputation as the strip club capital of the country seems poised to prosper as well.

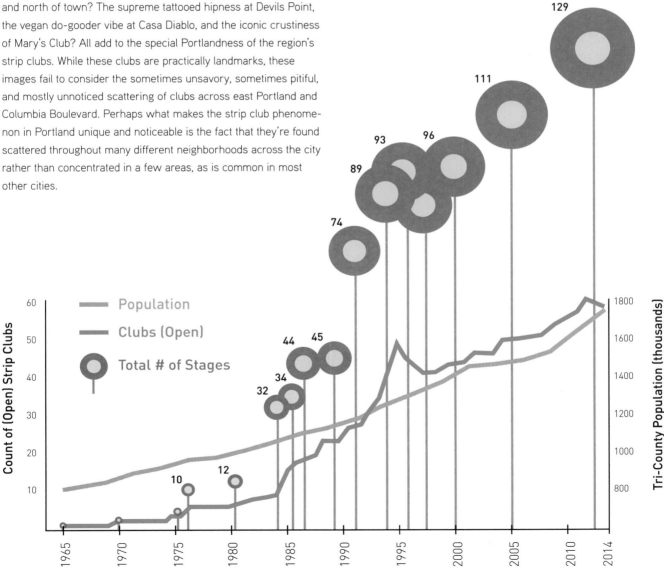

II.   THE ONCE AND FUTURE CITY

Usually we come to know a place for what's there, but sometimes what's missing is at least as important as what's present in terms of how we relate to that place. Considering what's lost invites our geographic imaginations to engage with the past of a place. Certainly much of the natural environment has been lost, but so has much of the built environment—houses, schools, churches, and industrial sites. Considering what's missing invites us to imagine not only what's gone but what could've been.

In many parts of the city, Portland's urban landscape is changing quickly. In this land of transplants it can be hard for new arrivals to imagine anything other than the current landscapes. Sometimes faint imprints of the past are left in place names, churches, and building stock. Ross Island, a local source for sand and gravel for decades, is roughly half the size it was when Portland was founded. In other places, it's almost impossible to see what used to be there. For many residents it's difficult to imagine the Jantzen Beach Amusement Park, which closed in 1970, through the thicket of strip malls that occupy that space now.

The urban landscape that seems so fixed and permanent is in fact constantly changing, and with each change comes loss. People established the city because of the favorable connection of land to water. Forested lands gave way to streets and buildings which came up to, into, and over the Willamette River. The economic landscape of warehouses that originally dominated the riverfront largely disappeared and was replaced with a highway. In the 1970s the city "reclaimed" the river by building a waterfront park over the highway. Portland is celebrated for this reconnection to the river, and thus the city is known in part for what it's lost. In some cases, parts of the urban landscape have existed only in the minds of planners and on their maps and design charrettes and never came to be, such as Portland's failed bid for the 1968 Olympics. In this chapter, we examine elements of the city that are no longer present or never came to be.

TOWNSHIP AND CHANGE

ANNEXATIONS

Beginning with thirty-six square blocks in 1845, the city of Portland grew up along the west bank of the Willamette River. By 1866 Portland was bounded by the West Hills to the west and the river to the east. In 1891 East Portland and Albina were consolidated with old Portland on the west side. Two years later Sellwood was annexed.

Many visitors to the 1905 Lewis and Clark Centennial and American Pacific Exposition and Oriental Fair were impressed with the city and decided to move there. During the decade from 1900 to 1910, the geographical boundaries enlarged by 33 percent to almost fifty square miles. As less expensive, rural land became easily accessible, the area's small farming towns grew and turned into bedroom communities.

Many peripheral populations were incorporated through a series of annexations, including Montavilla (1906), Mount Scott-Arleta (1908), Lents (1912), Linnton (1915), and St. Johns (1915). This increased the geographic size of Portland by 25 percent. Between World War I and World War II the city's growth plateaued.

Between 1950 and 1980, suburban Clackamas and Washington Counties saw their populations triple and quadruple, respectively, while Multnomah County saw only a 20 percent increase in population. Large areas of East Portland were annexed between 1980 and 1998, when Portland reached its current boundaries.

FOUNDING TO PRESENT DAY

1845–1851

1852–1887

1888–1893

1894–1907

1908–1915

1916–1954

1955–1964

1965–1974

1975–1983

1984–1993

1994–Present

Believed to be named for John W. **York**. Born in Georgia to English and Scottish parents, York was a Methodist episcopal minister who travele

Robert Bruce **Wilson** was born in Virginia and went to California for the gold rush before arriving in Portland. He was a physician ar

George W. **Vaughn** was a New Jersey-born merchant who served as mayor from 1855–1856. He constructed the first steam-power

Abel Parker **Upshur** was a Virginia politician who served as secretary of state under President John Tyler. He advocate

G. William **Thurman** was a telegraph executive and close friend of Douglas Taylor, the city engineer who prepared the street name changes in 1891. It is not certain th

Thomas A. **Savier** was born in Norfolk, Virginia. He went to California for the gold rush before arriving in Portland. He was a merchant and business partr

A. E. **Raleigh** was born in Ireland, moved to New York, and then settled in Portland. He was deputy superintendent of streets in 1891 when the names chang

L. P. W. **Quimby** was born in Vermont and arrived in Portland in 1862. He was one of the first hotel proprietors and later ra

Francis W. **Pettygrove** was one of Portland's founders. Born in Maine, he left for Oregon in 184

William **Overton**, along with Lovejoy, obtained the donation land claim that became Portlar

Edward J. **Northrup** was born in Albany, New York. He began a business deali

John **Marshall** was born in England. He was a riverboat captain who worke

Asa **Lovejoy** was born in Massachusetts and came by wagon to Oregon

Edward Smith **Kearney** was born in Philadelphia and lived

Arthur H. **Johnson** was born in London. He was a butcher wl

William **Irving** was a Scottish-born steamboat capta

Richard **Hoyt** was born in Albany, New York. A riverbo

Dr. Rodney **Glisan** was a medical officer in t

Captain George H. **Flanders** was bc

Colonel Edward **Everett** established

Anthony L. **Davis** came

Daniel W. **Burnside** w

THE STREETS SPEAK THE LANGUAGE OF THE PAST

As Portland grew in the late nineteenth and early twentieth centuries, the naming of streets was generally left to whoever platted out each subdivision. At times streets have later been renamed for reasons practical or political. The first major round of street renaming occurred from 1891 to 1892 as Portland absorbed the eastside cities of Albina and East Portland, and duplicate names were changed.

The current system, in which each street name is prefixed by its part of the city (N, NE, NW, SE, SW), was put into place in 1931 and was accompanied by a round of street renaming. Parts of Southeast Portland had numbered avenues running east-west, all of which were given names. A new citywide system of address numbers, allotting one hundred numbers to each block, was put in place at that time as well.

ughout the country for work.

ried Caroline Couch, eldest daughter of John H. Couch.

mill in the city on the corner of Front and Madison.

Oregon's admittance to the United States but never lived here.

et is named for him, but in 1921 a local paper received a letter suggesting so.

W. Burnside and operated a general store on Front street called Savier and Co.

street may also be named for Patrick Raleigh, a merchant in Portland's formative years.

ge trucking business. Quimby was the first state game warden. He is buried in Lone Fir Cemetery.

bought half of the land claim that would become Portland. He left in 1848 for Port Townsend, Washington.

old his interest to Pettygrove in 1844 and left for Texas. He spent less than three years of his life in Oregon.

er and wagon supplies, but died after falling twenty feet through a trapdoor in his office. He is buried in Lone Fir Cemetery.

he rivers of the Portland area for fifty years. The street may also be named for a Captain George Marshall or a Thomas Marshall.

. He obtained the land that became Portland with Overton, then founded the city with Pettygrove. He is buried in Lone Fir Cemetery.

burg before coming to Portland, where he was a prominent businessman and US marshal for Oregon. He is buried in Riverview Cemetery.

a large meat market and a land developer who owned many blocks of real estate in early Portland. He and his wife Cordelia had fourteen children.

business partner of Captain Hoyt. In 1859, he moved to British Columbia. His land claim became the Irvington neighborhood of Northeast Portland.

ain, he established the Columbia Steam Navigation Company in 1857. His two brothers later joined him in Portland. He is buried in Lone Fir Cemetery.

Army and became a professor at the Oregon Medical College, Oregon's first medical school. Glisan married Elizabeth Couch, daughter of John H. Couch.

Massachusetts and came to Portland with his brother-in-law and business partner John H. Couch. They developed wharves along the Willamette River.

ran an insurance firm in Portland during the late 1800s. In 1891, he led the parade which celebrated the consolidation of Portland, East Portland, and Albina.

tland from Indiana. Elected Portland's first justice of the peace, he helped to establish the first public school. His daughter Mary Jane married Daniel W. Burnside.

John H. Couch was a Massachusetts-born sea captain and Flanders's business partner. He developed the area that would become the Alphabet District.

ominent businessman in the city's formative years. Born in Vermont and drawn to California by the gold rush, Burnside settled in Portland in 1852.

Captain Alexander P. Ankeny opened the New Market Theater, Portland's first theater.

ALPHABET DISTRICT

Willamette River

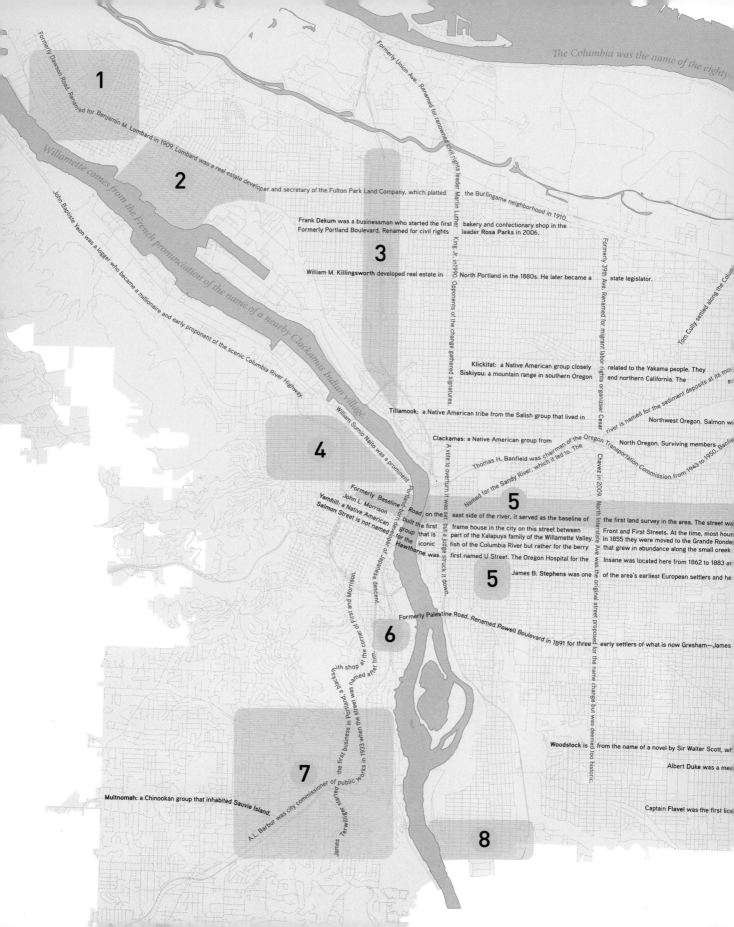

1

Formerly Dawson Road. Renamed for Benjamin M. Lombard in 1909. Lombard was a real estate developer and secretary of the Fulton Park Land Company, which platted the Burlingame neighborhood in 1910.

2

John Baptiste Yeon was a logger who became a millionaire and early proponent of the scenic Columbia River Highway.

Willamette comes from the French pronunciation of the name of a nearby Clackamas Indian village.

The Columbia was the name of the eighty-

Formerly Union Ave. Renamed for renowned civil rights leader Martin Luther King Jr. in 1990. Opponents of the change gathered signatures.

Frank Dekum was a businessman who started the first bakery and confectionary shop in Formerly Portland Boulevard. Renamed for civil rights leader Rosa Parks in 2006.

3

William M. Killingsworth developed real estate in North Portland in the 1880s. He later became a state legislator.

Formerly 39th Ave. Renamed for migrant labor rights organizer Cesar Chavez in 2009.

Tom Cully settled along the Colu

Klickitat: a Native American group closely related to the Yakama people. They
Siskiyou: a mountain range in southern Oregon and northern California. The

Tillamook: a Native American tribe from the Salish group that lived in Northwest Oregon. Salmon w

Clackamas: a Native American group from North Oregon. Surviving members. Banfie

William Sumio Naito was a prominent

4

Thomas H. Banfield was chairman of the Oregon Transportation Commission from 1943 to 1950.

river is named for the sediment deposits at its mou

Named for the Sandy River, which it led to. The

5

A vote to overturn it was the first land survey in the area. The street wa
but a judge struck it down. Front and First Streets. At the time, most hous

Formerly Baseline Road, on the east side of the river, it served as the baseline of

John L. Morrison built the first frame house in the city on this street between
Yamhill: a Native American group that is part of the Kalapuya family of the Willamette Valley. In 1855 they were moved to the Grande Ronde
Salmon Street is not named for the fish of the Columbia River but rather for the berry that grew in abundance along the small creek

Hawthorne was first named U Street. The Oregon Hospital for the Insane was located here from 1862 to 1883 an

developer for the iconic

James B. Stephens was one of the area's earliest European settlers and he

5

Portland-town developer who built the first

North Interstate Ave. was the original street proposed for the name change but was deemed too historic.

6

Formerly Palestine Road. Renamed Powell Boulevard in 1891 for three early settlers of what is now Gresham—James

A.L. Barbur was city commissioner of public works in 1933 when the street was named after him.

James Terwilliger started the first business in Portland, a blacksmith shop at the corner of First and Morrison.

Woodstock is from the name of a novel by Sir Walter Scott, wh

7

Multnomah: a Chinookan group that inhabited Sauvie Island.

Albert Duke was a mea

Captain Flavel was the first lice

8

There are a few parts of the city with distinct themes to their street names, although some are too obscure for most of us to recognize.

...long ship Captain Robert Gray was sailing when he entered the river in 1792.

...ted as early as 1881.

...ated trade between coastal ...in the original Irvington plat of 1887.

...who held the land claim of the area in the 1850s and for whom Sullivan Gulch is named. *and Eastern Oregon tribes. They ceded their land in 1855.*

to their culture and economy.

...rsially chosen over Timothy Sullivan, *were moved to the Grande Ronde Reservation in 1855.*

102nd was originally

122nd was originally

...d for Benjamin Stark, who operated the first ferry across the Willamette and was later a US Senator.
... His tenure in Portland was brief and he later moved to Washington.
...tion. This was one of the first street names chosen in Portland.
...to the Willamette down a draw where the street is now located.

130th

...was known as Asylum Avenue. It was renamed in 1888 for the founder of the hospital, Dr. James C. Hawthorne.
...on land claim that now makes up part of Southeast Portland. He originally worked for the Hudson's Bay Company.

named Craig Road.

112th was originally

named Buckley Road.

named Clarnie Road.

was originally named

Prune Road.

Powell, and Dr. John P. Powell. None of them were related, but all came from the east by wagon.

in the late 1800s.

s.

a River bar pilot.

1. The most prominent theme to St. Johns's street names is cities. These include Baltimore, Philadelphia, Pittsburgh, Chicago, New York, Syracuse, Charleston, Richmond, Reno, Olympia, and Salem. New York place names, many of Native American origin, are most common, including Oswego, Seneca, Mohawk, Hudson, and Allegheny.

2. The University Park neighborhood streets bear the names of prestigious colleges: Amherst, Berkeley, Bowdoin, Buffalo, Butler, Cambridge, DePauw, Drew, Harvard, Morgan, Oberlin, Princeton, Stanford, Syracuse, Vanderbilt, Wabash, Wellesley, and Yale. Another thirty-two streets are named after famous educators, theologians, authors, and important figures in Methodist history.

3. The north-south streets between North Interstate Avenue and North Albina Avenue are named after states that begin with the letter M: Maryland, Montana, Minnesota, Missouri, Michigan, and Mississippi. Massachusetts Street is just west of Interstate.

4. Northwest Portland's Alphabet District—see previous page.

5. Portland has two centrally located areas where streets are named after trees. Just south of East Burnside are Ash, Pine, Oak, and Alder. In Ladd's Addition are Birch, Cypress, Hazel, Hemlock, Hickory, Holly, Larch, Lavender, Locust, Maple, Mulberry, Orange, Palm, Poplar, Spruce, and Tamarack.

6. There are ten Southwest streets named after Oregon governors of the mid-1800s, in more or less chronological order from Abernethy at the south end to Woods at the north end.

7. Southwest Portland has an area of streets named after states that follows no discernible pattern. To the south a botanical theme emerges with streets named Garden Home, Lobelia, Marigold, Orchid, and Plum. A few streets named after women are scattered through this area, but it's hard to tell which particular women they are named after, as they are first names only.

8. Sellwood's southernmost streets are named after places in Oregon and Washington, most derived from Native American words: Nehalem, Tacoma, Tenino, Umatilla, Clatsop, Ochoco, Marion, and Linn. Nehalem, Tenino, Umatilla, and Clatsop are indigenous peoples of Oregon. Tacoma is the Native American name for Mount Rainier. Ochoco is a Paiute word meaning willow or tall pine.

ETHNIC IMPRINTS

In the late nineteenth and early twentieth centuries, European immigrants flooded into the United States, most famously through New York's Ellis Island. Portland, too, had a significant influx of immigrants during this era. Many found work with the railroads and settled in the Albina area of North and Northeast Portland. The combined Scandinavian population was the largest group, and a number of churches in the area were built for Swedish, Danish, and Norwegian congregations. The St. Stanislaus Polish Church served the small Polish community nearby. Mt. Zion Baptist Church catered to the Russian immigrant population, which lived in a great enough concentration nearby to earn the area the name "Little Russia." In Southeast Portland, early Italian immigrants settled in areas with large plots of land where they could grow vegetables, and St. Philip Neri Catholic Church was built there in 1913.

Portland's ethnic enclaves were largely transitional stopover neighborhoods where immigrants lived just as long as it took them to get on their feet. The transition could happen quickly and leave very little trace. For example, Northwest Portland's Slabtown neighborhood was first Irish and then Croatian. In Albina European immigrant populations assimilated and dissipated throughout the city's middle-class neighborhoods and were replaced by African American residents. Most of the Scandinavian churches transitioned to predominantly black congregations. One remnant of Portland's Scandinavians is the Norse Hall at Northeast Eleventh and Couch. St. Stanislaus Church remains a center for the Polish community, hosting a festival each year.

Albina neighborhood along North Killingsworth, 1913

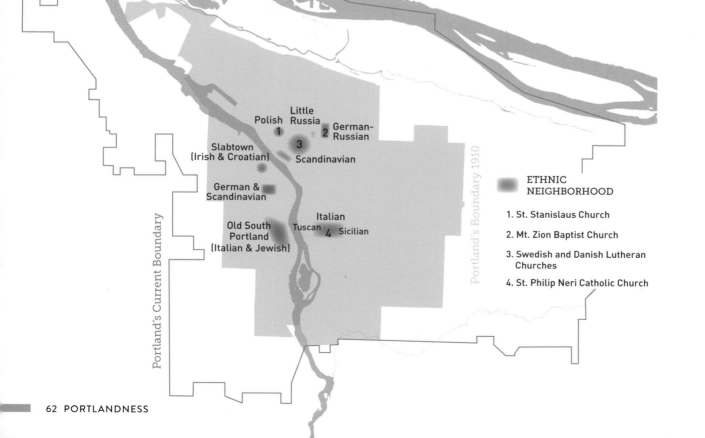

Little Polish Russia
German-Russian
Slabtown (Irish & Croatian)
Scandinavian
German & Scandinavian
Italian
Old South Portland (Italian & Jewish)
Tuscan Sicilian

Portland's Current Boundary

Portland's Boundary 1910

ETHNIC NEIGHBORHOOD

1. St. Stanislaus Church

2. Mt. Zion Baptist Church

3. Swedish and Danish Lutheran Churches

4. St. Philip Neri Catholic Church

The area known as South Portland was home to Italian and Eastern European Jewish immigrant communities. Between 1900 and 1910 the Jewish population doubled to about 2,300 while the Italian population grew five times as large to about 3,000. The first stop for many Jewish immigrants was Neighborhood House, currently in operation at a different location. Jewish immigrants tended to live in families, while the Italian immigrant population was 75 percent male (in 1910), most of whom were single. The majority of business owners and store clerks in the area were Jewish. Italian men usually worked as laborers or peddlers, boarding their horses and wagons at stables in Marquam Gulch and doing business with junk stores on Southwest First. Children attended the Shattuck School, now PSU's Shattuck Hall, and the Failing School, whose original building is now the National School of Naturopathic Medicine. Many Italian Catholic children attended the academy at Saint Lawrence Church. There were several synagogues in the neighborhood; Kesser Israel remains. St. Michael the Archangel Catholic Church, originally serving the Italian population, is still there too.

In 1955 the city of Portland chose the area for urban renewal and the proposed site for Memorial Coliseum. They declared it blighted, citing the fact that one third of residents were over the age of sixty and many of them lived alone. Voters chose an eastside location for the coliseum, but demolition in South Portland went ahead anyway. Office buildings and higher-value apartments went in, and eventually I-405 cut through the old heart of the neighborhood. Most of the old neighborhood was lost. Portland is quite rare in that so much from these immigrant groups is absent from the contemporary landscape. Compared with many East Coast cities, very little remains of Portland's European immigrant neighborhoods.

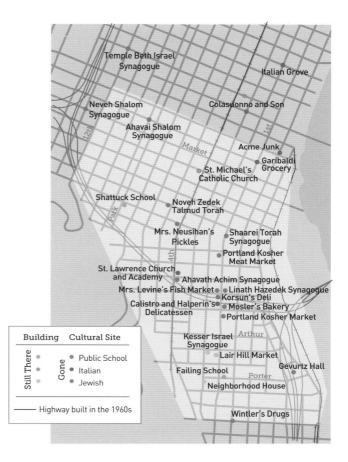

Building / **Cultural Site**

Still There / Gone

- Public School
- Italian
- Jewish

— Highway built in the 1960s

South Portland during the construction of I-405, 1963

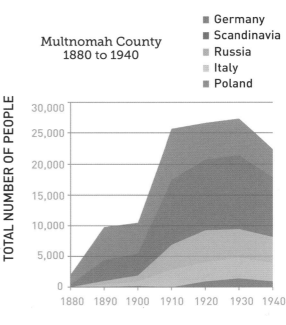

PLACE OF BIRTH FOR SELECTED FOREIGN-BORN RESIDENTS

Multnomah County
1880 to 1940

- Germany
- Scandinavia
- Russia
- Italy
- Poland

TOTAL NUMBER OF PEOPLE

30,000
25,000
20,000
15,000
10,000
5,000
0

1880 1890 1900 1910 1920 1930 1940

HISTORIC CHINATOWN

- Chinese Gardens
- Block with Chinese Business or Residence
- Streets ca. 1910
- Tanner Creek

1879

Chinese immigrants settled downtown and along Tanner Creek, where they practiced traditional farming. The vast majority of Chinese immigrants were single men who were served by boarding houses, laundries, and entertainment in Chinatown.

1889

The Chinese Gardens reached an extent of twenty-one acres and provided produce to much of the city. There were over one hundred Chinese businesses downtown, distinguished by balconies, paper lanterns, and colorful signs.

1901

The Gardens lost land to the Multnomah Athletic Club. At this time Chinatown included thirty-eight gambling houses, thirty-six brothels, three theaters, and six temples. The great flood of 1894 catalyzed a migration of Chinese businesses to the north of Burnside Street.

1908

Increasing downtown property values and a large fire at Second and Alder caused more Chinese businesses to move north of Burnside. Japanese immigration increased, and Japan Town formed in the same area.

1926

By 1926 several major changes had occurred in the Chinese community. In 1910 the city of Portland banned produce sales by peddlers downtown. The Chinese Gardens were no longer economically viable and soon disappeared.

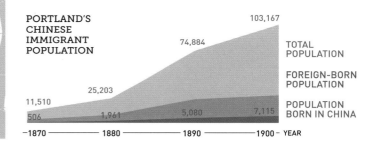
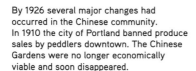

PORTLAND'S CHINESE IMMIGRANT POPULATION

- TOTAL POPULATION
- FOREIGN-BORN POPULATION
- POPULATION BORN IN CHINA

103,167
74,884
25,203
11,510
506
1,961
5,080
7,115

—1870 —— 1880 —— 1890 —— 1900 — YEAR

The very first Chinese-owned business in Portland, a restaurant and boarding house, opened in 1851, the year of the city's founding. The Chinese community grew with, and in many ways built, the booming late nineteenth-century city from the sustenance provided by the Chinese vegetable gardens to labor provided by the residents of Chinatown. Like other immigrants and US citizens, Chinese men were drawn to California by the 1849 gold rush. Both the United States and China had open-door immigration policies at the time. New job opportunities on the railroads drew Chinese immigrants north to Oregon in the following decades. From the late 1800s through the early 1900s, many ships from China came directly to Astoria or Portland, and the Chinese became the largest foreign-born population in the city.

From the beginning, Chinese immigrants on the West Coast faced prejudice and violence. The Oregon state constitution of 1859 specifically prohibited Chinese and African Americans from voting or achieving state citizenship. In the 1870s certain labor unions

Chinese Gardens circa 1890

blamed high unemployment on their presence, and pressure from these groups led to the first federal Chinese Exclusion Act of 1882. It prohibited the immigration of Chinese laborers and in later versions prohibited the immigration of laborer and merchants' wives. Men already vastly outnumbered women in the Chinese immigrant community, and this only served to increase the gender gap. The Exclusion Act remained in place until 1943.

Anti-Chinese riots in Seattle, Tacoma, and other parts of Washington and Oregon in 1885 and 1886 forced many Chinese to relocate. In Portland such incidents were avoided largely due to the vocal opposition of Mayor John Gates and the *Oregonian* newspaper. It wasn't that the mayor and the editors of the *Oregonian* abhorred racism; it was more that they wished to avoid mob violence and promote a civil, law-abiding society in Portland. In their view the Chinese were a necessary evil, essential to the rapid growth of the city but inherently inferior and unable to assimilate. Portland's Chinatown became a safe haven for refugees from around the region, and they were aided in their resettlement by successful local Chinese entrepreneurs.

In 1890 Chinese-born persons were nearly 10 percent of Portland's total population—a significant presence in the city of about 46,000. While there was much public discussion of restricting the Chinese

to one small part of the city as had been done in San Francisco, the effort was never entirely successful. Chinese residents already occupied buildings throughout downtown. The standard practice was to charge them much higher rent than that of white residents, an incentive for many building owners to take on Chinese tenants and for those tenants to modify buildings in order to fit more people or businesses inside.

Due to the lack of traditional Chinese family structure and the racism of white society, alternative social structures developed in Chinatowns across the country. District associations were composed of people from the same province in China; family associations or clans were composed of members with the same surname, and secret societies, or tongs, were anti-establishment and often criminal organizations. These groups met the financial, legal, social, and educational needs of Chinese in the United States. The Chinese Consolidated Benevolent Association (CCBA) was a national organization whose branch in Portland was known as the Jung Wah Association. It hired lawyers, negotiated labor contracts, and served as a link to the Chinese government. The tongs were often opposed to the decisions of the CCBA and were responsible for the underworld activities that gave Chinatown its unsavory reputation, such as opium dens, gambling, and prostitution.

MODERN CHINATOWN

In more recent decades, immigrants arriving in Portland from China and other parts of Asia have usually settled far from downtown. The Chinatown of the 1920s is still officially known as the Chinatown neighborhood; it's history memorialized by the Chinatown gate, the Lan Su Chinese Gardens, and decorative light posts, but there are few Chinese businesses left there. Most Chinese restaurants, groceries, and other businesses are found along Southeast Eighty-Second in the area recently named the Jade District, the heart of a community whose heritage includes many other parts of Asia and the world.

The Jade District, a new business district along Southeast Eighty-Second between Division and Powell, has quite a few things in common with Portland's earliest Chinatown. It's located in an area with a reputation for being dangerous and undesirable (as much for motor vehicle traffic and pollution as for the drug traffic and prostitution). Local residents and entrepreneurs have taken it upon themselves to create a thriving community. Some have chosen to redevelop property in a way that draws inspiration from the culture and architecture of their home country. There are even plans for a community garden in which residents will be able to grow the vegetables used in their traditional cuisine, much as Portland's first Chinese immigrants did.

The neighborhood surrounding the Jade District began to see an increase in Asian immigrants after 1970. In 1970 the foreign-born, Asian-born, and Chinese-born populations in the area were all basically the same relative size as in the city as a whole. By 1990 the total foreign-born population was only slightly above the city-wide percentage, but 85 percent of those immigrants were from some part of Asia, with nearly half being from China. The relative number of Chinese immigrants has been over three times the Portland average ever since.

With the new residents came a number of new businesses. Some, such as the well-known Hung Far Low restaurant, relocated from the traditional Chinatown in downtown. Fubonn, the large Asian shopping center that includes a large grocery store, opened in 2006 and is one of the main anchors of the district.

After an effort by the local business owners and other community members, the area was given a Neighborhood Prosperity Initiative (NPI) designation from the Portland Development Commission (PDC) in 2011. The NPI program focuses on commercial districts in underserved areas of the city, particularly those with large populations of low-income residents and people of color. With grants

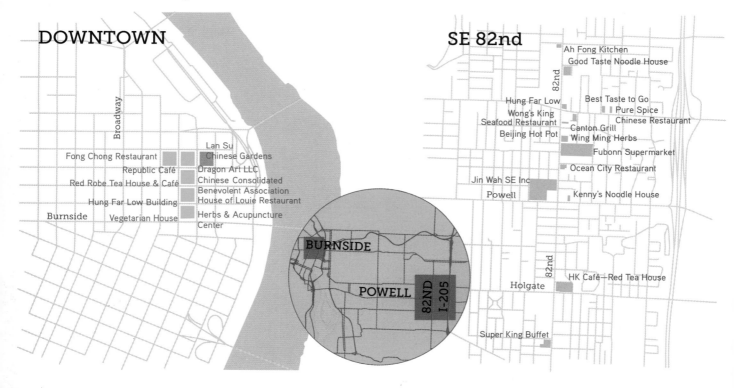

DOWNTOWN

Broadway

Fong Chong Restaurant
Republic Café
Red Robe Tea House & Café

Hung Far Low Building

Burnside   Vegetarian House

Lan Su Chinese Gardens
Dragon Art LLC
Chinese Consolidated Benevolent Association
House of Louie Restaurant
Herbs & Acupuncture Center

BURNSIDE

POWELL   82ND I-205

SE 82nd

Ah Fong Kitchen
Good Taste Noodle House

82nd

Hung Far Low   Best Taste to Go
Wong's King   Pure Spice
Seafood Restaurant   Chinese Restaurant
          Canton Grill
Beijing Hot Pot   Wing Ming Herbs
          Fubonn Supermarket
          Ocean City Restaurant
Jin Wah SE Inc
Powell   Kenny's Noodle House

82nd

          HK Café—Red Tea House
Holgate

Super King Buffet

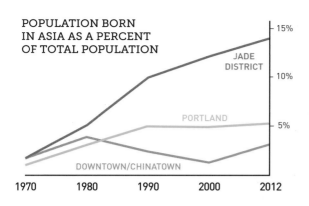

POPULATION BORN
IN ASIA AS A PERCENT
OF TOTAL POPULATION

JADE
DISTRICT

PORTLAND

DOWNTOWN/CHINATOWN

15%

10%

5%

1970   1980   1990   2000   2012

Sign for the iconic Hung Far Low Restaurant

and support provided by the PDC and the leadership of a board of directors and a district manager, the Jade District organization collaborates with residents and community groups to create economic opportunities and improve health, and well-being for the diverse population of the neighborhood. The Asian Pacific American Organization of Oregon was contracted to help with community outreach in 2013.

Wing Ming Plaza is one of the commercial lots that has benefited from the Jade District project. Business owner Ken Yu, who grew up in China, designed and implemented the construction of the plaza, in which businesses and homes cluster around a large tree in a parking lot offset from busy Eighty-Second Avenue. On a recent city-led walking tour of the area, he mentioned that he'd been inspired by the urban forms and walkability of his hometown.

In addition to commercial development, the Jade District has plans to hold cultural events such as Lunar New Year celebrations. An Asian-inspired night market is planned for the summer, most likely on the newly rebuilt Portland Community College campus. The community garden broke ground on June 21, 2014, at Harrison Park Elementary School.

Sign for Wing Ming Square, Southeast 82nd and Taggart

Chinatown Gate, West Burnside

Fubonn shopping center, Southeast 82nd

EXPO TO INFILL

Bandstand, US Government Building, and Guild's Lake

GUILD'S LAKE

The 220-acre marsh that once occupied the lowlands between present-day Forest Park and the Willamette River has historically been the site of much change. The Donation Land Act allowed nineteenth-century settlers Peter and Elizabeth Guild to claim 598 acres of pristine swampland in 1847, which included a crescent-shaped lake and the surrounding vacant waterfront property.

Guild's Lake, as it would later be called, was an oxbow lake disconnected from the Willamette River. After Peter Guild's death in 1870, Elizabeth Guild and her nine children inherited the land that housed peripheral aspects of the growing city, including immigrant farmers, a garbage incinerator, dairies, and sawmills.

In 1903 John Charles Olmsted was contracted to design a public parks plan for the rapidly populating city. He chose Guild's Lake as the site for the Lewis and Clark Centennial and American Pacific Exposition and Oriental Fair, despite general feelings that the area was a blight on forest scenery. The Exposition drew some 1.6 million people and promoted Portland as a progressing metropolis, not a distant lumber-manufacturing outpost.

After the fair, Guild's Lake again became a landfill, but could no longer adequately process the waste from the expanding city. Lafayette Pence proposed to clear the land, fill the lake, and redevelop the area for residential and industrial use. By 1907 he'd spent several hundred thousand dollars with only a murky lake and partially built houses to show for his efforts. He abandoned the project, leaving the city of Portland to find new investors.

LEWIS AND CLARK EXPO

1. Fine Arts
2. Forestry
3. Oriental Palace
4. Foreign Palace
5. Agriculture
6. Manufacturers
7. Mining
8. Electricity & Transportation
9. Fisheries
10. Bandstand
11. Hungarian Chalet
12. Swiss Chalet
13. Experimental Gardens
14. Carnival of Venice
15. Streets of Cairo
16. Haunted Castle
17. Japanese Village
18. Animal Show

State buildings labeled with state abbreviations (OR)

In 1909, the Lewis-Wiley Hydraulic Company successfully filled fifty acres of Guild's Lake with hillside dirt and fifty-six new industrial lots. A push for a larger industrial district began, which was supported by the Northern Pacific Railway Company. The area became an important switching yard for trains. In the early 1920s the Port of Portland funded development to fill in the rest of Guild's Lake and the surrounding wetlands using dredge from the Willamette River. To this day, the transportation epicenter built over Guild's Lake is still in use despite advances in commercial distribution.

In 1920 Portland annexed the Guild's Lake area, although the Depression impeded further growth of industry. During World War II the nearby Kaiser Shipyards brought an influx of workers who lived in temporary housing called the Guild's Lake Housing Project. Heavy industry became centered in the former lake circa 1950.

After the war, chemical, petroleum processing and storage, metals manufacturing, and other large industries grew dramatically. The area, now the Northwest Industrial District, is a hub for semiconductor fabrication, large-scale printing, and transnational distribution. In 2001 the city of Portland adopted the Guild's Lake Industrial Sanctuary Plan to protect its "long-term economic viability as an industrial district." Today Guild's Lake is a remnant of Portland only preserved in historical documents and used to name area businesses. The lake itself is buried beneath acres of dirt.

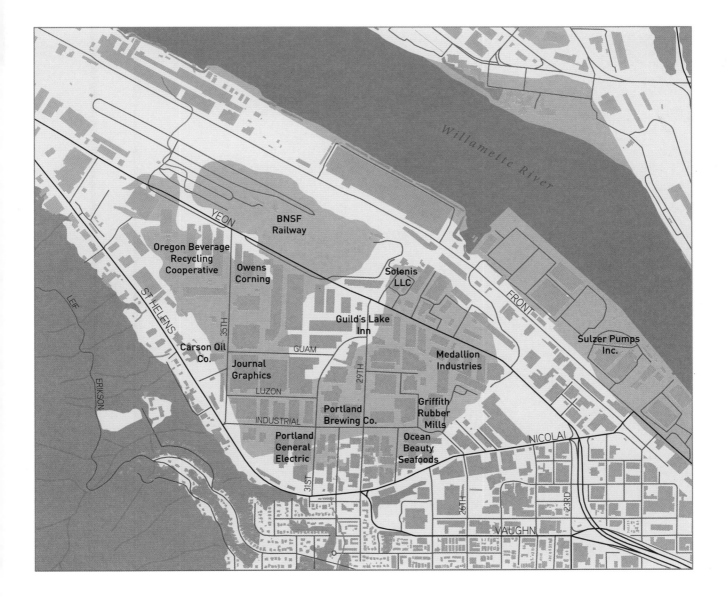

Aerial photo of Swan Island Municipal Airport 1935

FROM ISLE TO PENINSULA

SWAN ISLAND

Swan Island has been many things: an island, a peninsula, a ship-building site, an airport, a shipbuilding site again, a large grove of oaks, and a Superfund site. When it was first charted on a map in 1844, the industrial peninsula that juts out from the east bank of the Willamette River looked quite different than it does now. The island was the base of operations for a group of fur trappers and traders who were soon to become the region's first European shipbuilders with the support of Lieutenant Charles Wilkes, the commander of a six-vessel worldwide exploration sponsored by the US government.

While at Swan Island, Wilkes became enamored with the groves of oaks that populated the island; in fact, Wilkes called the island "Oak Island" in his journal. Upon his return from the mission, Wilkes changed the island's name to Willow Island for the atlas report to the US government. While it's not known exactly why or when the name of the island was eventually changed to Swan Island, the importance of the island in Oregon's history was tied to the shipbuilding group's success in building and launching the ship that Wilkes had helped to secure materials for. The ship, called the *Star of Oregon*, launched in 1841.

RUNWAYS

Swan Island Municipal Airport, 1929
Portland International Airport, Current

The story of Swan Island's transition to peninsula involves a bar in the river that surrounded it. This bar created headaches for ship captains trying to navigate the Willamette and required frequent dredging on both sides of the island to keep the shipping routes open. Annual dredging began as early as the 1870s but was costly to maintain. In 1927 the Port of Portland, which had bought Swan Island in 1922, was granted permission to close the east side of the island and begin dredging a wider path to the west of the island.

With the east channel closed and demand for an airport on the rise, the southern edge of Swan Island was filled in—converting the island into a peninsula—and runways constructed. Swan Island was a natural location for an airport: it was centrally located and flat, and by 1926 the US Postal Service was already using it as a center for its airmail operations. Shortly after his record-setting transatlantic flight in 1927, Charles Lindbergh flew into Portland to dedicate the newly opened Swan Island Municipal Airport, despite the fact that the airport didn't begin to handle passenger service until 1929.

The Swan Island airport proved a popular destination, operating at capacity almost right away and usually packed with weekend crowds that had come out to watch stunt pilots and aerial shows. The airport's success was not long lived, however, as new developments in the aviation industry led to the introduction of planes that were too big for Swan Island's runways. Expanding the airport was not an option, either, since the island could not be extended any farther. By 1935—just eight years after the airport opened—it was clear to officials that Portland's airport could not be on Swan Island. A larger airport, which eventually became Portland International Airport, was soon constructed to the northeast. Swan Island Municipal Airport was closed for good in the early 1940s.

Immediately after the airport's closure the island became a ship-building center. When the United States entered World War II in late 1941, Henry Kaiser located one of his seven major shipbuilding sites at Swan Island to fill the demand for wartime ship production. Kaiser's company, the Oregon Shipbuilding Corporation, famously churned out these ships, producing roughly one quarter of all ships built during World War II.

Although Swan Island has become quite industrial over the years, it continues to be a maritime site. Vigor Industrial runs three dry docks and fifteen cranes there, building and repairing ships to this day. Swan Island also hosts McCarthy Park, a virtually unknown greenway trail that offers access to the Willamette River. Along this trail one can photograph the Fremont Bridge, relax among the driftwood on one of a few sandy areas along the water, take in views of the tallest 30 percent of downtown Portland, or peruse the myriad posted warnings about trespassing or eating fish caught in the river. At the south end of Channel Avenue one can contemplate all this over a Woody Royale burger at Tilt—hipster culture's lone contribution to Swan Island.

1852 General Land Office Cadastral Map

Swan Island shipbuilding circa 1943

Swan Island Industrial Park, 2014

THE ONCE AND FUTURE CITY 71

THE CITY THAT NEVER WAS

1903 OLMSTED PLAN
☐ Proposed Park or Boulevard

1912 BENNETT PLAN
— Proposed Boulevard
☐ Proposed Park
☐ Included in both Bennett and Olmsted Plans

1966 COMPREHENSIVE DEVELOPMENT PLAN
— Proposed Freeway

1962 OLYMPICS BID
☐ Rose City Olympic Center Area

1988 CENTRAL CITY PLAN
▲ Water Taxi Stop

CURRENT
— Street
— Freeway (Year Completed)
☐ Parks

RIVERGATE FREEWAY

COLUMBIA FREEWAY

ST. HELENS FREEWAY

MINNESOTA FREEWAY

I-5 (1967)

I-205 (1975)

PRESCOTT FREEWAY

52ND FREEWAY

I-84 (1957)

STADIUM FWY.

I-405 (1973)

BANFIELD FREEWAY

I-205 FREEWAY

MT. HOOD FREEWAY

BALDOCK FREEWAY

JOHNSON CREEK FREEWAY

1903 Olmsted Plan

In the first years of the twentieth century, the city of Portland's new board of parks commissioners hired landscape architect John Olmsted, the stepson of the well-known designer of New York's Central Park. His 1903 plan of parks and boulevards incorporated the already existing city parks, such as Macleay, Washington, and Columbia, into a network of green spaces and tree-lined boulevards. Although the city didn't have the funds to see it to completion, it continues to influence planners up to the present day. Perhaps the most notable difference between Olmsted's vision and reality is that the large parks he planned for marshy areas along the Willamette and Columbia Rivers were all developed for industry. Of his meandering boulevards, those on the west side came to pass, while there's no trace of those planned for the east side.

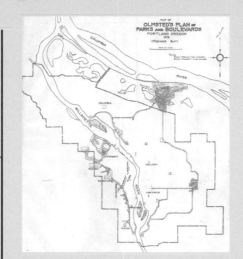

1912 Bennett Plan

The Greater Portland Plan of Edward Bennett was inspired by the grand boulevards and parks of European cities, particularly Paris. Bennett proposed the addition of diagonal boulevards crisscrossing the city. His plan for a civic center along Chapman and Lownsdale parks corresponds to the modern location of government buildings, although they are not housed in the kind of building he envisioned.

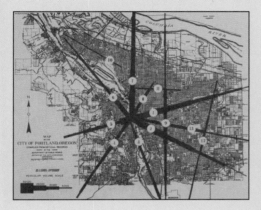

1943 Moses Report

In the 1940s and '50s, a man named Robert Moses reshaped American cities from coast to coast. He's best known for his highways, particularly for his penchant for bisecting poor and working-class neighborhoods with high-speed interstates. His plan for Portland, approved by voters in 1944, included sewers, docks, schools, and a suburban loop of scenic drives.

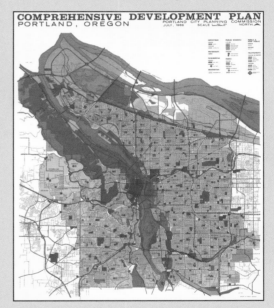

1955 Freeway and Expressway System Portland Metropolitan Area Report

This document proposes a network of fourteen new highways (above) to connect Portland to outlaying suburban areas. The following year the federal government put forth a plan to pay for the construction of most freeways nationally.

1962 Rose City Olympic Center

Mayor Terry Schrunk led Portland's bid to host the 1968 Olympics. The plan revolved around the construction of an Olympic stadium, a 60,000-seat outdoor natatorium, and an Olympic Village for athlete housing in Delta Park (below). The US Olympic Committee picked Detroit instead, and ultimately the games were held in Mexico City.

1966 Comprehensive Development Plan

The 1966 Comprehensive Plan (above) was the first planning document to conceptualize each neighborhood as a "unit" that should have its own school, park, and retail. Neighborhood names corresponded with the main elementary school in the area. Some neighborhood names have endured and continue to be used today. Others, including Applegate, Beach, Binnsmead, Chief Joseph, Hollyrood, Lesser, and Sacajawea, have fallen out of favor.

1988 Central City Plan

The 1988 Central City Plan, with its emphasis on balancing economic development, livability, and environmental conservation, is one of the things that's contributed to Portland's national reputation as a paragon of good urban planning. Many of the ideas proposed in it, such as the Eastbank Esplanade, OMSI, etc., have since been built. Perhaps the most notable proposal that never came to pass is the water taxi system meant to crisscross the Willamette between downtown and the Inner Eastside. The city is still trying to get a constructed but never used water taxi dock off its hands.

HAUNTED

Portland is known for its natural surroundings but could just as easily be known for its supernatural environment. The ghostly aura of the map reveals the density of spooky landscapes—locations of murders, fatal crash sites, and creepy old buildings. Cemeteries and ghost sightings are also inscribed.

One of the most elegantly creepy cemeteries in the city is Lone Fir Cemetery, located on thirty acres in Southeast Portland. It serves as the final resting place for over 25,000 bodies. Of that number, approximately 10,000 have no headstone—so watch where you step! One notable name to be found etched on a tombstone is James C. Hawthorne—founder of the Oregon Hospital for the Insane. Many of Hawthorne's patients are buried here as well.

The picture behind the map is of Cathedral Park under the St. Johns Bridge. In 1949, a teenage girl was murdered nearby, and her killer was later sentenced to death in the gas chamber. Over the years, people have contacted the police after hearing screams for help rise from the park at night. As the authorities have found nothing, some believe the sounds emanate from the phantom of that young soul who haunts the park beneath the bridge.

R.I.P.

Ghost Sighting

Lone Fir Cemetery

Cemetery

LEGENDARY SCARINESS LEVEL

(Murders, Fatal Crashes, Creepy Old Buildings)

Hair raising — Eyebrow raising

MAYWOOD PARK

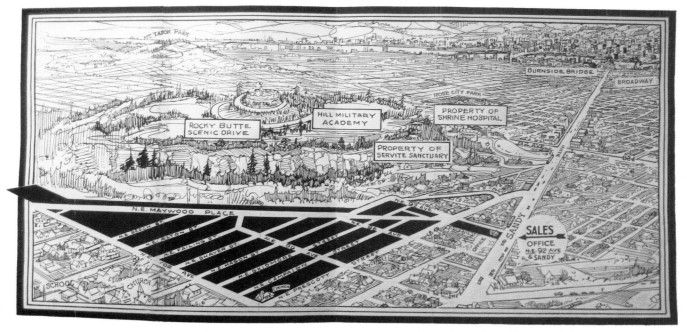

Image From Maywood Park brochure, circa 1930

Maywood Park is a small, incorporated "island" of a city completely surrounded by Portland. A pie slice of a parcel of less than one-fifth a square mile, it has a population of 750 who live in just over 300 houses. It is similar to Portland in many ways—its racial and ethnic makeup is about the same as Portland, as is its population density. Most people in Portland probably don't even know there's another city nested within their own. How did this tiny area become its own city?

The story begins in the 1920s when Portland's population passed 250,000, and the city continued to grow outward via Streetcar lines and automobile-oriented subdivisions. At that time, Sandy Boulevard was the only viable roadway through the outer portions of Northeast Portland. In the 1920s this roadway was widened and extended to connect with the Columbia River Highway. The triangular plot that became Maywood Park was bought by the Columbia Realty Company in 1926.

At the time of purchase, the parcel was Parkrose District farmland. The tract was quickly platted for development as a subdivision. Early promoters of Maywood Park emphasized that the area lay in the "eastern shadow" of Rocky Butte (an extinct volcano), was in the center of a thick stand of conifer forest,

and—most importantly—was connected to the Sandy Boulevard expansion. In 1930 property developers Commonwealth Inc., took ownership of Maywood Park with the intention of building a stylish subdivision similar to Laurelhurst. The Great Depression derailed plans for the intended upscale houses, but in the 1940s housing construction took off in the subdivision. Most of the modest Cape Cod and English bungalow houses currently in Maywood Park were built during this period. These quaint and nicely landscaped homes must have seemed a dramatic contrast to the World War II surplus housing built in the surrounding Parkrose.

The incongruence between Maywood Park and the surrounding areas might have offered its residents a sense that they belonged neither to Parkrose nor Northeast Portland. This sense of seclusion helps explain why it became an incorporated city rather than just another neighborhood in Portland. I-5 was built in the wake of the 1956 Federal Aid Highway Act. Soon thereafter, the I-205 bypass was planned and slated to run through Maywood Park. The people of Maywood Park thought they might have a better chance of halting construction of this freeway through their homes if they incorporated as a city. This idea was based on an understanding, whether right or wrong, that the state of Oregon doesn't want to run freeways through incorporated areas. With the objective of halting freeway development through their "city," Maywood Park residents sought incorporation in 1967, which the state granted based on the principle of "home rule."

In the end, Maywood Park failed to have the I-205 freeway rerouted in spite of its city charter. However, residents saved many of the houses that would've been lost, had the freeway elevation sunk to minimize noise and proximity to traffic, and had a sound berm installed along the side of the highway. Nevertheless, part of Maywood Park was destroyed.

At the time Maywood Park became incorporated in 1967, the large unincorporated area between Portland and Gresham was known as Mid-County until the 1990s. Maywood Park sat in the center of the northwestern quadrant of Mid-County as the only incorporated city in the area until annexations by Portland and Gresham in the 1980s and 1990s.

In 1983 there was an effort to incorporate all of Mid-County into a proposed city called Columbia Ridge. This proposal failed, and nearly all of the Parkrose, Parkrose Heights, and Woodland Park neighborhoods were annexed to Portland from December 1983 to November 1985. These neighborhoods surround Maywood Park to the north, south, and east. Thus, in the span of a few years, Maywood Park went from being isolated from Portland to an "island" city surrounded by Portland. This is the Maywood Park story: apart from Portland even though it seems a part of Portland.

I-205 freeway bypass. This was the west edge of Maywood Park and there were houses along the right edge here until 1978.

Current west edge of Maywood Park. This photo was taken twenty feet east of the freeway photo (to left).

III.   WILDNESS

Portland is widely known for its green spaces and its connection to the natural environment. For example, Portland is home to the largest urban natural forested area in the country—Forest Park. An extensive network of parks reaches most parts of the city. Towering elm, oak, and maple trees line the Park Blocks downtown, and there are statues of animals all over the place. So for many, the line between city and wilderness is intentionally blurred in Portland. There's evidence for this. Here we use terms like "the urban canopy." Portland anchors a region that holds both rural reserves, which are largely farm and forest land deemed protected for fifty years, and urban reserves, which are areas deemed suitable for urban development and protected as such for fifty years.

Portland also has a conflicted relationship with the natural environment. City residents seem to pine for a more direct preindustrial relationship with the natural environment while simultaneously expecting the comforts and mobility of the modern era. Amidst this tension, there are many concerns and conversations about the speed at which the city is growing and about not letting the city get too big or turn into (gasp) another San Francisco or Seattle. To guard against urban creep, Oregon law mandates that each city and urban area in the state have an urban growth boundary that limits development in both natural areas and productive agricultural land.

Yet in many ways, it's the wild that keeps creeping into and resurfacing in Portland. Here, moss routinely envelops entire cars. Grass and other plants sprout from nearly every impermeable surface in the city. Concrete sidewalks are deformed and split by tree roots. Thorny blackberry vines alone seem capable of covering most of the city if left unchecked by goats, Weedwackers, and loppers for a few years. In this chapter we explore the idea that in spite of renowned planning initiatives, multimodal transportation nodes, manicured public parks, and mushrooming condo developments, Portland is also wild.

STUMPTOWN

Stumptown is arguably Portland's oldest nickname, hailing from the early 1850s. For some, this moniker evokes a deforested landscape, a history which Portland is now trying to "green" its way out of. Others wear Stumptown like a badge of devil-may-care ruggedness, with businesses and even sport franchises lauding the area's logging past with nicknames such as Timbers and Lumberjax. But what's really in a name?

Originally, Stumptown referred to actual stumps littering the rapidly expanding Portland streets rather than the state of the local forest. Indeed, much of the land immediately surrounding the new city was heavily forested, with one early settler recalling "cougar and panther waiting to drop down out of the dark firs." Neither was the early Portland landscape an unbroken primeval forest. Land survey data recorded in 1851 provides a picture of what the place looked like before the changes brought about by pioneer settlement. The city's landscape was far more open than popularly imagined expanses of endless old-growth forest. Landscape dynamics were predominantly driven by wildfires, often intentionally set and managed by Native Americans.

Fast forward to the present. Portland is considered one of the country's ten best cities for urban forests by the organization American Forests. Unlike most places across the United States, citywide tree canopy cover is increasing, even in commercial and industrial zones, reaching 30 percent in 2010. But this is a different kind of forest. The urban forest now consists of 236,000 trees that

FOREST & WOODLAND
(includes riparian & wetland forest)

PRAIRIE

SAVANNA

SHRUBLAND

EMERGENT

WATER

BURNED

Looking south along Front St (now Naito Pkwy)

Looking south along Naito Pkwy

line streets, 1.2 million park trees, and who knows how many private property trees. Broadleaf deciduous trees—not old-growth fir and cedar—predominate, accounting for 85 percent of street trees and 77 percent of park trees. Fifty percent of those trees are less than six inches in diameter and less than 10 percent are greater than thirty inches in diameter.

Tree canopy averages, such as the 33 percent number for residential areas, obscure large spatial differences. West Hills neighborhoods, such as Hillside and Arlington Heights, have 60 to 70 percent

canopy cover, while their neighbors to the south, such as Hayhurst and Hillsdale, have 30 to 40 percent canopy cover. Seemingly leafy eastside neighborhoods, such as Eastmoreland and Laurelhurst, hover around the average, while most East Portland neighborhoods have about 20 percent. Hosford-Abernethy neighborhood, home to Ladd's Addition (one of the most beautifully treed neighborhoods in Portland), has some of the lowest tree canopy cover in the city because the neighborhood includes substantial industrial and commercial land.

Views over Portland from locations such as Council Crest and Mount Tabor suggest the city is almost completely covered by trees, which of course is not quite the case. And although it may not bear much relationship to the presettlement landscape, the city is by no means the concrete jungle that the numbers suggest.

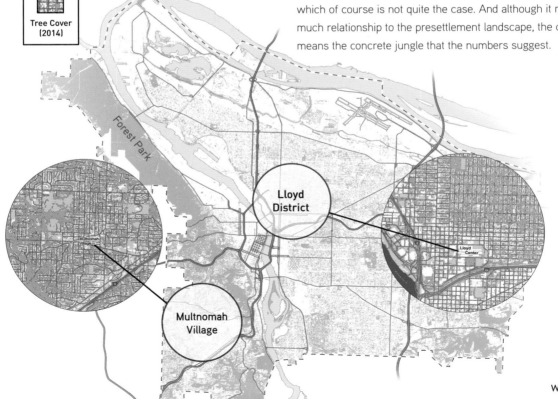

Tree Cover
(2014)

Forest Park

Lloyd District

Multnomah Village

SCATTERED SHOWERS AND SUNBREAKS

Despite its reputation for rain, Portland doesn't even crack the top ten for US cities with the highest annual rainfall, coming in with a mere thirty-nine inches of rain per year. However, Portland ranks third on the list of cities with the most rainy days in the country with 164 rainy days a year. So it's not that Portland gets a lot of rain; it just rains all the time.

For the newcomer, the weather forecast in Portland may appear to be pointless or inaccurate or both. Although it's not true that Portlanders have forty different words for rain, there seem to be many euphemisms for general wetness. Measurable precipitation, traces of rain, mist, drizzle, showers: these terms may all mean the same thing. And does a 20 percent chance of rain mean it'll most likely be dry, or does it mean that it'll almost certainly rain for 20 percent of the day? *Sunbreaks*—moments when the sun comes through on a cloudy day—seems to be a term unique to the Pacific Northwest. *Oregon Sunshine* is both a flower and a light rain.

Highest Number of Rainy Days
The top ten US cities range from:

- 135 days/year (Detroit and Miami) to
- 167 days/year (Rochester and Buffalo)

Highest Average Annual Rainfall
The top ten US cities range from:

- 47.3 inches/year (Nashville) to
- 62.7 inches/year (New Orleans)

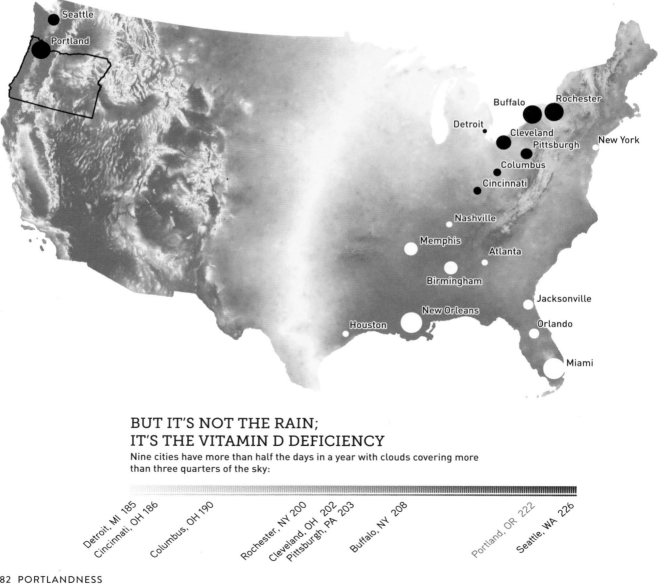

BUT IT'S NOT THE RAIN; IT'S THE VITAMIN D DEFICIENCY
Nine cities have more than half the days in a year with clouds covering more than three quarters of the sky:

Detroit, MI 185
Cincinnati, OH 186
Columbus, OH 190
Rochester, NY 200
Cleveland, OH 202
Pittsburgh, PA 203
Buffalo, NY 208
Portland, OR 222
Seattle, WA 226

OREGON RAINFALL

In Oregon, average annual rainfall varies from under seven inches in the eastern part of the state to over 200 inches in parts of the Coast Range. Oddly enough, considering its reputation for rain, Portland lies in the rain shadow of the Coast Range and is protected from cold, dry continental air by the Cascades range to the east.

METRO AREA RAINFALL

Portland is not the rainiest place in the metro area. Parts of the metro area receive sixty-four inches per year—fifteen inches more than Portland's official rainfall measurements, which are taken at the airport, one of the driest spots in town.

THE PORTLAND WEATHER FORECAST

Mon 45°/45°	Tue 45°/45°	Wed 45°/45°	Thu 45°/45°	Fri 45°/45°
PARTLY CLOUDY	RAIN	CHANCE OF RAIN	SCATTERED SHOWERS	OVERCAST
Chance of Rain: 10%	Chance of Rain: 80%	Chance of Rain: 60%	Chance of Rain: 40%	Chance of Rain: 20%

LOST WATERS AND PHANTOM STREAMS

"Disappeared" Water Features from 1852 Survey

Lake   Stream   Wetland

Computer-Modeled Stream Channels

2014 Water Features

Lake   Stream

Like many cities, Portland enclosed and buried most of the streams and creeks that meander through the city and filled many wetlands connected to the rivers. Much of this water is now unseen and thus forgotten. Historic photographs, government surveys, and old maps can be combined with computer modeling to get a sense of the city's hydrologic landscape when white settlers first arrived.

In the flood plain of the Columbia River north of the Columbia Slough, extensive wetlands and lakes have been lost to various other purposes with the notable exception of Smith and Bybee Lakes. The same is true for certain areas along the Willamette River. Intermittent streams still cut through the West Hills, just not as many as in the past. In the generally flat lands east of the Willamette, only Johnson Creek on Portland's southern edge and its tributary Crystal Springs Creek survive as urban streams. Old maps suggest that others did exist, but how many? Certainly they existed in the Eastmoreland area of south Portland, west of Laurel-hurst Park, and through Sullivan's Gulch, which is now filled with Interstate 84.

But complicated computer models of the landscape suggest the existence of many other creaks and tributaries of flowing water not mapped by pioneer surveyors. These are the phantom streams that

only exist in theory. The map above indicates various historic and modeled water features that hint at the stories behind Portland's lost and imagined waters. One such story can be seen in the history and hydrology of Tanner Creek, named for the tannery that used to occupy a site near the location of the present-day Timbers/Thorns stadium.

In the late 1800s Tanner Creek flowed from the Central West Hills down to shallow Couch Lake between the Steel Bridge and the Fremont Bridge. The creek's course was marked by a prominent gulch that was fifty feet deep and several blocks wide in places. Accounts from as late as 1921 remember Tanner Creek as "a beautiful trout stream" and a place to catch catfish and crayfish, and it was noted that local children enjoyed running the rapids that passed under the trestle bridge where Burnside Street (1) is now.

As Portland's population grew during the late nineteenth-century, Tanner Creek was rerouted underground through a system of pipes and culverts to the Willamette River. Couch Lake (2) and the surrounding wetlands were filled in, making way for industrial development and what eventually became the Pearl District. Over the years, an enormous amount of infill from Portland's ever-expanding network of streets was used to erase

Tanner Creek's course through the city. The most obvious legacy from the formerly city-spanning gulch can now be found in the Goose Hollow neighborhood where Vista Bridge (3) spans Jefferson Street. Originally, many of the pipes in the Tanner Creek system were combined with sewer overflow pipes. The city completed the Tanner Creek Stream Diversion Project between the early 1990s and 2011, which removes about 165 million gallons of stormwater annually from the combined system (shown on the map below in red).

There are several places where one can still encounter Tanner Creek. It's been said Tanner Creek can be heard rushing below a manhole cover on the east side of the King's Hill light-rail station. The Pearl District's historically inspired Tanner Springs Park (4) has no physical connection to the original creek, but instead uses primarily recycled rainwater for its constructed urban wetland. But for all the impact Tanner Creek has had on Portland over the years, once its water enters the pipe network high in the West Hills, it doesn't see the light of day again until draining unceremoniously into the Willamette River from the unremarkably named Outfall 11 (5).

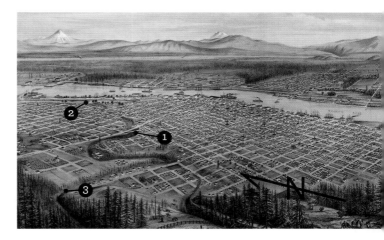

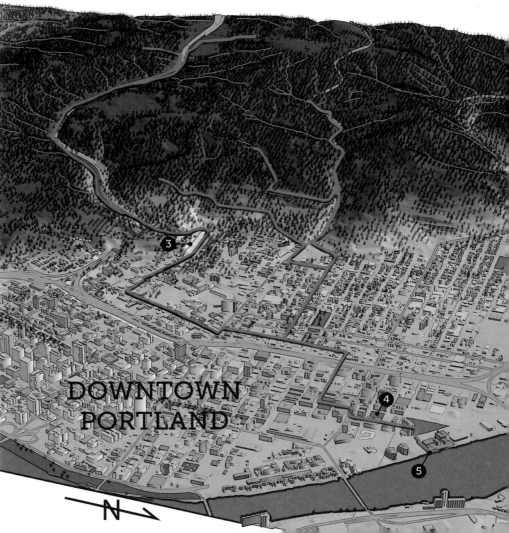

DOWNTOWN
PORTLAND

N

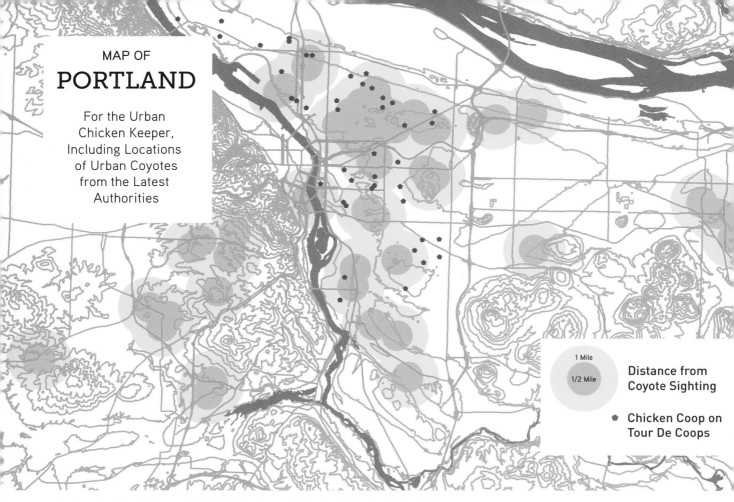

MAP OF PORTLAND

For the Urban Chicken Keeper, Including Locations of Urban Coyotes from the Latest Authorities

1 Mile
1/2 Mile

Distance from Coyote Sighting

Chicken Coop on Tour De Coops

THE CITY CHICKEN AND THE COUNTRY COYOTE

Something that a lot of people like about Portland is that it has "the best things about a city" and "the best things about living in the country." Portland has urban amenities, while at the same time you can take a city bus, get off at the last stop, and be in a forest. Or on a farm. The city's award-winning urban plazas are just a few miles away from the largest forested park in the United States.

This best-of-both-worlds situation isn't just an appreciation of the physical environment but also of the cultural differences between city and country life. The urban values of high-tech connectivity and sleek, simple design are said to meet the rural virtues of community and responsible stewardship of the land. The popular view of Portland's cultural identity seems to dwell somewhere on the frontier where urban and rural not only meet but get along.

You can, for example, raise chickens here. Some cities don't let you do that. In Portland, it's not uncommon to see a "Lost Chicken" sign with a photo of the bird and the cell number or Facebook page of the owner posted on a utility pole.

Of course, the best-of-both-worlds image is just that—an image. There's no free lunch. Except maybe for the coyotes, which is exactly the point. Yes, the rural and the urban meet in Portland, as they do in most cities,

Missing chicken sign, SE Portland, November 2012

but it's seldom a tension-free convening. There are arguments and discussions about issues including the Urban Growth Boundary and the extension of public transportation lines into neighboring towns. Many political issues continue to reveal a strong urban-rural divide. There are also ethical considerations on a wider scale—what are our obligations to other species? What's the best way to live—in a city or in closer contact with the natural world? Can we have both? Coyote sightings seem to be on the rise. Better watch your chickens.

Northeast Portland's Alameda neighborhood has many features that might be attractive to the urban coyote. It's a gorgeous neighborhood with quiet, tree-lined streets and lovely older homes. Alameda Ridge provides a stunning view of Portland and the West Hills. Alameda is a popular and prestigious community with a strong sense of neighborhood pride. Two lovely parks, as well as an elementary school and middle school, are all within walking distance. Along with a classy neighborhood and lovely homes, Alameda offers the cool, funky, and trendy businesses that make

Portland such a fun place to live in. Coffee shops, a brewpub, and some nice residential and commercial areas for strolling can all be found nearby. Alameda is served by TriMet buses, and the MAX light rail is an easy jog away for the young urban coyote.

The coyote sightings shown on this map were collected in about a two-week period in 2010 by second graders at Alameda Elementary in conjunction with Portland State University's Urban Coyote Tracking Project.

One of Portland's urban coyotes, NE Portland, October 2014

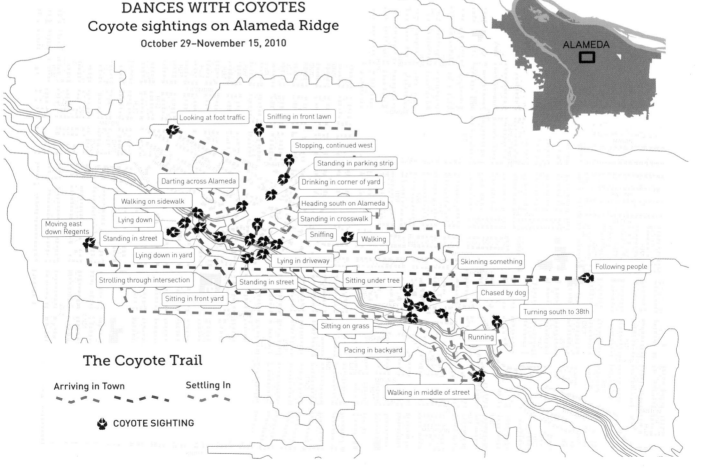

DANCES WITH COYOTES
Coyote sightings on Alameda Ridge
October 29–November 15, 2010

ALAMEDA

Looking at foot traffic

Sniffing in front lawn

Stopping, continued west

Standing in parking strip

Darting across Alameda

Drinking in corner of yard

Walking on sidewalk

Heading south on Alameda

Lying down

Standing in crosswalk

Moving east down Regents

Standing in street

Sniffing

Walking

Lying down in yard

Lying in driveway

Skinning something

Following people

Strolling through intersection

Standing in street

Sitting under tree

Chased by dog

Sitting in front yard

Turning south to 38th

Sitting on grass

Running

Pacing in backyard

Walking in middle of street

The Coyote Trail

Arriving in Town

Settling In

COYOTE SIGHTING

PLIGHT OF THE HONEYBEE

Bees pollinate the majority of fruit and vegetable crops that people depend upon for their food supply. Since 2006, both commercial and backyard beekeepers across the country have witnessed an increase in deaths of their colonies from a mysterious disease termed Colony Collapse Disorder. The adult bees simply never

Average Flight Radius from Hive

2 Miles
1.5
1
0.5

Average Hives per Square Mile

6+ 5 4 3 2 1

Spring 2014

return to their hives, leaving the young bees who care for the queen and brood to die without nutrients and overnight heat generation.

When comparing Portland's honeybee loss numbers to those nationally, local bee enthusiasts realized there's a different urban story itching to be told. The geographical data for these maps were collected as part of the 2014 Portland Urban Beekeepers annual survey, because the growing buzz in the field is locating just how many healthy overwintered hives there are. Also included here is a map of average flight radius to give some indication of the foraging range of bees—most of the city.

The data indicates that the once imagined safe haven for honeybees in urban neighborhoods offering plenty of their preferred nutrition of exotic flora may be an illusion, but why? What is it that keeps the decreasing percentage of urban bees from living through the long, wet winters of Portland?

Fall 2013

Members of the bee community discuss many hypotheses. Explanations include pesticide use, beekeeping practices, and lack of ample forage throughout the seasons. Could it be in part that bees have replaced chickens as the urban homesteading creature of choice? If so, is the loss merely the new beekeepers' learning curve? Out of those surveyed, only four in ten Portland beekeepers have kept bees for more than three years, and less than one in ten

A beekeeper inspects hives

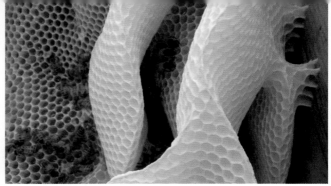

Honeycomb when unattended to by a beekeeper

has over ten years of experience. Or are new beekeepers convenient scapegoats for a large set of problems?

By looking at the participants' years of experience keeping bees, it seems there are definitive pockets of knowledge surrounded by inexperience. There's certainly a lot to be said for pairing the energy of new beekeepers willing to diligently open, inspect, and potentially help a bee colony with the support and assistance of an experienced mentor. If this is just another new trend, then let's hope the bees' resilience endures long after their popularity has faded.

According to this data, winter survival seems to be a larger problem in the urban backyard setting. While nationwide beekeepers have suffered a 23 percent hive loss from 2013 to 2014, the statewide beekeepers' loss was 48 percent. For this same period, Portland backyard beekeepers experienced a 68 percent loss. As the maps illustrate, Portland entered fall with a peak of four to seven hives per square mile, yet came out in spring with a peak of only two to three.

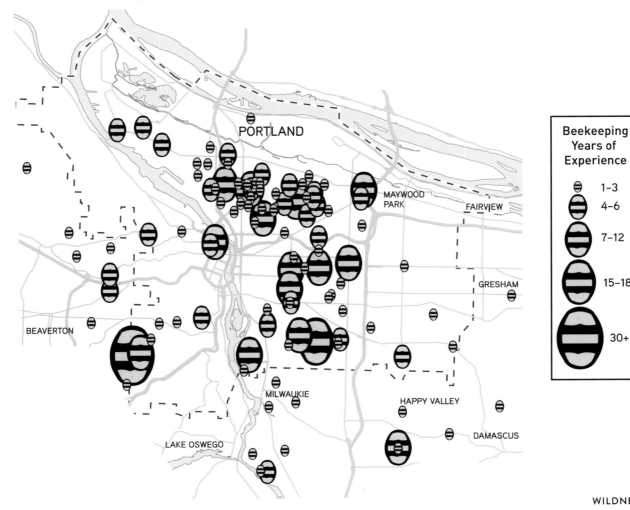

OAKS BOTTOM

THE MAKING OF AN URBAN WILDLIFE RESERVE

SUGGESTED PLAN
FOR THE DEVELOPMENT OF THE
SELLWOOD - OAKS AQUA PARK
& TRANSPORTATION MUSEUM

While Forest Park garners so much attention for being Portland's largest park, it was Oaks Bottom that became the city's first official urban wildlife refuge. The story of how this came about illustrates how direct action from local people can sometimes trump seemingly inevitable city plans. Over time, a network of local individuals can remake places in the city.

At the turn of the nineteenth century, the Bottoms had been cut off from the Willamette River by the railroad fill for the interurban rail line. The City of Portland acquired most of the Bottoms in the late 1950s, naming it Oaks Pioneer Park. In the early 1960s, the south

area become a landfill. The Park Commissioner later lobbied for the site to become a parking lot, which triggered the formation of a coalition of conservation groups, including the Sellwood Moreland Improvement League (SMILE), and soon there was local interest in recognizing the place as a wildlife refuge.

In 1963, The Nature Conservancy put forth the idea that the area should be called Wapato Marsh, although the proposal was dismissed out of hand. Although the city lacked the funds to initiate development plans, the new parks commissioner envisioned establishing museums, a motocross course, and even a gondola

Mural on Portland Mausoleum above Oaks Bottom

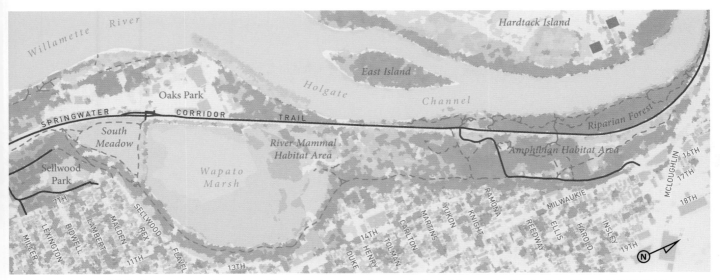

Current extent of Oaks Bottom area—planned road below the lagoon on the map to the left is now a trail indicated with red dashes above

that would transport people into the Bottoms from the adjacent Sellwood neighborhood. Public reaction against those plans was strong, and Oaks Bottom became a defining battleground for the larger issue of city responsibility for retaining wildlife and their habitats in the urban core.

The Bottoms was well underway in its conversion from wetland to buildable upland by the mid-1970s. The stadium (I-405) freeway rubble had been deposited in the north end of the wetlands, forming what became known as the North Fill, and after more recent restoration efforts became the North Meadow. Due primarily to the insistence of community groups, the Park Bureau backed off from their development plans.

"By Any Means Necessary," a credo born of the 1960s, inspired some guerrilla action in the face of the city's refusal to recognize the Bottoms as a wildlife refuge. In that spirit, Mike Houck, currently director of the Urban Greenspaces Institute, and Jimbo Beckmann decided to force the issue in 1985. Houck knew that the Oregon Department of Fish and Wildlife had large yellow signs with "Wildlife Refuge" printed in large impossible to miss black text. He obtained forty signs and cut off any markings that could be traced to the agency. He replaced the identifying information with a handmade stencil reading "City Park" and spray-painted that onto the bottom of the signs.

Houck and Beckmann then took a tall ladder, nails, a hammer, and a fifth of Jim Beam and posted all forty signs around the perimeter of the Bottoms, high enough that no one could remove them. Within a couple weeks, the *Oregonian* began referring to Oaks Bottom

Wildlife Refuge in stories related to the Bottoms. It was only a matter of time until the general public began referring to Oaks Bottom as a wildlife refuge.

By May of 1988, momentum had shifted entirely from a development-oriented future to a preservation and restoration mode, a management plan was adopted, and restoration work began. Next came installation of a weir, designed to manage water levels to control mosquitoes, manage vegetation, and provide habitat for migratory shorebirds and waterfowl.

In 1991, Mark Bennett painted a seventy-foot-high and fifty-foot-wide great blue heron mural on the Portland Memorial Mausoleum. In 2009 Bennett and his son Shane collaborated with others to expand the mural to cover eight west- and south-facing walls on the mausoleum. At 55,000 square feet, it's the largest hand-painted mural on a building in North America.

In the mid-1990s and into the early 2000s, significant budget increases then allowed the bureau to transform what had been an all-volunteer, community-led effort in the mid to late 1980s to a much more effective professional management team, which developed strategies for future restoration efforts at the refuge.

In 2004 the City Nature Division was created to combine management of the city's natural areas, forestry program, and environmental education under a unified natural area program, thereby elevating the importance of the city's natural areas portfolio—which accounted for more than 75 percent of the city's park land—to an equal status with recreational facilities.

RODENTS OF UNUSUAL SIZE
THE NUTRIA

The nutria, *Myocastor coypus*, is a large, semiaquatic, herbivorous rodent indigenous to South America. Smaller than a beaver and larger than a muskrat, nutria live in burrows on lakeshores, riverbanks, or wetlands. Entrepreneurs imported nutria to Oregon to be bred for fur production, but the promised riches for nutria ranches never materialized. Escaped and released animals established wild populations that continue to thrive today.

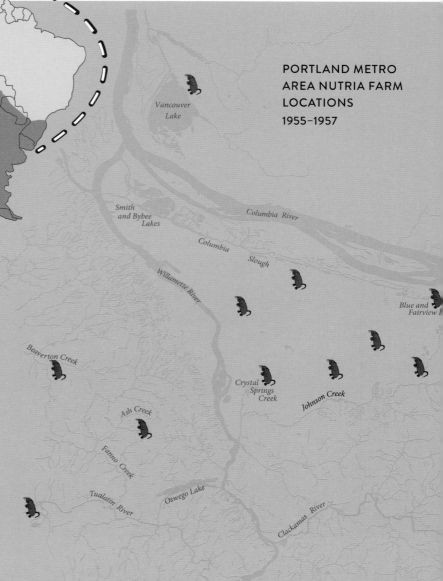

On August 10, 1931, ten pairs of nutria arrived in Portland on a steamer ship from Uruguay. They were imported by La Pine Fur Traders, Inc., one of the largest fur companies in the state, and taken to the company's facilities near Coos Bay on the Oregon coast. In 1943, the *Oregonian* reported that a number of the animals had escaped and made their way into the Willamette. By 1950, feral populations seem to have been well established in western Oregon. Despite their plentiful presence in the wild, in the mid-1950s nutria breeding and farming experienced a sudden boom in the Portland metro area. Following a promotional exhibit in 1954, it was reported that about fifty Oregon fur farmers bought breeding animals. The price for a pair was as much as one thousand dollars at the height of the craze. Their spread through the metro area seems to have been driven largely by one farm in southeast Portland, Purebred Registered Nutria of America, which placed ads in the classifieds every single day in 1955 selling pairs of "purebred" nutria. Advertisements claimed pelts would sell for forty dollars, while reports in the *Oregonian* at the same time reveal they were going for closer to seven dollars per pelt.

PORTLAND METRO AREA NUTRIA FARM LOCATIONS 1955–1957

Vancouver Lake

Smith and Bybee Lakes

Columbia River

Columbia Slough

Willamette River

Blue and Fairview L

Beaverton Creek

Crystal Springs Creek

Johnson Creek

Ash Creek

Fanno Creek

Tualatin River

Oswego Lake

Clackamas River

Beaver Creek

NUTRIA RUN WILD

Many fur entrepreneurs failed to find buyers for their breeding stock and released them into local waterways. As a result, research suggests that Oregon's freshwater marshes have the highest density of nutria in the world today. They feed on native plants and agricultural crops, and contribute to erosion damage by burrowing into stream banks and pastures. They can also carry and transmit parasites and diseases. As of this date, there's no coordinated nutria management plan in the Pacific Northwest.

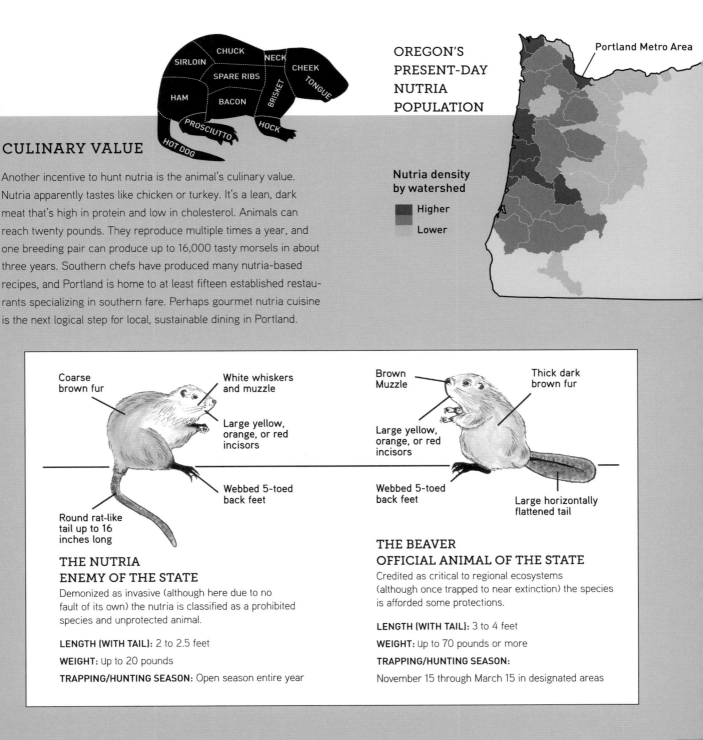

CHUCK
NECK
SIRLOIN
CHEEK
SPARE RIBS
TONGUE
HAM
BACON
BRISKET
PROSCIUTTO
HOCK
HOT DOG

OREGON'S PRESENT-DAY NUTRIA POPULATION

Portland Metro Area

Nutria density by watershed

■ Higher
■ Lower

CULINARY VALUE

Another incentive to hunt nutria is the animal's culinary value. Nutria apparently tastes like chicken or turkey. It's a lean, dark meat that's high in protein and low in cholesterol. Animals can reach twenty pounds. They reproduce multiple times a year, and one breeding pair can produce up to 16,000 tasty morsels in about three years. Southern chefs have produced many nutria-based recipes, and Portland is home to at least fifteen established restaurants specializing in southern fare. Perhaps gourmet nutria cuisine is the next logical step for local, sustainable dining in Portland.

Coarse brown fur

White whiskers and muzzle

Large yellow, orange, or red incisors

Webbed 5-toed back feet

Round rat-like tail up to 16 inches long

Brown Muzzle

Thick dark brown fur

Large yellow, orange, or red incisors

Webbed 5-toed back feet

Large horizontally flattened tail

THE NUTRIA
ENEMY OF THE STATE

Demonized as invasive (although here due to no fault of its own) the nutria is classified as a prohibited species and unprotected animal.

LENGTH (WITH TAIL): 2 to 2.5 feet

WEIGHT: Up to 20 pounds

TRAPPING/HUNTING SEASON: Open season entire year

THE BEAVER
OFFICIAL ANIMAL OF THE STATE

Credited as critical to regional ecosystems (although once trapped to near extinction) the species is afforded some protections.

LENGTH (WITH TAIL): 3 to 4 feet

WEIGHT: Up to 70 pounds or more

TRAPPING/HUNTING SEASON:
November 15 through March 15 in designated areas

HETEROTOPIA: THE COLUMBIA SLOUGH

The nineteen-mile-long collection of brackish freshwater channels and wetlands sitting along Portland's northern edge known as the Columbia Slough has been pivotal in the ongoing effort to define Portland's identity.

At the turn of the twentieth century, planners saw the Columbia Slough as an essential component in developing a far-reaching network of parks. That vision is at odds with the grim reality that later developed. Industrial development in the slough brought economic growth to the city but that came with horrendous environmental and social costs. Yet today the Columbia Slough, like Portland itself, is neither Verdant Utopia nor Industrial Dystopia but rather an inextricably intertwined heterotopia.

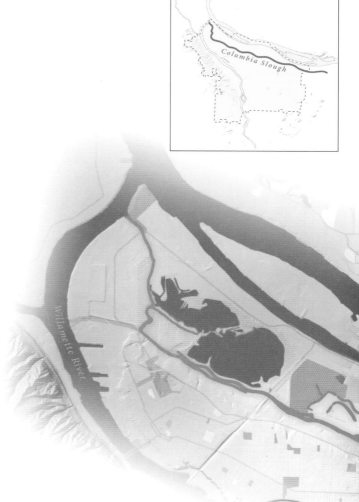

UTOPIA

Coined by sixteenth-century humanist philosopher Thomas More, *utopia* described an imaginary island that was simultaneously goodplace (eu-topia) and no-place (ou-topia).

A 1903 report for the City of Portland Park Board written by John C. Olmsted identified the importance and promise of the area, "The remaining great landscape feature of the city is that of the Columbia Sloughs which border the eastern part of the city on the north. . . . It is therefore to be hoped that a much larger park of the meadow type than can elsewhere be afforded will gradually be acquired here by the city. . . . While there are many things, both small and great, which may contribute to the beauty of a great city, unquestionably one of the greatest is a comprehensive system of parks and parkways."

Olmsted's report represents a codification of the city's most durable utopic vision. The plan anticipated the creation of present-day parks such as the Park Blocks, Mount Tabor, and Forest Park, as well as many of the other parks that are beacons of Portland's green image. The final, and to this day unrealized, recommendation was for the establishment of a Columbia Slough Park.

Today, the Intertwine Alliance embodies the essence of the Olmsted plan. A regional multientity coalition dedicated to "ensuring the vision for the world's greatest parks, trails, and natural areas system for the Portland-Vancouver metropolitan region," the Alliance continues to build on utopian ideals.

DYSTOPIA

The other side of the visionary coin, *dystopia* represents a counter utopian society or the fatal flaw in an otherwise idealized utopia. From the Portland Housing Authority's distress at the "negro problem" following the Vanport flood in 1948 to the city's use of the slough as an extension of its sewer system, the landscape lying between Columbia Boulevard and the Columbia River is the dystopian reflection of Portland's progressive and environmentally conscientious image.

Ellen Stroud, in her study, "Troubled Waters in Ecotopia: Environmental racism in Portland, Oregon," describes the history of environmental and racial abuses coincident with the Columbia Slough: "As late as 1970, Pacific Meat [Company] was dumping

150,000 gallons of blood and animal particles directly into the slough every day. Incredibly, the Oregon Department of Environmental Quality had given the company a permit to do just that."

Over the years, studies commissioned by agencies such as the Oregon Department of Environmental Quality and Portland's Bureau of Environmental Services have detailed the accumulation of toxic materials in the slough's sediment, as well as in the fish that are caught there to this day.

HETEROTOPIA

For philosopher Michel Foucault, *heterotopia* (other-place) is a space outside the orderings of society, which nevertheless reflects all existing social spaces. Heterotopia mirrors the spaces around it, juxtaposing utopian and dystopian relationships and exposing the messy realities that undergird space and place.

Ultimately, no place is reducible to a philosophical label; all places perpetually change. So, the Columbia Slough is a space born from utopian dreams and dystopian nightmares of human society, where "natural" restoration and preservation efforts clash with the industrial and economic engines powering much of our existence. This is also an important place in the daily lives of many people and animals. This place is rain and gravity, algae and soil, Army Corps of Engineers pump stations and asphalt, and turtles, snakes, and raccoons.

Various spaces along the Slough mirror Portland's changing priorities. Places like Cully Park, a onetime quarry and industrial landfill, represent multiethnic, community-driven metamorphosis away from a landscape dominated by industry.

The Slough is Portland's heterotopic reflection, but it's also just a slough, a continuously changing heterotopia that's never quite what we expect. And tomorrow it will be something different.

UTOPIA   DYSTOPIA   HETEROTOPIA

IV.   VIEWS OF THE CITY

Senses are key to the way we experience cities and places within them. The sense most people rely the most heavily on is vision. Yet when we navigate cities, we unconsciously engage all of our senses, which catalyze feelings and emotions within us. The sounds, smells, tastes, and textures of a place play powerful roles in how people relate to that place. The act of remembering places is rooted in the senses as well. For instance, a smell—burning wood, cotton candy, freshly cut grass—can sometimes instantly trigger the actual feeling of being in a particular place at a particular time. There's a strain of geography called psychogeography that examines what places feel like, something we experience all the time but rarely talk about.

One of the reasons there's little talk about how we experience places is that sensory experience isn't easy to describe or quantify. Experiences are laden with emotions, feelings, and ideas that are difficult to represent and thus tricky to map. Furthermore, everyone experiences the city differently, so what resonates with one person about a particular park, street, or neighborhood might not compel others. Differences in how people see places can lead to conflicts about how places should look, how they should be used, and whom they should serve.

Most people engage with small parts of the city. Home, work, and recreation might overlap or they might not, but most people don't know the entire city. And yet it's easy for our own experiences to define the entire city. A closer look at places we might pass through occasionally reveals just how different the city is from place to place. The better we understand how other people connect to places, the better chance we have of making places that accommodate the needs and desires of many different people. To that end, this chapter examines the city from perspectives that aren't often represented or heard in struggles over what the city looks like or how it operates.

IMAGINED POPULATION DENSITIES

There's a lot of buzz about dense development in Portland. The Urban Growth Boundary and Metro's development goals encourage it. Academic studies laud it. However, by the standards of much of the world and even the United States, Portland isn't a very dense city. Of course, population density varies across the city. While the densest parts of Portland approach New York City and the least dense are closer to Salt Lake City, nowhere in Portland comes close to the 115,200 people per square mile of the world's densest city, Dhaka, Pakistan. This map shows the actual population density across the city of Portland and its suburbs.

POPULATION DENSITY OF PORTLAND
One Dot = 20 People

PORTLAND POPULATION: 609,456
PORTLAND LAND AREA IN SQUARE MILES: 133.43
PORTLAND PEOPLE PER SQUARE MILE: 4,375

PORTLAND METRO AREA POPULATION: 2,314,554
PORTLAND METRO LAND AREA IN SQUARE MILES: 467.38
PORTLAND METRO AREA PEOPLE PER SQUARE MILE: 4,956

OREGON POPULATION: 3,930,065
OREGON LAND AREA IN SQUARE MILES: 95,988
OREGON PEOPLE PER SQUARE MILE: 40

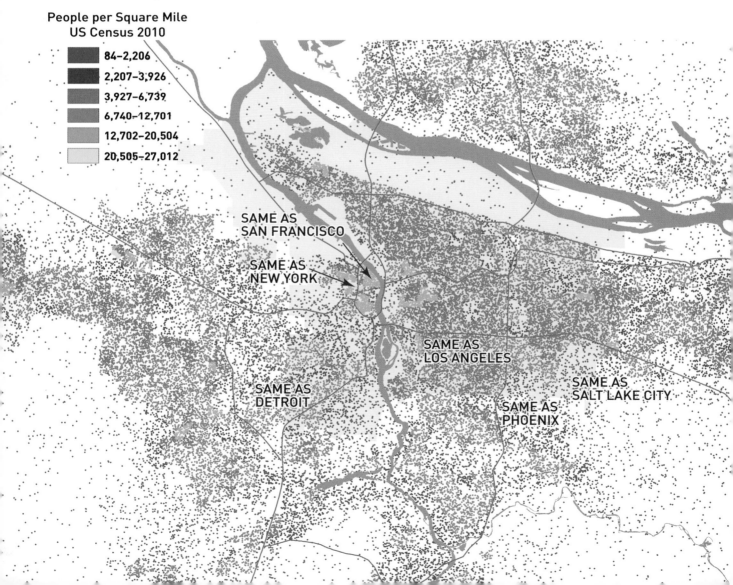

People per Square Mile
US Census 2010

- 84–2,206
- 2,207–3,926
- 3,927–6,739
- 6,740–12,701
- 12,702–20,504
- 20,505–27,012

SAME AS SAN FRANCISCO

SAME AS NEW YORK

SAME AS LOS ANGELES

SAME AS DETROIT

SAME AS PHOENIX

SAME AS SALT LAKE CITY

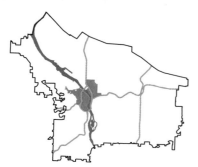

Dhaka, Pakistan

If Portland's population were as dense as the densest city in the world, Dhaka, Pakistan, all of our city's current residents could live within downtown, inner North Portland, and the Inner Westside—an area of about five square miles.

Mumbai, India

At the population density of Mumbai, India, we would have to expand into part of inner Southeast Portland for a total of seven square miles, or about 5 percent of Portland's actual area.

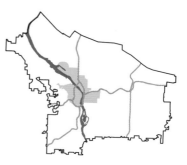

Bogota, Colombia

The densest city in the Americas is Bogota, Colombia. If we added the Overlook neighborhood in North Portland, we could all live at Bogota's estimated population density of 56,300 people per square mile.

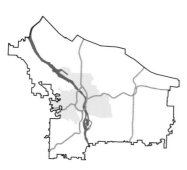

New York City, New York

The most densely populated city in the United States is New York City, at 27,000 people per square mile. We would live within twenty-one square miles of inner Portland if we had the same population density.

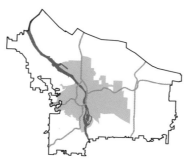

San Francisco, California

San Francisco is the most densely populated city on the West Coast. If Portland was composed of just downtown and its inner ring of neighborhoods, all the city's residents could live at a density of 17,000 people per square mile.

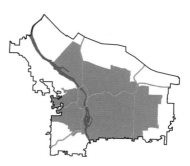

Los Angeles, California

Los Angeles is known for its sprawl, but the city is significantly more densely populated than Portland. At 54 percent of Portland's actual area, we would be as dense as LA.

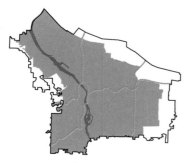

Detroit, Michigan

Detroit has gained a reputation for empty lots, abandoned houses, and a deserted urban center. Yet it has a slightly higher population density than Portland at 5,144 people per square mile.

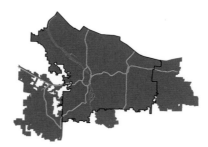

Phoenix, Arizona

Most US cities west of the Mississippi are not densely populated. To reach the lower population density of Phoenix at 2,798 people per square mile, some of Portland's residents would have to displace the residents of Gresham, Milwaukie, and Beaverton.

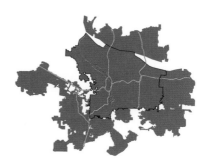

Salt Lake City, Utah

One of the country's least dense cities is Salt Lake City. Portland's current population would have to be spread out over most of the metro area, including Vancouver, to equal Salt Lake City's density of 1,678 people per square mile.

ISLANDS OF DIVERSITY

The Portland metropolitan area population is approximately 76 percent white (down from 90 percent white in 1990), making it one of the most homogeneous in the country. According to 2010 census data, of the top twenty-five largest metropolitan areas, only Pittsburgh and Minneapolis (in that order) have whiter metro areas. Of the fifty largest cities in the country, Portland itself ranks as the sixth whitest. The area shown on the map is inside the Urban Growth Boundary, rather than the metropolitan area, and is approximately 72 percent white.

Racial diversity does exist, just not quite where one might expect. Communities that contain a greater mix of races form "islands," which are located in the peripheral neighborhoods of Portland and in the east and west suburbs. The deeper sections of the less diverse "ocean" are generally located in the central-city core and the well-to-do suburbs along the Willamette River. This pattern of racial diversity is an inverted version of what one sees in the large cities in the East.

In the past fifteen years, most central Portland neighborhoods have seen a rise in the percentage of white residents. Many African American neighborhoods in North and Northeast Portland have gentrified and seen a dramatic increase in the number of white residents.

By block group, the highest percentage of African Americans in the city of Portland is 38 percent in Humboldt, the highest percentage of Hispanic Americans is 41 percent in Cully, and the highest percentage of Asian Americans is 28 percent in Powellhurst-Gilbert.

Of the twenty-two block groups with a white population of 90 percent or more, three are on Alameda Ridge, three are in Sellwood, two are in Eastmoreland, one is in Laurelhurst, and the remaining thirteen are in the West Hills. Within the city, the area west of the Willamette River is 83 percent white. The area east of Eighty-Second Avenue is 62 percent white.

More Diversity

Less Diversity

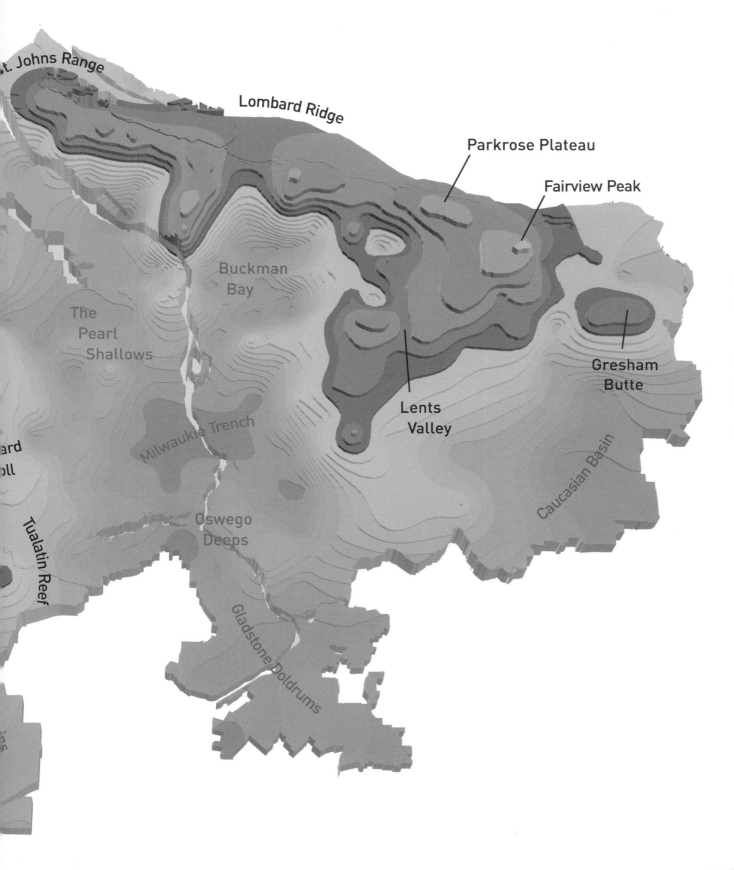

St. Johns Range

Lombard Ridge

Parkrose Plateau

Fairview Peak

Buckman Bay

The Pearl Shallows

Lents Valley

Gresham Butte

Milwaukie Trench

Caucasian Basin

Tualatin Reef

Oswego Deeps

Gladstone Doldrums

PSYCHOGEOGRAPHY

Psychogeography. It sounds like a twist on an Alfred Hitchcock film, but it's actually a recognized field of study that draws from geography and psychology. The approach focuses on how human senses and emotions relate to places and environments, typically in urban areas. In 1955, Guy Debord defined it as "the study of the precise laws and specific effects of the geographical environment, consciously organized or not, on the emotions and behavior of individuals." Esoteric in nature, psychogeography is meant to inspire your senses and draw you into places that are off the paths people usually travel.

The Situationists, an organization of intellectuals and artists in 1950s Paris, believed that cities have a psycho-spatial relief that forces people in some directions and deters them from others. The study of psychogeography forces people to pay closer attention to the finer details of a city, including smells, sounds, feelings, and recognition of things that are no longer there. Walking through a city to stumble upon unique experiences is the true nature of the discipline—in practice, this is called the dérive (drift). For a dérive, one ambles aimlessly through a place aware of how different places attract or repel. The maps on the next several pages were created in this vein—through purposeful wandering.

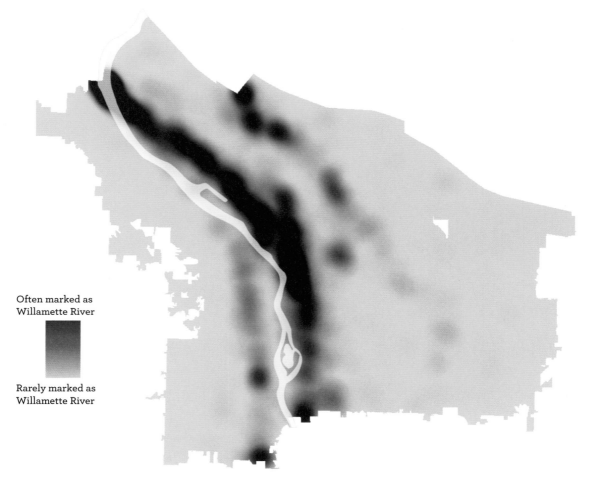

Often marked as
Willamette River

Rarely marked as
Willamette River

Composite of students' mental maps of the Willamette River

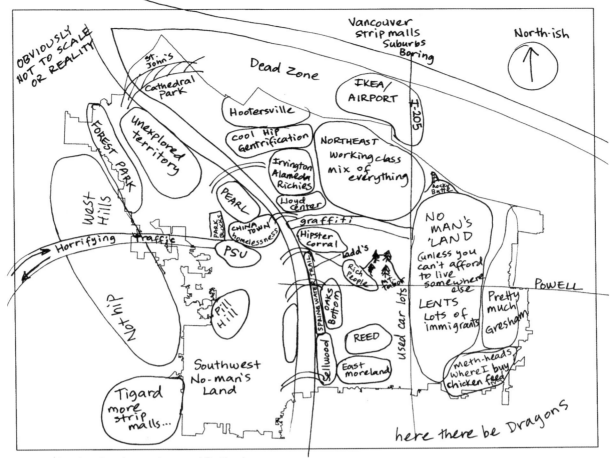

Composite of students' mental maps of Portland

What's a Mental Map?

A mental map, sometimes called a cognitive map, is a representation of how an individual sees and understands places and the connections between them. It's a tangible form of someone's geographic imagination. Mental maps may reveal the locations a person thinks is important, the routes a person often uses to move about the city, the places the person avoids, and attitudes toward different neighborhoods. Often what's missing from a mental map is as telling as what is included. Mental maps and psychogeography both privilege individual experience, cognition, and perception.

In geography, mental mapping is sometimes used as a methodology for research and a tool for teaching. The mental map of Portland shown above is a composite map that takes elements from individual mental maps created by students in a Maps and Society class at Portland State University. The other map depicts the actual location of the Willamette River compared with a composite of where students in the Maps and Society classes placed the river in

their own mental maps of Portland. Note that with the exception of a few phantom tributaries, the students as a group were remarkably accurate in placing the river. This is all the more impressive considering they were given no reference points other than the outline of the city.

Pyschogeography and mental maps figure prominently in the next eight pages of the book—Street Emotion, Sounds of the City, City of Noses, and Third Graders Illustrate the City. Each of these topics highlights the important role of perception and the senses in how people experience and understand places.

STREET EMOTION
DOWNTOWN

As an exercise in pyschogeography, three Portland Community College students mapped their emotions on a sunny spring Saturday at three different times of day. To more fully absorb the emotional impact that people can have just walking around a city, the students conducted a variation of a dérive.

This is a mental map of their experiences, a spatial record of their emotional journeys. It displays the three times of day the students visited (morning, afternoon, and evening), as well as an average of all three. A selection of observations that influenced emotional states of being is highlighted.

Several common themes emerged. The waterfront park blocks were the most pleasant. There was a stark contrast between the east and west side of the river—the east side is more industrial and therefore felt cold and isolated. Most noises (sirens, people yelling, buses, honking, and cursing) and smells (urine, old beer, throw up, and garbage) were generally negative.

Time of day was a major factor influencing emotion. The morning was calm as the day was getting started. The few encounters with people were mostly pleasant. The sounds of children chasing Canadian geese on the waterfront park were comforting.

High energy, from tourists and locals alike, characterized the afternoon. The park was filled with runners, bikers, sightseers, and sunbathers. Unpleasant feelings stemmed from foot and vehicle traffic, as well as the pain felt for the people living on the streets in obvious agony.

The evening was met with stress and anxiety. The students were deterred at one point on the west side due to a crime scene that police were investigating, and the dreariness of some areas around Burnside became suddenly more apparent. On the east side, the students encountered a homeless "village" under the I-84 and I-5 overpass, which brought on feelings of sadness.

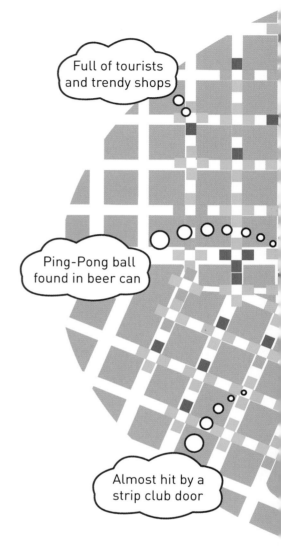

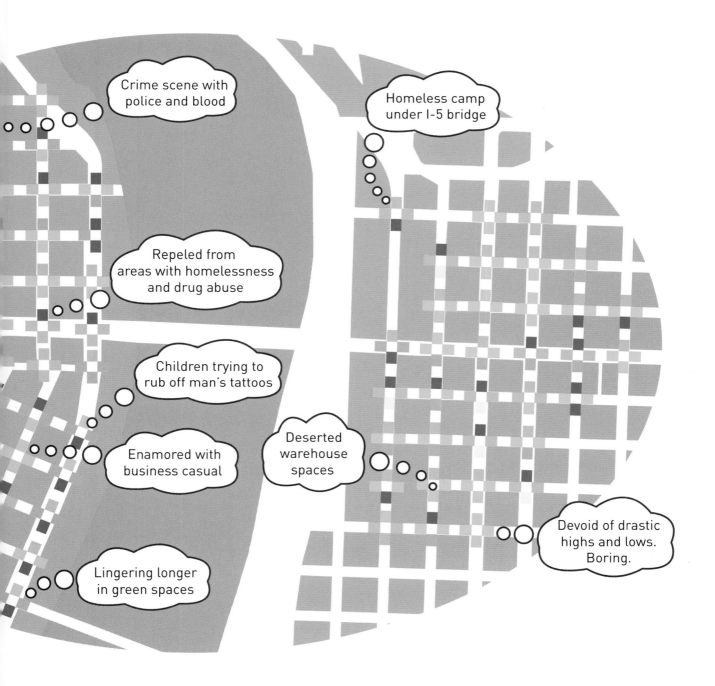

What We Felt . . .

Eew! Meh... OK Pleasant Giddy

. . . And When.

Daily Composite | Morning | Early Afternoon | Late Afternoon

SOUNDS OF THE CITY

The city pops, clangs, whines, and sputters all around us. These sounds coalesce into a homogeneous din that's easy to ignore. In this map, we took a walk in the city, listening closely, in an attempt to break apart the blended noise—to rehear the sounds of the city.

A sound walk is a different way of experiencing the city. So often we default to our vision for observing and evaluating places. Many of us move through the city with earbuds or headphones that provide our own personal soundtrack to life but divorce us from fuller sensory experiences of place.

When we take the time to disconnect from iPods and phones, we encounter an audible world—one that becomes hard to disregard once you start paying attention to it. You can shut your eyes, but shutting your ears (without the help of earphones) is nearly impossible.

This map is a sound bite of Portland, Oregon, from busy West Burnside to the (relative) quiet of Washington Park—an auditory snapshot of Portland in winter at dusk.

A car whooshes by.

Fresh rain drains in the gutter.

Squeaking and clanging intermittently, cars whoosh by in both directions.

BURNSIDE

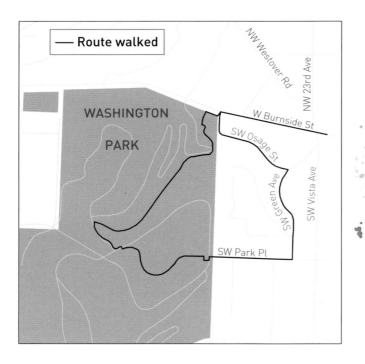

— Route walked

NW Westover Rd

NW 23rd Ave

WASHINGTON PARK

W Burnside St

SW Osage St

SW Green Ave

SW Vista Ave

SW Park Pl

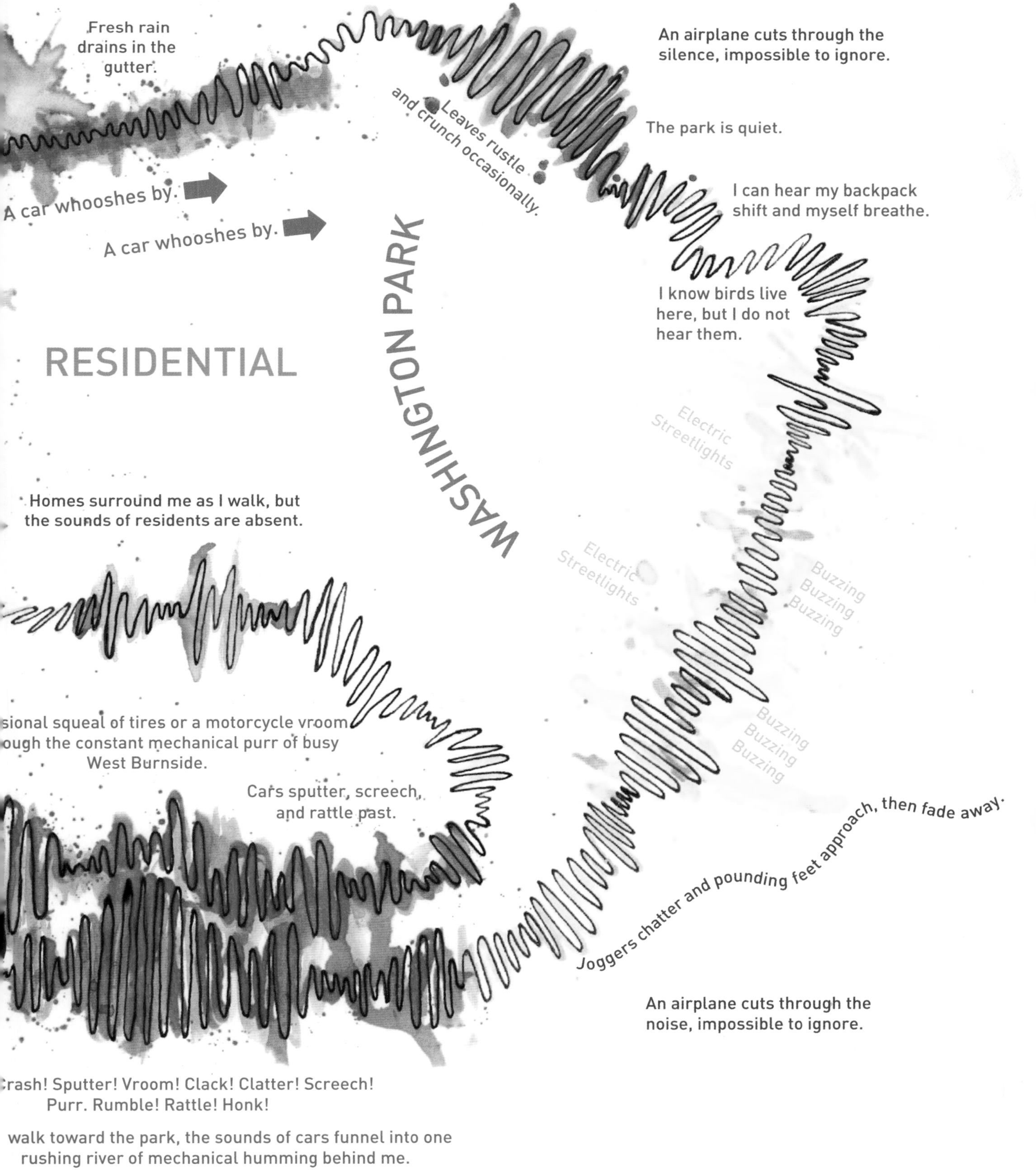

Fresh rain drains in the gutter.

Leaves rustle and crunch occasionally.

An airplane cuts through the silence, impossible to ignore.

The park is quiet.

A car whooshes by. →

A car whooshes by. →

I can hear my backpack shift and myself breathe.

I know birds live here, but I do not hear them.

RESIDENTIAL

WASHINGTON PARK

Electric Streetlights

Electric Streetlights

Buzzing
Buzzing
Buzzing

Homes surround me as I walk, but the sounds of residents are absent.

Buzzing
Buzzing
Buzzing

...sional squeal of tires or a motorcycle vroom ...ough the constant mechanical purr of busy West Burnside.

Cars sputter, screech, and rattle past.

Joggers chatter and pounding feet approach, then fade away.

An airplane cuts through the noise, impossible to ignore.

...rash! Sputter! Vroom! Clack! Clatter! Screech! Purr. Rumble! Rattle! Honk!

...walk toward the park, the sounds of cars funnel into one rushing river of mechanical humming behind me.

CITY OF NOSES

The original definition of London's Cockney population was anyone born within hearing distance of the bells of St. Mary-le-Bow Church. What if Portland's neighborhoods were defined by the sensory experience of living in them, like the things you can hear or smell? Most strong smells around Portland originate from particular types of pungent businesses, such as coffee roasters, breweries, bakeries, or (less pleasantly) heavy chemical industries or roof tarring. These smell districts are formed around odors collected from observation and from complaints to the Department of Environmental Quality.

One can't necessarily smell the local odor in every part of the district or at all times. Also, people perceive smells differently. The boundaries suggest which scent is usually dominant. The more time you spend walking around a place, the more attuned you become to the smells and the smaller these odor districts become.

Tulip Pastry
Heights

Soggy Bottoms

Willamette
Superfund
Toxic Corridor

Daimler Trucks
Downwind District

Metro Dump
District

Esco Foundry Flats

Grand
Bread

The Fragrant Forest

Nuvrei P
Distri

Oregor
Printi
Pres

International
Rose Test
Garden

Packy Dookie

The Smell of Money Hil

Slough Belt

Camas Paper
Mill Cloud

larkey
hingle
facturing
Mile

Nabisco
Cookie Zone

Boeing Aircraft
Paint Plains

Wood Waste
Mulch Meadows

Alberta Park
Tree Town

Peninsula
Rose Park

Alberta Coffee
Mile

The Mash Tun
Beer District

Cully Built-on-a-Landfill Park

Popeyes
Fried Chicken
District

Widmer
Brewery
Bottoms

Mystery
Plastic Zone

Broadway
Cigar Neighborhood

Crematorium
Corners

port
Blocks

Franz
Bread
Barrio

Voodoo
Too District

I-84 Highway
Fumes Corridor

82nd
Avenue
Greasy
Food
Strip

's Bread
Town

Voodoo
Doughnut
Town

Tazo
Tea

Portland
national
d Zone

Portland
Bottling
Soda

Perfume
House
Hollow

Greater
Trumps
Cigar Cove

Mt. Tabor
Evergreen
Zone

Distillery Row
Mash Mile

Patchouli

Little T's Bakery

Stumptown Coffee
Neighborhood

Freeway
Convergence
Diesel Downs

Chinese
Food
Corner

An Xuyen Bakery

Recology
Compost District

Train Yard
Creosote

THIRD GRADERS ILLUSTRATE THE CITY

This map is a compilation of fifty-seven individual hand-drawn mental maps of Portland, created by the third-grade students of Jason Lee K–8 School in Northeast Portland. To begin this project, the students viewed different maps of Portland and then brainstormed places they felt were important to include on their own maps. They were instructed to include at least five points of interest but were free to include any places, streets, and details that reflected their own perception of the city. Creating mostly from intuition, each student made an illustrated map in Sharpie and watercolor pencil.

The authors of this atlas often give adults similar exercises and find that many native Portlanders are often paralyzed and unable to write anything on the map at all, afraid to misrepresent their place. These kids, the only people the authors could find willing to illustrate a map of Portland, did not have that fear.

This map includes a redrawn portion of every student's map. Each illustration has been placed where the student originally drew it on his or her map, and the original colors employed by the student have been matched as closely as possible. However, the scale of many of the students' drawings has been altered. The student work was redrawn by Jason Lee art teacher Nicole Penoncello.

Jason Lee K–8 School is located in the Madison South neighborhood, just east of Eighty-Second Avenue. It's a part of the Portland Public School district and serves over 400 students.

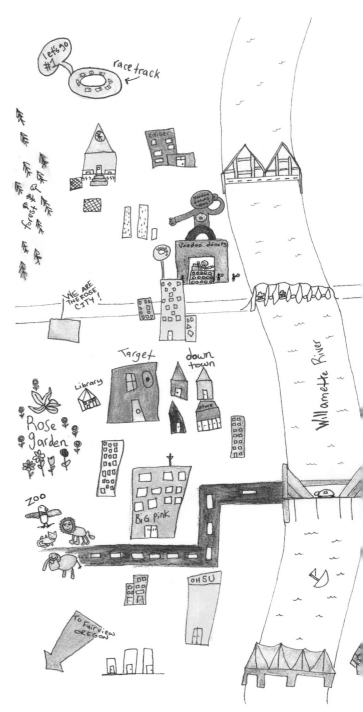

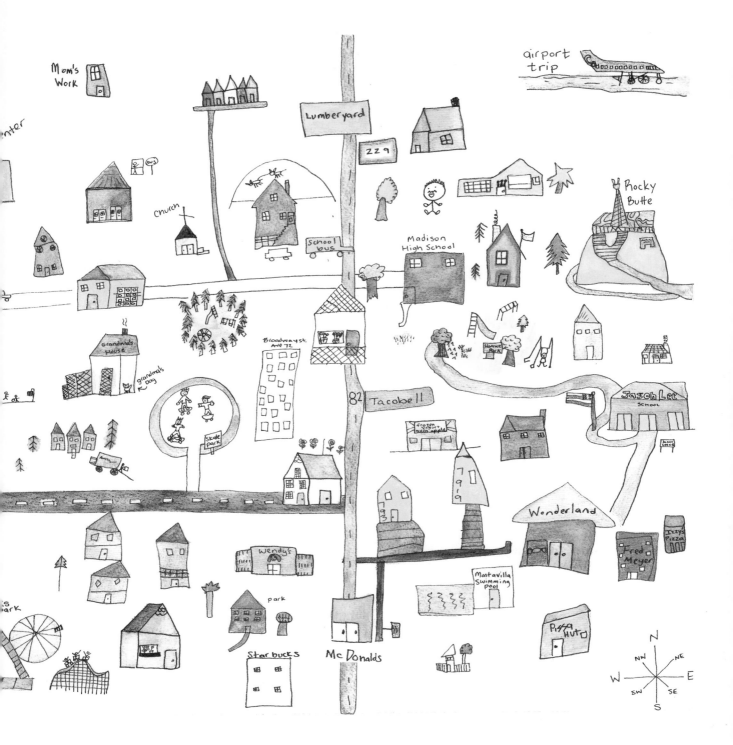

TALES FROM OUTSIDE THE DOUGHNUT HOLE

Some of Portland's neighborhoods seem to get all the attention. On the west side it's the Pearl, Downtown, and NW Twenty-Third. On the east side it's many close-in Southeast and Northeast neighborhoods and a couple in North Portland. What to even call the neighborhoods seems to be in flux. Traditional neighborhoods as delineated by the city are still used by many—Buckman, Sellwood, Tabor. But increasingly, the traditional designations seem to be disregarded in favor of referring to neighborhoods by the dominant commercial arterial—Mississippi, Alberta, Burnside, Belmont, Hawthorne, Division.

Whatever they're called, these somewhat central neighborhoods on either side of the Willamette seem to dominate many popular imaginations of the city as a whole. Yet for many who live in Portland, this so-called core is largely absent from their daily lives. The parts of the city that might seem peripheral from the perspective of downtown or Laurelhurst are the very centers of life for many people. In this section, we profile some of the neighborhoods that are often absent from the limelight that seems to bathe the middle of the city.

About This Doughnut

One of the lead cartographers of this atlas has friends at the legendary Voodoo Doughnut. She told them we were making an atlas of the city and they made us this Portland-shaped doughnut. It's composed of enough dough and pink glaze to make a dozen regular doughnuts. After this image was taken, the doughnut was eaten at the Lucky Labrador Brew Pub on Hawthorne (which normally prefers no outside food).

The doughnut is a perfect metaphor for our focus in this section. Where doughnuts are concerned, all the substance is in the ring around the center, which is in fact empty, a void.

To PDX Airport

PDC Airport Way
Urban Renewal Area

Union Pacific Railroad   Columbia Blvd

Colwood
National
Golf
Course

NE 42nd Ave

Cully Blvd

NE 82nd Ave

NE 42nd Ave
NPI Area

Cully Blvd
NPI Area

**Community Advocates
and Businesses**

Hacienda CDC
Investment

NAYA

Verde
Investment

Columbia Biogas
Renewable Energy

**Urban Agriculture
Sites**

Urban Farm

Community Garden
or Garden Collective

Teaching Farm

Block with
Urban Farm(s)

**Zoning and
Land Use**

Industrial

Commercial

Parks and
Open Space

CULLY

Cully has always existed on both the geographic periphery of Portland and on the edge of the city's conscience. Bifurcated by Columbia Boulevard and the railroad, Cully's industrial north and residential south have long been reputed for boasting Portland's largest collection of unimproved streets, a scarcity of sidewalks, and a surplus of crime. Annexed by the city in 1985, Cully is home to some 14,000 people in approximately three square miles. Parts of the neighborhood lack fundamental amenities; many streets are unpaved and lack effective street lighting. Only 34 percent of the streets have sidewalks.

However, Cully is emerging from the historical neglect; it's now being recognized for its cultural and ethnic diversity and as a vestige of affordability west of Eighty-Second Avenue. There's a cautious optimism for the city's Neighborhood Prosperity Initiatives (NPI) targeting Cully Boulevard and Northeast Forty-Second Avenue. Affordable housing advocates representing the Native American (NAYA) and Latino (Hacienda CDC & Verde) communities as well as several grassroots urban farmers, all anchored in Cully, also have a vested interested in the neighborhood's future. Just west of Cully is Alberta Street, often considered a cautionary

example of city-sponsored urban renewal. Alberta's reduction in crime and economic revitalization is obvious, but so is the accompanying gentrification and tensions related to it. For this reason, in 2013 the Living Cully Ecodistrict, a partnership of Hacienda, NAYA, and Verde, worked with students from PSU's Urban and Regional Planning program to develop a set of antidisplacement strategies for the neighborhood.

Cully's urban farmers are changing the landscape of the neighborhood and promoting another identity: the Cully Garden District. Big but affordable lots have been the catalyst for this in Cully. These Portlanders have established a number of working farms, community gardens, CSAs, and businesses that extoll the urban homestead ethic and farm-to-table food movement for which Portland is widely known.

The question is: Will the NPIs complement these grassroots efforts to establish Cully as a diverse and vital area of the city, or will the current residents be further marginalized and forced to the new periphery of the city as economic refugees of the neighborhood's success?

FOSTER-POWELL

Foster-Powell, or "FoPo," is bounded by Foster Road, Powell Boulevard, and Eighty-Second Avenue and traces its beginnings to the early 1890s. It wasn't until the early 1900s that the area then known as the Kern Park streetcar subdivision connected with the eastward-expanding city of Portland.

Today, FoPo seems to be both on the verge of hipster cool and box-store bland. The neighborhood is collectively charting a path . . . but to what? The answer, for now, is captured in the micro-cosm of food choices at the intersection of Southeast Fifty-Second Avenue and Southeast Foster Road, where your appetite could lead you either to the thirteen food carts at the Carts on Foster pod, or the Subway, Little Caesars, Burger King, and Taco Bell all to the west of the intersection.

It's a place that has more overgrown lawns than manicured flower gardens and more unspectacular strip malls than funky artisan bou-tiques, and yet some areas of Foster-Powell seem to be carved out of trendy inner Southeast. Of the old buildings along the commercial districts on Foster between Fifty-Second Avenue and Sixty-Seventh Avenue, about half have been converted to foodie eateries and bars, while the other half house older businesses—gun shops and auto parts stores with sun-faded lettering and outside walls with count-less layers of graffiti covered by poorly color-matched bucket paint.

The neighborhood's diversity extends beyond its built environment. Foster-Powell's relative affordability, combined with its proximity to the inner Southeast and downtown areas of Portland, has made it attractive to immigrant communities as well as young families and postcollege singles. Prominent ethnicities in the area are Russian, Vietnamese, and Chinese. The Portland Mercado, a highly anticipated Latino-themed economic development project, will

open in 2015 on Foster. The area is well served by TriMet bus lines, and both streetcar and light-rail lines down Foster and Powell have been proposed.

Like many neighborhoods in Portland, FoPo bears the traces of a place in transition. There's plenty of old, a little new, and a lot of in-between. For now, however, it still has the feel of a hungry bystander deciding between food carts and fast food.

MULTNOMAH VILLAGE

Multnomah Village is typically described as quaint, comfortable, family friendly, and safe. It's like Portland's grandparents—predictable and historical. To the people who live there, it's as close in to the center of the city as it gets. To those who don't, it's a suburb somewhere between Beaverton and Tigard. The neighborhood has suburban appeal, yet allows one to keep a Portland address.

What it doesn't have is any edginess. When people put out their yellow bins full of beer bottles, soda cans, and plastic water bottles, they actually get picked up by Waste Management. When an unknown person spends too much time in one place, multiple residents call the police to report suspicious activity. When you spot a crowd hanging out at the Lucky Lab or Village Coffee, it's full of families and white-collar professionals.

It's also missing sidewalks—not just from the residential streets, but from the main pedestrian thoroughfares: Capital Highway, Garden Home, and Multnomah Boulevard. This hinders pedestrian access and gives the residents something to complain about in an otherwise picture-perfect place. A grocery store is a valued

component of urban neighborhoods, yet there are none directly in the Village. There are five in less than two miles, including the mainstream Safeway and Fred Meyer, the quirky and owner-based co-op, the independent and local stores, and a specialty world market. It might not be possible to walk to any of them, but you have plenty of choices.

Yet there are many attractions that bring residents from all over the city: John's Market with its large selection of beers; Thinker Toys, for the perfect, unique, and eco-friendly toy; Annie Bloom's Books and its resident cat; Marco's Cafe, with its umbrella collection on the ceiling; Northwest Wools for the DIY and knitting enthusiasts; Gabriel Park, catering to the skaters, dog lovers, outdoorspeople, and gardeners; Multnomah Arts Center, which served as the neighborhood school up until the late 1970s; and the Southwest Community Center and pool. In the future, "outer" Southwest Portland, including Multnomah Village, just might be distinct enough to be considered Portland's sixth major sector—South Portland, so to make it distinct from downtown.

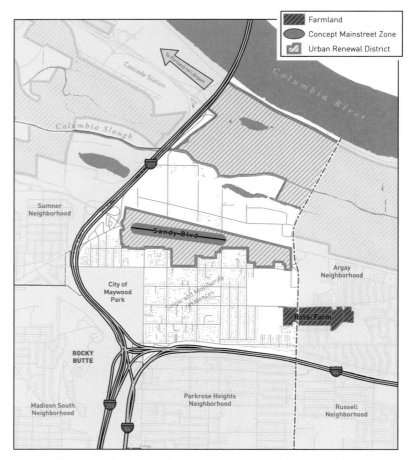

Legend:
- Farmland
- Concept Mainstreet Zone
- Urban Renewal District

Columbia River

To Portland Int'l Airport

Cascade Station

Columbia Slough

Sumner Neighborhood

Sandy Blvd

Argay Neighborhood

City of Maywood Park

Single and Multifamily Residences

Rossi Farm

ROCKY BUTTE

Madison South Neighborhood

Parkrose Heights Neighborhood

Russell Neighborhood

PARKROSE

Parkrose is the type of neighborhood that some may be jealous of while others take pity on it. Take its location, for example. Because it's situated near the airport, the freeways, and the Columbia River, escaping the city isn't hard. Furthermore, if you have a thing for disposable furniture or gigantic packages of toilet paper, IKEA and Costco are right around the corner. But Parkrose's location is also cordoned off from the rest of Portland by the awkward I-84/I-205 exchange and the airport, somewhat preventing the neighborhood from fully connecting to the center of the city. Not everyone in Portland is an IPA-drinking hipster, though, and some people are probably happy to be separated from all the hipness. At least that keeps the neighborhood affordable.

As should be obvious to the reader of this atlas, contradictions are right at home in Portland. Take, for example, the 2007 redevelopment recommendations offered to Parkrose by a group of planners: among their suggestions was the enhancement of the appearance of Sandy Boulevard by replacing graffiti with commissioned murals (Parkrose's old graffiti must have been really bad). The stretch of Sandy Boulevard in question is a blink-and-you-might-miss-it commercial district that's unspectacular but also ungentrified, a rarity for Portland commercial districts.

A good part of Parkrose has been under urban renewal for a long time, but the feeling of the place suggests a developmental staleness, as if the people of the neighborhood are either happy with the way it is or are already too invested in nearby Cascade Station (full of shiny new Targets, Best Buys, and Red Robins) to care about Sandy Boulevard anymore. Yet plans still exist to transform part of Sandy into a tree-lined, café-strewn business district.

The small, modest houses and Senn's Dairy Park to the south of the commercial district do give the neighborhood a cozy, rural, almost Midwestern feel. Rossi Farms, a working farm just to the east of the commercial district, has been in operation in Parkrose for over 130 years and utilizes a good deal of the land east of 122nd Avenue. But before people can feel too bucolic in Parkrose, an approaching jumbo jet buzzes overhead in preparation for landing at Portland International Airport; the hum of two freeways full of rush-hour traffic—as well as 122nd Avenue, a constantly busy street—also reminds people that they are, in fact, still smack in the middle of a major American city.

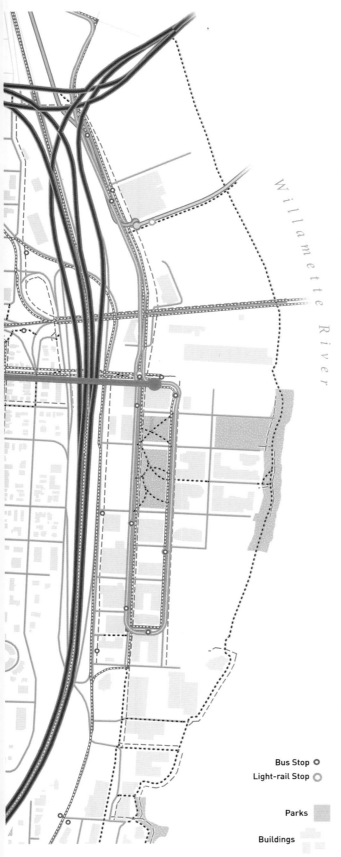

SOUTH WATERFRONT

Almost inexplicably, Portland's South Waterfront neighborhood has the feel of an off-the-beaten-path place. It sits right across the Willamette from super-trendy inner Southeast Portland, the Streetcar rolls through every ten to fifteen minutes, it's a twenty-minute walk from downtown, and it's one of only two neighborhoods in the United States served by an aerial tram. None of these points should nurture a feeling of isolation.

Yet it can feel quite isolated. It certainly lacks the hip and quirky vibe of the Inner Eastside. It's also isolated from the heavy traffic of other close-in neighborhoods, separated from the Eastside by the Willamette, from the Lair Hill and Corbett neighborhoods by I-5, and from every-where else by the spiderweb of interstate exchanges that segue into the Marquam Bridge.

But it's also *insulated* from the grittiness and other "problems" of quirky Portland. South Waterfront is immaculate; the streets and sidewalks have nary a gum spot, there's no graffiti (save for the backsides of the not-yet-torn-down machine shops that still populate the western edge of the neighborhood), and the closest power line adorned with hanging shoes is near the recently torn-down Greyhound station on Corbett Avenue—half a mile away.

South Waterfront's old landscape hasn't been completely wiped away, but what exists now is almost completely new. This area was never a neighborhood in the first place, and in that it's unlike other Portland neighborhoods undergoing change. When the high-rises, streets, and sidewalks were first built, a walk in the area was a bit eerie because the buildings were all unoccupied. The place was haunted by absence of human activity, human relationships, and human meaning.

Now, however, people live and work in these buildings. They eat in restaurants, attend violin performances, stroll by the river, and play with children in green spaces. Perhaps the South Waterfront doesn't yet hold a great deal of meaning for many Portlanders, but the people who live there and visit there are developing their own relationships with the place, and soon the meanings they give to the place will further transition this area from an abstract, industrial space to a meaningful, residential, and commercial place.

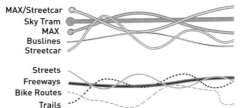

Bus Stop ⊙
Light-rail Stop ◎

Parks

Buildings

MAX/Streetcar
Sky Tram
MAX
Buslines
Streetcar

Streets
Freeways
Bike Routes
Trails

V. SOCIAL RELATIONS

One way of understanding a city is by looking at how people relate and get along . . . or how they don't. Relationships between people have a lot do with how cities are experienced and known. Examining relationships that are often hidden or obscured provides particularly useful glimpses at perspectives different from our own. In an age where we tend to connect online, personal relationships and social relations on the streets of the city are more important than ever. In the 1950s and 1960s, Jane Jacobs argued that the city was an urban ballet that was in part made safe by eyes on the sidewalks—a place where even strangers looked out for each other. Her ideas continue to be relevant today.

The role of governing authorities is important too. When people distrust the people who rule and police them, the tension can be easy to see and feel. The relationships between people and ideas also have a lot to do with how the city is experienced and understood. Many outsiders (and several insiders as well) know Portland for its hipster associations, the kinds lampooned on the television show *Portlandia* and written about with some frequency by the *New York Times*. The city's nicknames reveal bits and pieces of the identities people attach to the city. Little Beirut (coined by President George Bush) and the People's Republic of Portland both evoke particular narratives about Portland's identity. Stumptown and Bridgetown conjure other meanings. Rip City and Soccer City evoke local sport identities. The Rose City connotes yet something else.

The pages in this chapter explore relationships between people and people, people and authorities, and people and ideas. Several of the pages highlight how these relationships, both historical and contemporary, are sometimes very real to some people and invisible to others.

MISSION INVISIBLE

THE PATH OF LEAST SURVEILLANCE

UNION STATION

PATH OF LEAST SURVEILLANCE

SECURITY CAMERA

STREET LIGHT

← NORTH

CRAMER HALL, PSU

Living Under a Watchful Eye

In the months following the bomb explosion at Boston's 2013 Marathon, many people recognized the powerful role that video cameras throughout the city can play in identifying criminals, particularly ones who commit such horrible acts of violence. Video footage plays an increasingly important role in criminal cases of all kinds. This surveillance can also be used to track people. Advances in facial recognition software make it possible to sift through massive amounts of video in seconds. This will increasingly allow authorities to track individuals not only within a city, but from city to city and even internationally.

In the summer of 2013, news about the National Security Agency's comprehensive monitoring of phone calls made by American citizens brought attention to the potential for abuse surveillance systems bring. The American Civil Liberties Union filed a suit to have the phone monitoring stopped. Others call attention to the great expense of surveillance systems and the industries they support.

In Portland, people might not think much about being constantly monitored, but perhaps they should consider just how much they're being watched. With cameras on most blocks, the chances of being caught on film are high. Some people don't like to be watched. Sometimes people change their behavior when they know they're being watched. The map on the previous pages tells you how to navigate downtown with minimal exposure to surveillance cameras and street lights.

Often mentioned in discussions about the impact of surveillance on society is *1984*, George Orwell's novel about a future where every movement made by each person in society is monitored by Big Brother via the telescreen. Punishments aimed at targeting each individual's worst fears awaited those who stepped out of line. Orwell suggests that people alter their behavior to conform to what the state wants because people must always assume that they're being watched. And so people fall into line, afraid to act in any way that might be construed as independent. This was Orwell's fear for the future of urban civilization, and many believe that Orwell's nightmare is, in places, a lived reality. Michel Foucault discusses urban society in a similar way by evoking Jeremy Bentham's Panopticon—a prison designed to control its population's behavior through constant surveillance.

Most would be hard pressed to call Portland a Panopticon, yet people are probably being watched much more closely than they think. There are over 400 discernible surveillance cameras focused on the streets in downtown Portland alone. This doesn't include scores of video cameras on ATMs spread throughout downtown. This doesn't include video cameras that are completely hidden from view, and this doesn't include people walking down the street taking HD video with their phone and immediately posting the footage to YouTube.

How the security camera data for this map was collected

Members of the Cultural Atlas Production class collected this data on June 26, 2012. The downtown area was divided into seven sectors. Two researchers walked every street in each sector, recording the location of every identifiable security camera. This didn't include ATMs, most of which are equipped with cameras, nor did this include security cameras inside buildings that were focused on outdoor areas. On that field excursion, researchers also collected data on public art, billboards, and notable sounds and smells.

GREEN PARADISE

Across the country, Portland is known as a green paradise. In fact, the idea that Portland ranks as a leader in environmental and sustainable movements is often taken for granted. With that in mind, we designed this map to acknowledge the city's green credentials while also evoking the idyllic and cartoonish image that people seem to have of Portland. Some would say Portland engages in some degree of green-washing. And certainly greenness is not evenly distributed throughout the city. Taking a closer look reveals both positive and negative realities beyond this glossy caricature of popular imagination, and shows that, in Portland, there are shades of green.

There is certainly evidence to suggest that Portland is working hard to build a sustainable city. An array of metrics is used to crown Portland as the capital of sustainability: 250 miles of bike paths, 175 LEED-certified buildings, 288 public parks, and over 50 community gardens that collectively have some 2,000 plots. Additionally, 33 percent of all energy consumed in Portland comes from renewable sources, the city has the lowest percentage of coal usage (25 percent) in the country, over half of Portland's garbage is recycled or composted, and it was the first major US city to ban plastic bags. Portland also has the most residents whose vehicles are bicycles, the most parking spots converted into rainwater filtering stations, and the most vegans per capita.

Portland doesn't just stick its toe into the sustainability pool; it goes skinny-dipping in it. Back in the 1970s, the city created an Urban Growth Boundary to reduce sprawl, and it has one of the best public transportation systems in the country for a city its size. Forest Park is the largest urban natural forested area in the country.

Rivergate

St. Johns New Columbia
Housing Project
Three community gardens
CBWTP Operations Center
Two LEED apartment buildings
Bioswales

Toyota Motor Sales

Wildwood Nature School

Wastewa

Cathedral Park Place

University
How
Shi

NORTHWEST
LEED-certified buildings:
Jean Vollum Natural Capital Center
The Louisa Apartments
REI
Whole Foods
Bud Clark Commons Transitional Housing
The Brewery Blocks
Icebreaker
Oregon College of Oriental Medicine
The Hoyt Yards "Green Neighborhood"
Many condos and apartment buildings

Environmental Organizations:
Ecotrust
Solar Oregon
Oregon Environmental Council
Oceana

W Multnomah Soil & Water
Conservation District

Audubon Society

Providence Pa

Oregon College of Arts & Crafts

World Forestry Center

Downtown and PSU
LEED-certified buildings:
The Portland Building
Mosaic Condominiums
Hamilton West Apartments
Bureau of Environmental Services
Five buildings at PSU
The KOIN Center
Mercycorps Headquarters
Two banks
Two hotels
Many condos and apartment buildings
Five more buildings at PSU

Wetlands Co

C

Avalo

Ne

Hillsdale Library

Earth an

Environmental Organizations:
1000 Friends of Oregon
Waterwatch of Oregon
Northwest Environmental Advocates
Renewable Northwest Project
Sustainable Northwest
Western Ancient Forest Campaign
Friends of the Columbia Gorge
Trust for Public Land
Oregon Natural Desert Association
Green Empowerment
Climate Trust
River Network
Lower Columbia River Estuary Partnership
Western Rivers Conservancy
Oregon Forest Resources
Opal Creek Ancient Forest Center
Intertwine Alliance
Sustainable Oregon Schools Initiative
SOLVE

Lewis and (
Schoo
Robe

Friends of Tryon Cree

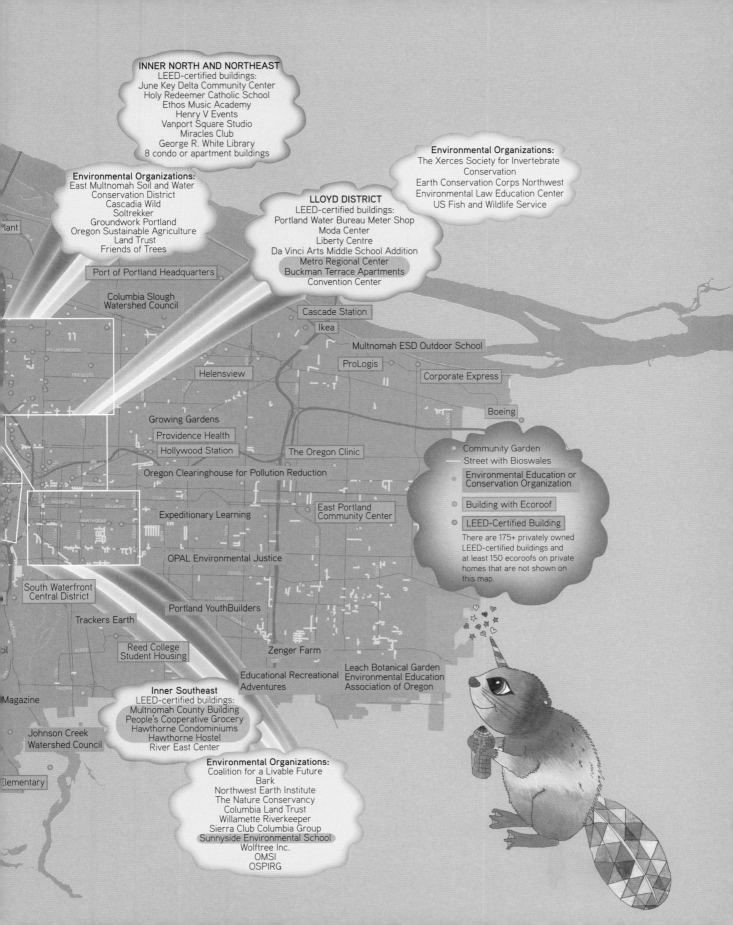

INNER NORTH AND NORTHEAST
LEED-certified buildings:
June Key Delta Community Center
Holy Redeemer Catholic School
Ethos Music Academy
Henry V Events
Vanport Square Studio
Miracles Club
George R. White Library
8 condo or apartment buildings

Environmental Organizations:
East Multnomah Soil and Water
Conservation District
Cascadia Wild
Soltrekker
Groundwork Portland
Oregon Sustainable Agriculture
Land Trust
Friends of Trees

LLOYD DISTRICT
LEED-certified buildings:
Portland Water Bureau Meter Shop
Moda Center
Liberty Centre
Da Vinci Arts Middle School Addition
Metro Regional Center
Buckman Terrace Apartments
Convention Center

Environmental Organizations:
The Xerces Society for Invertebrate
Conservation
Earth Conservation Corps Northwest
Environmental Law Education Center
US Fish and Wildlife Service

Port of Portland Headquarters

Columbia Slough
Watershed Council

Cascade Station

Ikea

Multnomah ESD Outdoor School

ProLogis

Corporate Express

Helensview

Boeing

Growing Gardens

Providence Health

Hollywood Station

The Oregon Clinic

Oregon Clearinghouse for Pollution Reduction

Community Garden
Street with Bioswales

Environmental Education or
Conservation Organization

Building with Ecoroof

LEED-Certified Building

There are 175+ privately owned
LEED-certified buildings and
at least 150 ecoroofs on private
homes that are not shown on
this map.

Expeditionary Learning

East Portland
Community Center

OPAL Environmental Justice

South Waterfront
Central District

Trackers Earth

Portland YouthBuilders

Reed College
Student Housing

Zenger Farm

Educational Recreational
Adventures

Leach Botanical Garden
Environmental Education
Association of Oregon

Magazine

Johnson Creek
Watershed Council

Inner Southeast
LEED-certified buildings:
Multnomah County Building
People's Cooperative Grocery
Hawthorne Condominiums
Hawthorne Hostel
River East Center

Elementary

Environmental Organizations:
Coalition for a Livable Future
Bark
Northwest Earth Institute
The Nature Conservancy
Columbia Land Trust
Willamette Riverkeeper
Sierra Club Columbia Group
Sunnyside Environmental School
Wolftree Inc.
OMSI
OSPIRG

Portland Parks and Recreation instituted its community garden program in 1974. The city now coordinates 50 community gardens, which contain some 2,100 plots. The program is very popular; in spring of 2014, only 8 of the gardens had plots available and there were about 1,000 people on the waiting list—almost as many people as are on the waiting list for affordable housing in the Pearl District.

Portland also leads the nation in sustainability-related words that most people would need to Google. For example, many street corners around the city have been ripped up and replaced with bioswales. These are either stormwater treatment areas or soldiers in Portland's war against cars, depending on the perspective. On the one hand, bioswales filter oil and other toxins from rain runoff before they reach the sewer system and eventually the Willamette River. On the other hand, some gobble up three to five parking spaces in densely populated neighborhoods already starved for parking. There are roughly 1,350 bioswales around the city to date.

The Bureau of Environmental Services' Grey to Green Initiative promotes bioswales and other components of what the city calls green infrastructure. These include ecoroofs, street trees, control of invasive plants, and land acquisition. Put simply, an ecoroof (or green roof or living roof) is a garden on top of a structure. These gardens are another hopeful weapon against climate change; they absorb carbon dioxide, filter rainwater and air pollutants, and reduce the urban heat island effect. The city of Portland promotes the installation of ecoroofs by offering assistance and financial incentives to building owners and developers. From the late 1990s to 2013, over 560 green roofs were installed in Portland, totaling more than thirty-eight acres.

There's a pretty good chance that an ecoroof sits atop a LEED-certified building, of which Portland has over 350. About half those buildings are business/government zoned and the other half are residential. To achieve LEED certification, the US Green Building Council (USGBC) must review the property in five categories: sustainable sites, water efficiency, energy and atmosphere, materials and resources, and indoor environmental quality. After review the property can be certified at the Silver, Gold, or Platinum level, depending on the number of points gained in the review. A more stringent measure of green buildings comes in the form of the Living Building Challenge (LBC) certification program, which claims to be "the most advanced measure of sustainability in the built

environment possible today." Portland has only one LBC-certified building, so it's losing this green battle to its Cascadian rival, Seattle, which has three.

Portland also plays host to a variety of environmental activist organizations, ranging from large international nonprofits to small environmental justice groups. These groups focus on everything from environmental racism to land-use policy to invertebrate conservation.

While Portland does have a great climate for gardening, so do many cities. In fact, Portland's 50 official community gardens really aren't all that many for a city its size. Boston, for example, has nearly 200 community gardens, some of which have as many as 500 plots. As for other cities, Kansas City has around 350, Atlanta has about 100, Seattle has around 90, and Brooklyn has at least 75. San Francisco, which has one third of Portland's land area, has about 40. Detroit is about the same size as Portland in terms of square mileage and population, but some estimates put the total number of community gardens in Detroit at over 1,000. Detroit and Portland are difficult to compare for many reasons, but which city has the green reputation?

The Willamette is probably not anyone's top choice for a swim. As a matter of fact, the lower twelve miles of the river (known as the Portland Harbor, roughly between Swan Island and Sauvie Island) are so polluted that the whole stretch was designated a Superfund site in 2000; the stretch of the river between Swan Island and the St. Johns Bridge includes at least twenty-four individual sites that the Environmental Protection Agency has listed as high-priority

Bioswale on Cully Boulevard

Ecoroof on top of Portland Hostel Hawthorne

Ecoroof on top of Portland Wastewater Treatment Plant

cleanup sites. Over the past one hundred years, at least 150 different offending parties (industry, government agencies, etc.) have dumped mercury, arsenic, PCBs, phthalates, DDT, and thousands of other carcinogens into the river. These chemicals have been collecting on the bottom of the Willamette the whole while and are currently still free to work their way into the groundwater. In response to this issue, Portland constructed giant underground tunnels and pipelines to divert overflows of wastewater and prevent raw sewage from flowing into the Willamette and Columbia Slough. The $1.4 billion project, known as the Big Pipe, concluded in 2011 after twenty years of construction.

Regarding green building, it's helpful to remember that green certifications, such as LEED, cannot be achieved without paying rather substantial fees to the proper green building agency (for example, the USGBC). LEED certification not only requires sustainable design, but also sufficient capital. Furthermore, critics of the LEED system have long pointed out that LEED certification is awarded before the building actually functions as a green building; the green features of the building might not actually work in practice. Some studies have shown that many LEED-certified buildings actually use *more* energy than other buildings. In fairness, LEED has addressed some of these cases with revisions to their certification process. Ultimately, if the developer or agency has the money to pay, they get their plaque; after that, it doesn't matter how much energy the building consumes—it still gets its green kudos as a LEED-certified building.

So yes, Portland is green. Setting aside the metrics, however, it becomes clear that in Portland there are shades of green. There's the sullen forest green of the Douglas fir, the native Oregonian tree that's been cut and converted into house frames and kitchen tables for the better part of two centuries. There's the proverbial green

light that allows developers to break ground on what seems like new apartment complexes every day. Or there's patent green, the color of the dollar in our pocket that we contemplate giving to one of the people sleeping on the sidewalk that we step over every morning on our way to the streetcar stop.

How green Portland is thus depends upon your criteria and whom you ask. It is easy to find all-or-nothing perspectives. Yet just labeling the city as green overstates the case and dismissing the city as green-washed is hyperbole. The lived experience of interacting with the natural environment doesn't always fit neatly in a box. The Douglas fir prominently featured on the Cascadia flag symbolizes the high standard of socio-environmental ethics by which Cascadians live, and also the accompanying contradictions. Portlanders hike among Douglas firs in Forest Park and picnic under the cool shade of Douglas firs at Laurelhurst Park . . . and then see great indie rock shows at the Doug Fir, a popular club on East Burnside.

LEED certification plaque

Megaton House
10124 NE Pacific
PotLuck starts at 4pm

July

Chesler
SeleneWines.com

RISK-OBLIVIOUS YOUTH

PUNK HOUSES AND CONDOS

Risk-oblivious youth is a term for the young mostly white artists, musicians, and other countercultural types who are drawn to live in low-income urban neighborhoods by the cheap rent and central location. Portland has long been attractive to folks like this. Since the '90s, more and more have made their homes in inner North and Northeast Portland—low-income neighborhoods that were home to almost 80 percent of the city's African American population in 1990. An already active local community of anarchists and punks saw an explosion in numbers after the 1999 World Trade Organization protests in Seattle, and with it came many of the punk houses seen here—shared dwellings that host basement punk shows, fundraisers, Food Not Bombs meetings, travelers, and political organizing. As condominiums and rent went up quickly in the early to mid-2000s, there began an exodus of people of color from the North and Northeast neighborhoods. Some would say the punk houses paved the way for the condos; some would say they represent another local culture lost. Perhaps it's a bit of both. Who doesn't love to hate on condos? Presumably the people who live in them.

But who are those people anyway? In this city of hundred-year-old, wood-frame, one- or two-story houses with generous yards, the construction of a new condominium building in the neighborhood can feel like the landing of a spaceship from the outer reaches of the galaxy. At the same time, as condos fulfill the city of Portland's mandate for high-density, transit-oriented, eco-friendly infill development, they're a powerful class symbol that's anathema to the self-image and ideals of many Portlanders. It doesn't help that their ground-level storefronts tend to fill up with Pilates studios, boutique shoe stores, and specialty salt vendors. For many, condo developments represent gentrification, the bourgeoisie, and capitalism. They're a reminder of the lack of affordable housing and the flight of families from the inner city. Also, most condos look exactly the same. Their presence contributes to the increasing blandness of the urban landscape.

RANCH
A HOUSE
K PiT
KEV
TUREGATE
LtiR GATE
RTY ISLAND
OLKET Sandwich
VACK Hause
PINK HOUSE
EUCKETTS
FAILING House

JU
KAR

SLUA

+ on
mo

09.22.
@ vulture
(3835 NE Cleve
INFO @

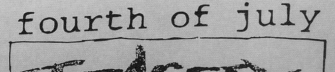

fourth of july

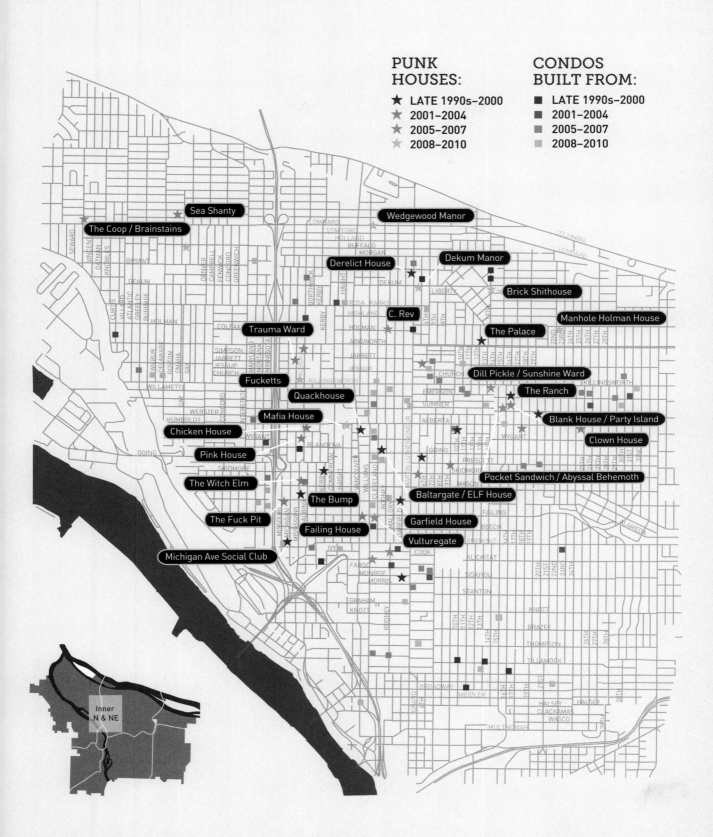

PUNK
HOUSES:

★ LATE 1990s–2000
★ 2001–2004
★ 2005–2007
★ 2008–2010

CONDOS
BUILT FROM:

■ LATE 1990s–2000
■ 2001–2004
■ 2005–2007
■ 2008–2010

Sea Shanty

The Coop / Brainstains

Wedgewood Manor

Derelict House

Dekum Manor

Brick Shithouse

C. Rev

Manhole Holman House

Trauma Ward

The Palace

Dill Pickle / Sunshine Ward

Fucketts

The Ranch

Quackhouse

Mafia House

Blank House / Party Island

Chicken House

Clown House

Pink House

Pocket Sandwich / Abyssal Behemoth

The Witch Elm

Baltargate / ELF House

The Bump

Garfield House

The Fuck Pit

Failing House

Vulturegate

Michigan Ave Social Club

Inner
N & NE

THE INVISIBILITY OF HOMELESSNESS

On January 30, 2013, 2,869 people were homeless in Portland. On that night, Multnomah County and Portland Housing Bureau officials counted 1,895 people on the streets and 975 sleeping in emergency shelters. According to estimates, a total of 15,563 people were on the streets, in shelters or transitional housing, or were sharing housing with friends and family.

RIGHT 2 DREAM TOO

Since the fall of 2011, Right 2 Dream Too has provided fifty people with a sheltered and safe place to spend the night. Unlike other shelters and transitional housing in the city, R2DToo allows pets and housing for couples. The city does not want to establish a transitional housing site at such a visible location.

UNHOUSED INDIVIDUALS (2013)

62   63–153   154–205   206–305   306–474

■ Shelter   ● Other site

DIGNITY VILLAGE

In 2001, advocates and homeless Portlanders camped under the Fremont Bridge and refused to disperse. The campers negotiated with city authorities. Eventually they accepted relocation to a permanent site next to the city's composting facility, near the Portland airport. Oregon Revised Statute (446.265) allows each Oregon municipality to establish two campground sites for use in providing transitional housing accommodations. Dignity Village is one of these. In its thirteenth year, Dignity Village is a successful model of democratic community that provides housing to about sixty residents. But the site's remote location means it's invisible too and forgotten by most Portlanders.

Race (compared to Multnomah County)

	Less than County	More than County
White	-12%	
Asian	-6%	
African American		+13%
Latino		+2%
Native American		+7%
Hawaiian/Pacific Islander		+3%

Length of Time Experiencing Homelessness

- >5 Years (22%)
- <1 Year (36%)
- 2–5 Years (24%)
- 1–2 Years (18%)

Unsheltered Sleeping Location

- Street or sidewalk
- Doorway or other private property
- Bridge/overpass/railroad
- Vehicle
- Woods/open space
- Park
- Abandoned building
- Other/unknown

Household Composition

- Individual adults (75%)
- Couples without children (18%)
- Familes with children (6%)
- Unaccompanied youth (<18) (1%)

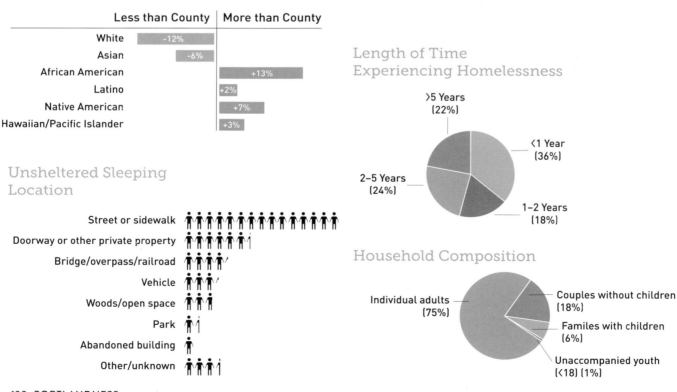

Right 2 Dream Too, 2014

Doors used as a fence, Right 2 Dream Too, 2014

Right 2 Dream Too is a community whose existence has generated strong reactions from the city of Portland, the Old Town neighborhood, surrounding businesses, and the greater public. Those who oppose the encampment located at West Burnside Street and Fourth Avenue suggest that such a place doesn't belong in downtown Portland, or at least, not in this particular place.

The land that Right 2 Dream Too resides on is privately owned and has a curious history. In the early 1980s its owner bought the building and opened an adult bookstore. The store closed in 2007 when the building, demolished the following year, was deemed unsafe. In 2011 the same owner attempted to fill the now vacant space with a food cart pod, but the city didn't allow this either and issued a fine for hosting food carts on an unpaved surface. The owner was restricted from paving a new lot because of zoning codes, and the lot remained empty.

Then in Autumn 2011, as Occupy Wall Street protests were beginning, houseless individuals in Portland unconnected with the protests set up tents on the lot. This was partially in response to a rhetorical question proposed to the public by the owner inquiring as to why, if a business would not work on this lot, shouldn't the houseless sleep there. Responding to this invitation, Right 2 Dream Too officially began on October 10, 2011. As of this writing, it remains on the same site in essentially the same presentation.

This space illustrates that there are alternatives to traditional channels for addressing homelessness. The centrality of this place has been critical to its sustainment. One reason is that within a quarter-mile radius of the site there are no less than ten different services used by those staying at Right 2 Dream Too and the larger houseless population in the city. For example, there are emergency shelters and missions; meal handouts at several locations; laundry and showering facilities; and clinics that offer medical assistance such as check-ups, mental health and substance recovery support, and job and skills training. For many, survival and their next steps to stability are contingent upon their proximity to these resources.

Right 2 Dream Too is also a resource for those who find themselves on the street for the first time and in need of direction in navigating unfamiliar circumstances. Its members make up a large support network containing a wealth of information about surviving on the street. It's an invaluable resource for those new to being houseless. Because of Right 2 Dream Too's visibility within downtown, it is a critical hub for resource support.

This space is a visual reminder that houselessness continues to be an issue in Portland. There simply aren't enough housing units and transitional housing spaces to shelter everyone who needs it. Right 2 Dream Too is not only a space that shelters the houseless looking for undisturbed sleep; its physical infrastructure—the doors that bound the place—projects statements of hope for the users of the space. Painted on these doors are calls for justice regarding issues such as social equality through affordable housing. The visible occupancy of this space draws attention to the severity of the issue and has been critical to its social support. There might not be a perfect place for Right 2 Dream Too to be located, but this community is certainly deserving of a place.

THE RED LINE . . .

Redlining is a term for discriminatory housing practices in which real estate agents, banks, landlords, and city government conspire to confine African Americans or other racial and ethnic minorities to certain neighborhoods. The redlined areas seen here are from a 1938 Portland residential security map. Redlining has been documented in Portland from the 1920s until as recently as the 1990s. Racially based housing discrimination persists in the Portland area to this day.

URBAN RENEWAL

Urban renewal refers to the urban planning practices initiated by the Federal Housing Act of 1949, which encouraged "the elimination of substandard and other inadequate housing through the clearance of slums and blighted areas." By the 1960s, it was popularly referred to as "negro removal."

3 Vanport 1942–1948

2

Albina 1940s

WOODLAWN

KILLINGSWORTH

LOMBARD

ROSA PARKS

HUMBOLDT

VERNON

KING

SABIN

BOISE

FREMONT

4 Guild's Lake Courts 1942–1945

YEON

ELIOT

IRVINGTON

MLK JR BLVD

21ST

5

LLOYD

BROADWAY

I-84

1 Census Tract 51 1883

NAITO

LOVEJOY

12TH

SANDY

GLISAN

BURNSIDE

STARK

GRAND

BELMONT

HAWTHORNE

CESAR CHAVEZ

20TH

MARKET

4TH

I-405

DIVISION

BARBUR

POWELL

33RD

COLUMBIA

I-5

INTERSTATE

GOING

42ND

PORTLAND

☐ Redlined Area: 1938

▨ Area of Displacement for Urban Renewal: 1950s–1960s

▨ Area of historically high African American population

ALBINA NEIGHBORHOODS

1 CENSUS TRACT 51 1883

In the late 1800s, the arrival of the Northern Pacific Railway and the Portland Hotel brought service and labor jobs to Portland's black residents. In 1900, the majority of the 1,105 African Americans in Oregon resided in Census Tract 51 in Northwest Portland. Black social life centered around the Golden West Hotel on Northwest Broadway.

2 ALBINA 1940S

The town of Albina was annexed to Portland in 1891. More than half of Portland's black population lived in Albina by 1940. It was home to the thriving jazz district known as Jumptown. After World War II, black shipyard workers displaced from temporary housing relocated to Albina, still limited in their housing options by racial discrimination. Most of the neighborhoods of Albina remained majority African American until the late 1990s or early 2000s.

3 VANPORT 1942–1948

During World War II, Portland's African American population increased significantly as people from all over the country were drawn to jobs in the shipyards. Two major housing projects were erected to house the influx of workers and their families: the independent town of Vanport and Guild's Lake Courts in Northwest Portland. These were racially mixed communities. Both decreased in population after the war, and Vanport was wiped out in a 1948 flood.

Aerial view of Vanport, 1943

4 GUILD'S LAKE COURTS 1942–1945

Guild's Lake Courts Housing, 1944

5 ELIOT & LLOYD NEIGHBORHOODS LATE 1950S–1960S

In the late 1950s, residents of the Eliot and Lloyd neighborhoods were displaced by Portland's Coliseum Urban Renewal Project, which demolished over 1,500 homes and businesses. In the late 1960s, the wrecking crew moved farther north up Williams Avenue, demolishing the heart of the Eliot neighborhood's black business district for an Emanuel Hospital expansion that never occurred. In both cases the rationale of the Portland Development Commission (PDC) was that these areas were "blighted."

REDLINING AND GENTRIFICATION

PAST: 1890–1990

The Northern Pacific Railroad arrived in Portland in 1883 and became one of the major employers of Portland's African American residents. Some found housing in Albina or other scattered parts of the city, but the majority lived in Northwest Portland, which was where the first black churches and black-owned businesses were located.

Racially based housing discrimination is first documented to have occurred in Portland with a 1919 rule of the Portland Realty Board that said it was unethical to sell property in a white neighborhood to a black or Chinese person. In 1935, the Federal Home Loan Bank Board asked the Home Owners Loan Corporation to create "residential security maps" for cities across the nation, such as the one for Portland shown on the previous pages. The term redlining, coined in the 1960s, refers to the red lines on these maps that marked the neighborhoods where banks were advised not to give loans. These were almost exclusively inner-city neighborhoods that were home to racial and ethnic minorities, particularly African Americans. Redlining came to refer more widely to the policies and practices of governments, landlords, real estate agents, and banks that restrict minorities to certain neighborhoods while preventing any financial investments in those same neighborhoods.

In the 1950s urban renewal came to Portland. The first to be affected were the majority-black Eliot and Lloyd neighborhoods, which were demolished for the construction of Memorial Coliseum and Interstate 5 in the mid- to late 1950s. In 1970 the population

of Boise was 84 percent black at a time when Portland as a whole was just 6 percent black. This was the heaviest concentration of African Americans in any neighborhood in Portland history and reflects the fact that Portland was one of the most segregated cities in the country.

Home ownership in the Albina neighborhoods had increased throughout the '60s and '70s, but assessed property values were low, and, despite the gains of the civil rights movement, banks continued discriminatory lending practices and refused to issue loans for properties in the neighborhood. This led to an increase in neglectful absentee landlords and predatory lending practices, with a corresponding decline in the quality of housing. It was this combination of racism, neglect, and the aftereffects of urban renewal that truly brought the "blight" the city had supposedly targeted over the preceding decades. In the 1980s the economic recession, the crack cocaine epidemic, and gang warfare hit the Albina neighborhoods hard. Those who could afford to leave the neighborhood did. The trend of increased home ownership was reversed, and the Boise neighborhood lost population, both black and white. By 1990 nearly one quarter of the housing units in the Boise neighborhood were vacant.

PRESENT: 1990–2012

When the recession ended in the early 1990s, the city of Portland targeted the neighborhoods of Albina—especially Boise and Eliot—for "redevelopment," which turned out to be a slightly more politically correct form of renewal's displacement. The Albina Community Plan of 1993 proposed the light rail-line on North Interstate Avenue as well as a network of bike routes through the neighborhood. It encouraged dense, multiuse development and the creation of local businesses. As plans for the MAX Yellow Line went forward, the PDC created the Interstate Urban Renewal Area in 2000. The plan, as adopted by the city, specified that increased tax revenues from rising property values in the area were to be used to benefit existing residents and protect against gentrification and displacement. However, during the post-9/11 recession, the plan's eighteen antidisplacement projects and small business assistance programs were suspended. Only one, the New Columbia housing development, was actually carried through. As the MAX line went in and other parts of the plan were implemented, property values did indeed begin to rise, and Boise's population increased.

The North Mississippi Avenue Historic Conservation District and Williams-Vancouver, which had been targeted in the plan, evolved into hip shopping and entertainment districts. The sudden appearance of four-story condominium buildings, boutique shopping, and bars was heavily subsidized by tax breaks to developers and grants to property owners. Since 2001, the PDC has given out $606,000 in storefront improvement grants to thirty-eight businesses along Williams and Vancouver alone. As of February 2012, 68 percent of the sixty-two retail spaces on black Portland's former Main Street had been there for less than five years.

The revitalization in Boise has led to a drastic demographic shift in the neighborhood. The number of black residents steadily decreased through the years, inverse to the rise in the number of white residents. The number of people aged eighteen to thirty-four increased while the number of children under age eighteen decreased. With the influx of new residents has come tension. In 1999, right around the time when Boise made the switch from majority black to majority white, neighbors organized to oppose the construction of new low-income housing units in the neighborhood.

As development on Mississippi peaked and leveled off, the stretch of Williams through the Boise neighborhood seemed to become one big construction zone. At least three big market-rate residential developments were initiated within a few blocks of each other in 2012. The recently completed Albert Apartments at North Williams and Beech, which was opposed by the Boise Neighborhood Association, received a $1 million transit-oriented development tax break but contains no low-income units. Some developers who want to build in Boise have admitted to keeping their plans under wraps to avoid opposition.

Street art made to look like a city sign, 2009

Perhaps partly because of this secrecy of the private developers, many residents feel they have little or no opportunity to influence the drastic reshaping of their own neighborhoods. It's the unmeasurable loss of such intangible things as a close-knit, mutually supportive community that's the greatest damage done by gentrification and that can be the hardest to restore as people who lived within a few blocks of each other find themselves on opposite edges of the metro area. Even as African American residents leave Albina by the thousands (7,700 between 2000 and 2010, according to the US Census), finding more affordable housing in Beaverton, Gresham, Vancouver, or East Portland, many institutions and businesses important to the black community remain in inner North and Northeast: restaurants, salons, barber shops, Jefferson High School, Portland Community College, and churches that have been there for over a hundred years. In order to shop and connect with friends and family, black Portlanders find themselves facing a long drive or bus ride. Churches spend mornings collecting their dispersed membership. Several have relocated or opened satellites.

Longtime residents who do remain in Albina might find themselves feeling unwelcome in their own homes. In addition to complaints about black bars and clubs, North and Northeast Portland neighborhood organizations have reported increased neighbor complaints about the noise from Sunday morning church services.

2013

LAS PRIMAS RESTAURANT
QUEEN BEE CREATIONS
GRIZZLY TATTOO
HOPWORKS BIKE BAR
SIDE BAR
KENNY AND ZUKE'S DELI BAR

LODEKKA

MYOPTIC OPTOMETRY

SCREW LOOSE STUDIO

CHOCOLATE CRAFT KITS

LINCOLN RESTAURANT
INK AND PEAT
RISTRETTO COFFEE
WAX ON SPA
EAT OYSTER BAR
SPIELWORKS TOYS
CHA CHA CHA TAQUERIA
YOGA SHALA
AKEMI SALON
TASTY N SONS
CHOP BUTCHERY AND CHARCUTERIE
ORO DI NAPOLI PIZZERIA
WHAT'S THE SCOOP ICE CREAM

ABRAHAM FIXES BIKES

NEW SEASONS

1956

WALLACE BAR-B-Q
RESTAURANT

WALNUT PARK
FURNITURE CO.

BINGO DETERGENT CO.

WILLIAMS SALES
AND SERVICE

ARCTIC FOOD
LOCKERS & MART

SMITHY'S GROCERY

RYDMAN'S BICYCLE STORE

MANNING'S SERVICE STATION

CUMA SALON FOR BEAUTY

PLUMBING AND HEATING
ENGINEERING CO.

MOZOROSKY GROCERIES

MIDWAY MEAT MARKET

TALLEY'S FURNITURE
EXCHANGE

IRISHER AND SWEDE,
WHOLESALE

CARTER RADIO SERVICE

ALBINA LUMBER CO.

ALBERT'S POULTRY MARKET

DELUX BARBER SHOP

FRANK'S SHOE REPAIR

DISABLED VETERAN'S STORE

WILLIAMS AVENUE
VARIETY STORE

...AND THE BOTTOM LINE

In the last five years or so, the section of North Williams Avenue between Fremont and Shaver has transformed from a row of empty lots and warehouses to a destination where condo dwellers live above gourmet foods, boutique shopping, and varieties of bars previously unknown to Portland (bike bar, deli bar, or oyster bar, anyone?).

Almost sixty years earlier and about six blocks south, a business district of a different nature was experiencing its heyday. This was the section of "Black Portland's Main Street," demolished in the late '60s for the expansion of Emanuel Hospital, which ran out of funding and left a gaping empty lot for four decades.

The North Williams Avenue of the 1950s was the type of walkable local business district that the North Williams of today is designed to be, but with a difference: back then, it was the kind of neighborhood any working-class person could live and shop in. Now such neighborhoods are more and more of an expensive privilege. How did North Williams go from Mozorosky Groceries to New Seasons? From Midway Meat Market to Chop Charcuterie? From Delux Barber Shop to Akemi Salon?

Those sixty years saw North Portland shaped by racism, disinvestment, and neglect followed by urban renewal and rapid gentrification. The Boise neighborhood, where both Williams and Mississippi are located, went from a thriving majority-black, majority-homeowner community to a neighborhood of abandoned houses and gang activity to a place where the young, white, and childless compete for scarce and increasingly expensive housing.

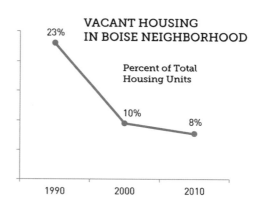

VACANT HOUSING IN BOISE NEIGHBORHOOD

Percent of Total Housing Units

23%

10%

8%

1990   2000   2010

1996

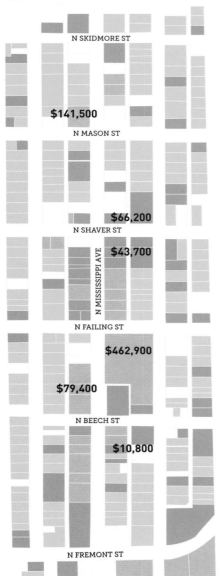

N SKIDMORE ST

$141,500

N MASON ST

$66,200

N SHAVER ST

$43,700

N MISSISSIPPI AVE

N FAILING ST

$462,900

$79,400

N BEECH ST

$10,800

N FREMONT ST

North Mississippi Avenue

North Mississippi Avenue was the Boise neighborhood's first commercial street to have developers seeing green. Assessed property values today are as much as ninety times what they were in the 1990s. It's no coincidence that the demographic makeup of the neighborhood has changed so drastically.

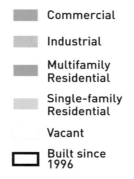

- Commercial
- Industrial
- Multifamily Residential
- Single-family Residential
- Vacant
- Built since 1996

2012

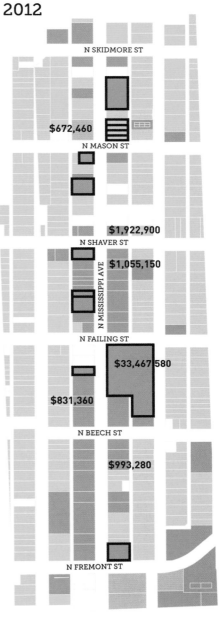

N SKIDMORE ST

$672,460

N MASON ST

$1,922,900

N SHAVER ST

$1,055,150

N MISSISSIPPI AVE

N FAILING ST

$33,467,580

$831,360

N BEECH ST

$993,280

N FREMONT ST

CHANGE IN RACE AND ETHNICITY OF RESIDENTS

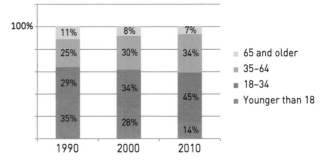

Number of People

- Black
- White
- Hispanic

CHANGE IN AGE OF RESIDENTS

	1990	2000	2010
65 and older	11%	8%	7%
35–64	25%	30%	34%
18–34	29%	34%	45%
Younger than 18	35%	28%	14%

N Gilbert and Sedro

N Wilbur and Hollman

NE 8th and Holland

NE 8th and Holman

NE 6th and Going

N Overlook and Failing

NE Rodney and Tillamook

SE 16th and Ash

SE 33rd and Yamhill

SE 15th and Alder

SE 130th Place and Ramona

SE 9th and Sherrett

SE 37th and Cora

POURING ART INTO THE STREETS

In 1996, architect Mark Lakeman erected a structure he called the T-Hows in his Sellwood front yard, a small kiosk he kept stocked with tea bags and hot water. It became a gathering place for neighbors, who soon organized a weekly neighborhood potluck. The illegal structure came to the attention of the city of Portland, but instead of requiring that it be torn down, the city issued a temporary permit. The T-Hows was dismantled at the end of the summer of 1996.

From this beginning emerged City Repair, which later held a block party to create a replacement community space for the T-Hows. This was the first manifestation of Share-It Square (Southeast Ninth and Sherrett Street), a painted intersection with a message board and a new small teahouse. The city issued a citation. Some of the people involved met with the city and made the case for how their project met the city's own goals, which resulted in the issuing of another temporary permit.

The processes and aesthetics of Share-It Square, as well as much of City Repair's work to come, were shaped partly by the life experiences of Lakeman. His father, architect Richard Lakeman, was the founder of Portland's Urban Design Division within the Bureau of Planning and was a driving force behind Portland's Pioneer Courthouse Square. His mother, architect and theorist Sandra Davis Lakeman, studied the characteristics of natural light and urban form in ancient villages, particularly the Italian piazza. Mark himself had spent many years traveling and learning from the practices and traditions of Native Americans.

The next manifestation of City Repair was a mobile T-Horse, which went from park to park serving donated tea and baked goods. Dozens of people would appear for these gatherings. There was a lot of cross-pollination between City Repair and other community-based artistic endeavors at the time, including Art Quake and Last Thursday. The T-Horse eventually evolved into the heavy and cumbersome Tea Palace.

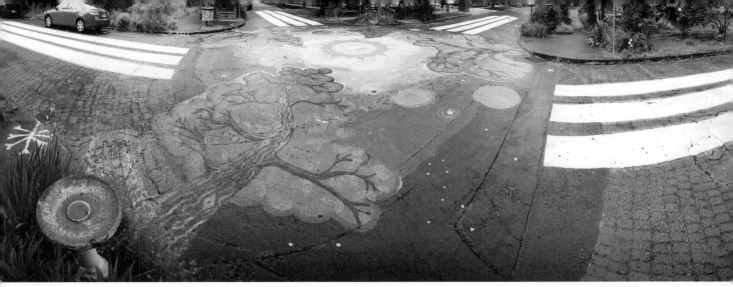

Intersection mural at Southeast 9th and Sherrett

These activities built enough popular support for City Repair that the city passed an ordinance in 1998 that established a process for legal intersection paintings. Originally, all neighbors within a three-block radius of the project had to weigh in on it, and if there was 90 percent approval, it could go forward. Today, a proposed intersection mural must have the support of 80 percent of residents within two city blocks of the project.

In 1999 City Repair became a nonprofit. Its mission centers on the idea of placemaking—the creative, environmental sustainability-focused reclamation of public space. The organization strives to link mainstream and radical processes by striving to change official policy, as well as working outside it.

The legal permit process didn't initially lead to a flood of intersection paintings. In 2001, Sunnyside Piazza (Southeast Thirty-Third and Yamhill) was the first project to follow the permit process for an intersection painting. Around this same time, City Repair became interested in natural building materials, particularly cob, as an accessible, participatory means of building structures. In 2002 they held a Natural Building Convergence in Portland. The next year, the Natural Building Convergence evolved into the first Village Building Convergence (called VBC3). It was based in the Southeast neighborhoods around the Sunnyside Piazza and around People's Food Co-op. At that time, the city's Office of Sustainable Development had small grants available for natural building projects and green roofs. They asked City Repair to research and create some example projects. In 2004, VBC4 took place in a larger area but was still confined to Southeast Portland.

In the years since, the annual VBC has expanded to include natural building projects, edible and native plant gardens, and other permaculture-focused projects. It's expanded geographically as well, first to other parts of Inner Eastside, then to west Portland, the outer eastside, and even a few sites in the suburbs. It's now a ten-day festival held every spring. During the day, volunteers participate in hands-on projects throughout the city. In the evenings there are food, speakers, and performances by local musicians. Although anyone in Portland can organize an intersection painting at any time, there are no examples of an intersection painting that has been created outside the framework of the VBC.

On Saturday, May 25, 2013, at Southeast 130th Place and Southeast Ramona, an intersection mural was painted as part of the VBC. The mural design is a book that turns into a butterfly, suggesting that a strong educational foundation helps one navigate the world. Two-year-olds and teenagers were equally excited to paint.

Intersection mural at Southeast 130th Place and Ramona

VI. FOOD AND DRINK

Food and drink are critical elements of how we experience places on a daily basis, and Portland is no exception. Regional variations in cuisine make places distinct. Here the environment is conducive to year-round produce, large variety, and a one-hundred-mile diet. Organic production, locally sourced ingredients, James Beard Award–winning chefs, and an explosion of food carts are some of what characterize Portland's distinction of foodie haven. The *New York Times* in particular seems smitten with Portland and its food scene.

Portland is in the midst of a renaissance in artisanal production of foods and beverages. Despite not having particularly large populations of many ethnic groups, the city features food from just about every corner of the world. Both coffee and beer are very big in a place with a good reputation for both—coffee and beer snobs are bountiful as well. Pork seems to have replaced salmon as the celebrated delicious protein of choice. Ice cream flavors involving balsamic vinegar, gorgonzola, and pear are already mundane here.

However, not everyone's eating kale salads with nettles and lavender-infused vinaigrette. Not everyone drinks locally branded coffee made one cup at a time. Portland is also a place with many chains at which foodies love to sneer. Starbucks, McDonald's, and Subway are everywhere for the simple reason that they're popular. The cuisine in Portland is, in many ways, as American as anywhere else. Furthermore, there are many in Portland who struggle to put food on the table at all. For those families and individuals, stretching their food dollar trumps anything else.

In this chapter, we take a closer look at some of the culinary and liquid dimensions of Portland.

ANY GIVEN SUNDAY

Few things are as certain as the fact that across Portland on weekend mornings, no matter how bad the weather, people will wait in line outside for up to two hours for brunch. Many things attract people to brunch, but foremost among them is the unspoken social contract involved which mandates that no matter how late into the afternoon you get a table, you can still get breakfast. And what is brunch, really, but breakfast with a five-dollar surcharge for waiting in line.

Putting in a long shift of waiting in line for the fried chicken and waffle at the Screen Door or the Reggie at Pine State Biscuits is a badge of honor in some circles here. And should anyone tire of the old standby dishes, the restaurant scene's obsession with in-season local food ensures an unrelenting cycle of innovative takes on beloved classics.

The brunch line says something about people in Portland and the left-coast priorities that exist here. Waiting in line disrupts the normal hierarchies of society and rearranges them according to who put their party's name on the clipboard first. Then again, perhaps just being in line is in itself a social marker, a declaration that one has three and half hours to spend on breakfast.

However, the Portland brunch line woefully endures a reputation in popular culture that emphasizes the well-worn hipster tropes of the city. Exhibit A: Waiting in line for brunch is spoofed with near weekly regularity on the situation comedy *Portlandia*. A similar satire that might hit close to home for many Portlanders ranks breakfast places as number thirty-six in a list of "Stuff White People Like." The ranking comes with the caveat that arriving late to a breakfast place might involve waiting in line for a significant period of time "with white people who cannot wait to get vegan pancakes, eggs benedict, waffles, or deluxe French toast. To a white person, there is no better way to spend a Saturday morning."

Table 1

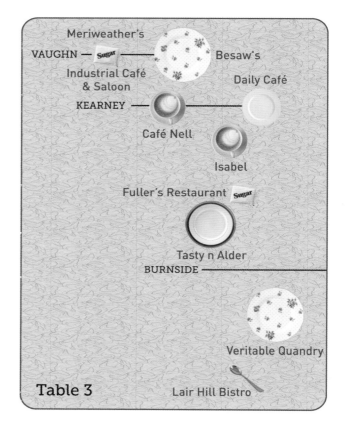

Table 3

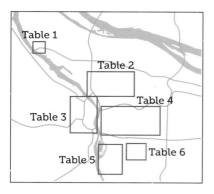

WAIT TO BE SEATED FOR SUNDAY BRUNCH

2 hours   1 hour   1/2 hour   No Wait

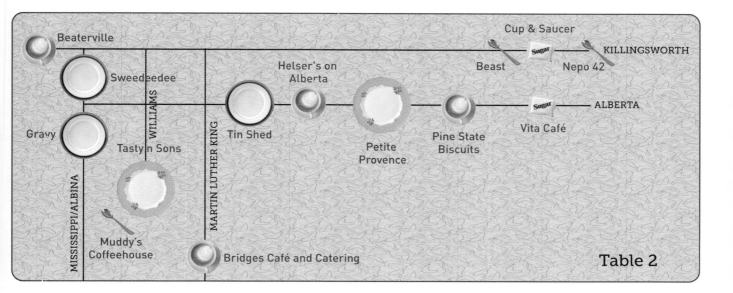

Table 2

Beaterville

Sweedeedee

Gravy

WILLIAMS

Tasty n Sons

MISSISSIPPI/ALBINA

Muddy's Coffeehouse

MARTIN LUTHER KING

Tin Shed

Bridges Café and Catering

Helser's on Alberta

Petite Provence

Pine State Biscuits

Cup & Saucer

Beast

Sugar

Nepo 42

KILLINGSWORTH

Sugar

Vita Café

ALBERTA

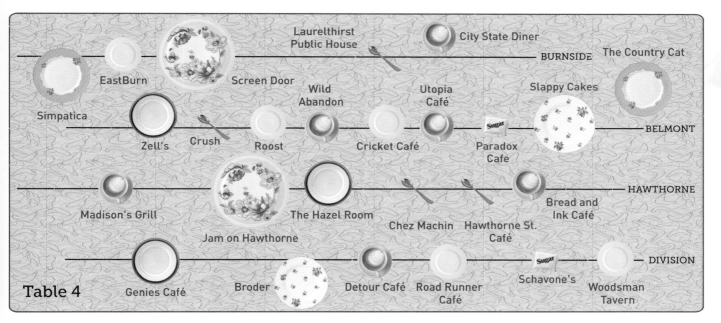

Table 4

Simpatica

EastBurn

Screen Door

Zell's

Crush

Roost

Laurelthirst Public House

City State Diner

Wild Abandon

Utopia Café

Cricket Café

Paradox Cafe

Sugar

Slappy Cakes

The Country Cat

BURNSIDE

BELMONT

Madison's Grill

Jam on Hawthorne

The Hazel Room

Chez Machin

Hawthorne St. Café

Bread and Ink Café

HAWTHORNE

Genies Café

Broder

Detour Café

Road Runner Café

Schavone's

Sugar

Woodsman Tavern

DIVISION

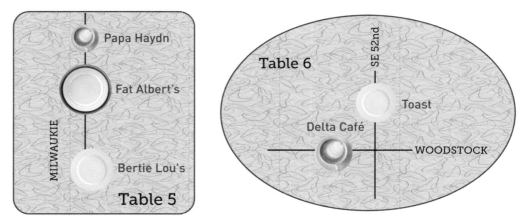

Table 5

MILWAUKIE

Papa Haydn

Fat Albert's

Bertie Lou's

Table 6

SE 52nd

Delta Café

Toast

WOODSTOCK

FOOD CART-O-GRAMS

A well-known and much celebrated aspect of Portland food culture is food carts, any collection of which is called a pod. Mapping the food cart scene in any comprehensive way is impossible. Mobile by nature, carts are constantly relocating from pod to pod. Furthermore, carts are always going in and out of business. The map to the side illustrates this dynamic at the Alder Street pod with data from two years, 2012 and 2014.

Part of the appeal of food carts is being able to roll up to a pod and have the opportunity to choose from a number of very different cuisines from across the country and different parts of the world. With that in mind, instead of mapping where carts are located in the city, we thought it would be interesting to map the origin of the cuisines featured in Portland food carts.

To do that, we opted to represent the data as a cartogram, a map style that is uncommon in standard media outlets. Instead of representing the area of different countries, we made the size of the country relative to how many food carts in Portland feature its cuisine. In this case, countries are represented by squares instead of the shapes of their borders. The largest squares belong to Mexico and Thailand because cuisine from those two countries is the most common among Portland food carts (outside of food associated with the United States).

Another cartogram represents carts associated with particular regional cuisines of the United States. At this time, barbecue and Southern cuisine have the largest number of carts, excluding the ubiquitous categories of burgers, hot dogs, and pizza.

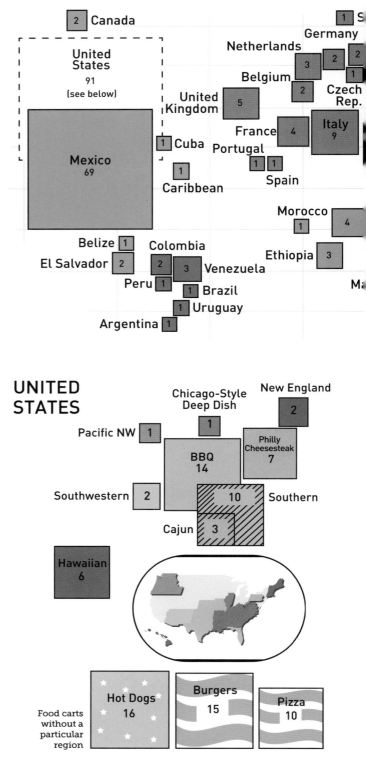

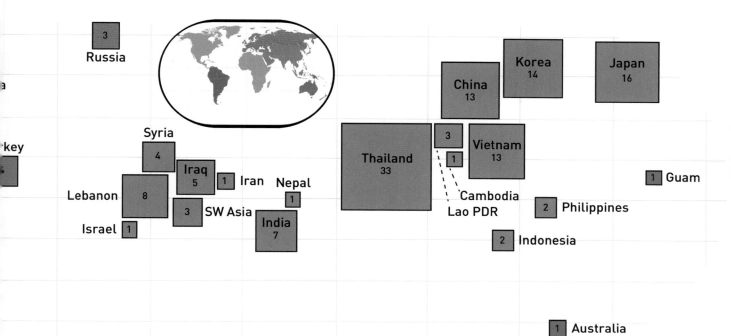

Russia 3	Korea 14	Japan 16
	China 13	
Syria 4	3	
Iraq 5	Vietnam 13	Guam 1
Lebanon 8	Iran 1	Nepal 1
Israel 1	SW Asia 3	Thailand 33
	India 7	Cambodia / Lao PDR 1
key		Philippines 2
		Indonesia 2

Australia 1

10TH & ALDER FOOD CART POD

Parking not for customers

East of the river, pods tend to be a bit smaller but configured in a more intimate and social way. These pods tend to serve a clientele that is off work and looking to eat on-site. The carts face inward, and instead of parked cars, the interior of east-side pods tend to have seating, planters, and areas for children to play. Most importantly, some of the east-side pods harbor little beer gardens too.

GOOD FOOD HERE FOOD CART POD

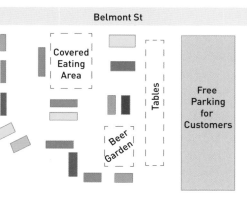

Belmont St

Covered Eating Area

Tables

Free Parking for Customers

Beer Garden

Food cart pods take decidedly different forms depending on which side of the Willamette River they are located on. West of the river, the pods tend to face the sidewalk and line the periphery of parking lots. Downtown pods such as the one on Alder Street provide many different possibilities for cuisine but very few options for seating. Vendors are generally serving a lunch crowd that must retreat to the office or eat on the curb.

Willamette River

A PALER SHADE OF ALE

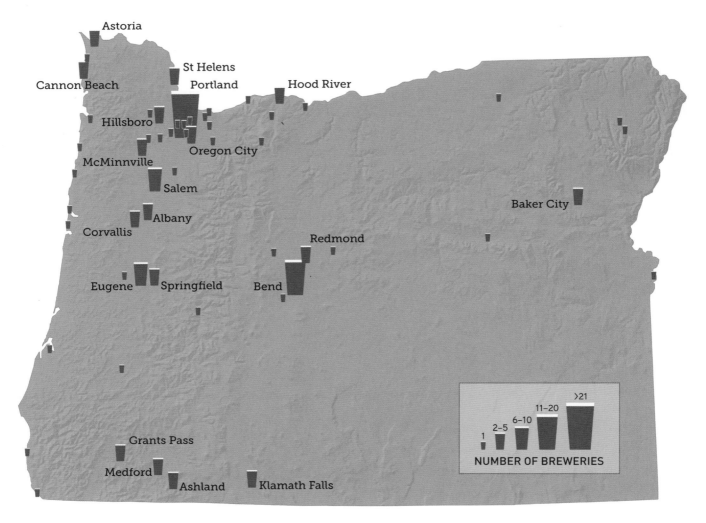

Oregon is for beer lovers. Home to over 220 brewing facilities in seventy different cities, the state ranks first in the United States for breweries per capita. Craft beer is enormously popular, and Oregon also ranks first nationally for percentage of dollars spent on it. Nearly 20 percent of all beer consumed in Oregon, and 53 percent of total draft beer, was made in-state.

The Oregon Brewers Guild, a nonprofit organization formed in 1992, coordinates a statewide brewery open house on President's Day weekend called Zwickelmania. The event is named for the spigot on the side of a fermentation tank used to draw beer for quality control sampling, known in brewing circles as a zwickel valve. The event is intended to directly connect the public with people who make craft beer—an example of the localism that tends to color much of the craft beer industry throughout Oregon. This localism is not only demonstrated by countless beer festivals and tastings, but in many other ways as well. For example, a Portland artist conducts a program called Beers Made by Walking, which involves brewers hiking in local areas, collecting edible plants and wild strains of yeast found along the way, and using them as ingredients in beers inspired by their journey.

Portland is renowned for its brewpubs and beer culture, and basks in that reputation. There are approximately fifty-six breweries in Portland and seventy-six in the metro area, which is more than any other city in the world. Portland leads the United States for percentage of dollars spent on craft beer. The Oregon Zoo Foundation used to host a beer festival fundraiser—Zoo Brew. Homebrew clubs abound. We put beer in ice cream here. Yes, Portlanders take their beer pretty seriously.

The story of Portland beer usually begins with Henry Weinhard, a German immigrant who moved to town, began brewing under his family name in 1856, and began what became the largest brewery in Cascadia by the end of the nineteenth century. The brewery operated for 135 years until it closed in 1999. By then, other ideas about Portland beer had already taken root.

Today, brewers seek out local ingredients; emphasize the importance of unfiltered, local water; and often choose names based on local places for their creations. Farm-to-glass sourcing and utilizing seasonal ingredients seems to be the Portland brewing credo. Every detail matters. Appreciating beer has many dimensions, but two of the most important aspects of experiencing a beer are color and taste, which are examined in these pages. We also compiled a list of beers with names that relate to the city, shown on the next pages along with color of each beer.

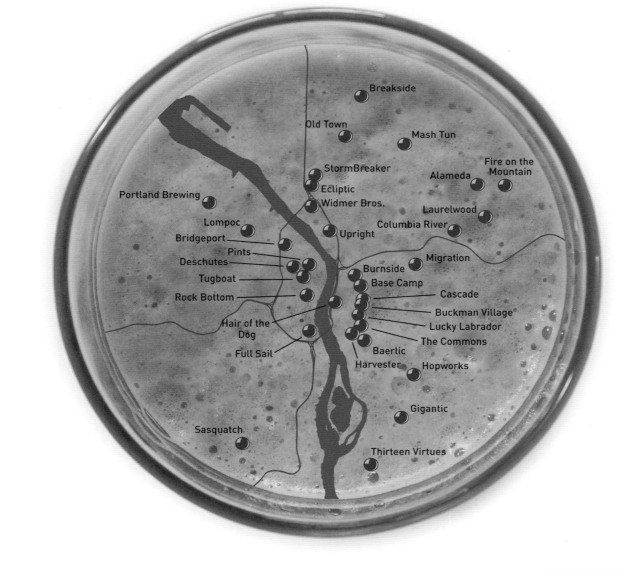

COLOR

Beer is nearly always served in clear glasses because color is so instrumental to the sensory experience of quaffing suds. The color of a beer is usually the first indicator of how a beer might taste. Deciding which beer to order often starts with the question—light or dark?

Beer color is largely determined by the malted grains used in making beer. The kinds of grains and length of time they are brewed are both key. The darker the malts and the longer they spend cooking, the darker the beer.

There are a number of technical approaches used around the world to discuss beer color. In the 1880s a color scale developed in Britain, Degrees Lovibond, matched beer colors to a set array of colored slides. In the mid-twentieth century a separate visual system emerged from the European Brewery Convention. The more modern Standard Reference Method involves using a photometer to measure the amount of light that passes though one centimeter of a particular beer. However, none of these scales have much traction in Portland, and people just describe beer colors by comparison—"This porter is even darker than Stumptown Espresso Stout!"—or relative opacity—"Sheesh, this lager is light enough to read through!"

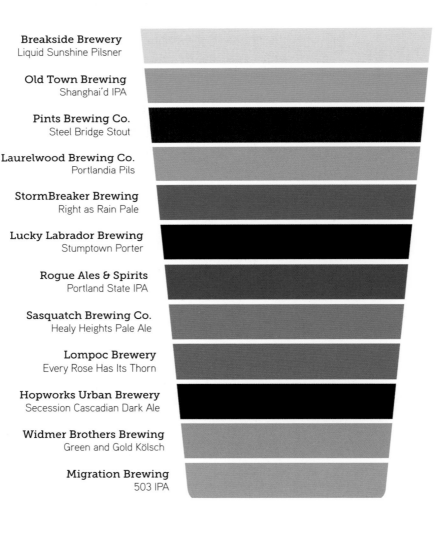

Breakside Brewery
Liquid Sunshine Pilsner

Old Town Brewing
Shanghai'd IPA

Pints Brewing Co.
Steel Bridge Stout

Laurelwood Brewing Co.
Portlandia Pils

StormBreaker Brewing
Right as Rain Pale

Lucky Labrador Brewing
Stumptown Porter

Rogue Ales & Spirits
Portland State IPA

Sasquatch Brewing Co.
Healy Heights Pale Ale

Lompoc Brewery
Every Rose Has Its Thorn

Hopworks Urban Brewery
Secession Cascadian Dark Ale

Widmer Brothers Brewing
Green and Gold Kölsch

Migration Brewing
503 IPA

BITTERNESS

Historians suggest that beer has been around for between 9,000 and 12,000 years, but apparently no one thought to add hops until about 1,200 years ago in Northern France, where written records suggest wild hops were first used for brewing. Probably around that same time, hops were also domesticated in Bavaria. Previously, hops had been harvested primarily for medicinal purposes.

Today, hops are king in the Portland brewing scene. Not accidentally, Oregon is currently the second largest producer of hops in the United States after Washington, which produces over five times as much. However, Washington doesn't have a professional baseball team named after this key brewing ingredient—Oregon and the Portland area do in the form of the Hillsboro Hops, a minor league affiliate of the Arizona Diamondbacks.

The top hop varieties grown in Oregon are Nugget, Willamette, and Cascade. Late summer marks the harvest and early fall is ushered in with a series of hop fests held throughout the region. Because hops grow so well in the Willamette Valley, brewers compete to make imperial India pale ales that stretch the tolerable limits of bitterness. Likewise, puns employed to articulate the extreme hoppyness of the bottle contents are brought to the edge of reason. Witness: Base Camp Brewing's Hoptastic Voyage, Sasquatch Brewing's Drop It Like It's Hop'd, and Laurelwood's The Audacity of Hops.

Another popular local hop-heavy favorite is the Cascadian dark ale (or black ale), a variety created in the area and one that wears its place identity on its label. To the point, Hopworks Urban Brewery calls their version Secession Cascadian Dark Ale, which features the Doug and the outline of Cascadia on the bottle. Cascadian dark ales, black in color and as hoppy as an IPA, date only to the 1990s.

The globally recognized gauge for measuring the relative bitterness of beer is the International Bitterness Units (IBU) scale. Unlike the classification schemes for color, Portlanders seem to embrace the IBU system. Bars and pubs across the city post the IBUs of each beer to aid savvy Portlanders who're either looking to indulge in or avoid the colossal hoppy bitterness that's so widespread.

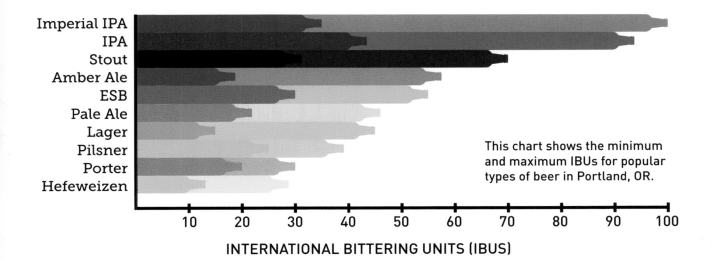

This chart shows the minimum and maximum IBUs for popular types of beer in Portland, OR.

INTERNATIONAL BITTERING UNITS (IBUS)

SMALL HALF-CAFF
SKINNY EXTRA-HOT
CARAMEL CAPPUCCINO
WITH EXTRA FOAM
IN A LARGE CUP

Distance from Independent Coffee Shops
(Miles)

.25   1   2   3   4   5   6   7

Starbucks Coffee Locations

● Company Owned
● Licensed

A Portland coffeehouse evokes images of industrial chic—somewhere on the decor spectrum between retro-modern and frumpy around the edges, located in a neighborhood serving cultural refugees from other parts of the United States who think any place with more than one location is "too corporate."

Closer inspection of the distribution of coffee in the city reveals quite a bit of diversity in the subcultures coffee shops serve and the neighborhoods where they cluster. One coffee shop is next to a hospital and police precinct, so in addition to the retired guys having coffee next to young parents briefly liberated while their kids are at school and couples out walking their dog, there's a larger than normal sprinkling of policemen and hospital workers taking a break. At another, hemp wallets and the daily astrological signs are prominently displayed at the cash register; in another part of town, the couple next to you has a baby stroller that costs more than your first car did.

This is just a sample from Portland proper; the shops in Gresham and Hillsboro, on the east and west flanks of the city, would represent a still more diverse clientele. One thing all coffee shops have in common, even Starbucks, is a coming together of people in the city to share conversation and engage the community. The United States has long been a place where the question "Do you want to have a cup of coffee?" means much more than a literal cup of coffee. It means "Do you want to sit down and talk, gossip, or catch up on what's happening in work and life?" The indie work ethic in Portland means that many people in coffee shops are still staring at their screens, but in a setting that allows for the opportunity to interact or observe.

Closest coffee sources for Portland

While the map to the left speaks to the everydayness of coffee shops in Portland, it also highlights the precious character of local coffee culture. Sprinkled among this array of places are a number of shops with coffee menus resembling a wine list at a chichi restaurant, where descriptions of coffee flavors include "buttery," "grapefruit," "olive," and "raspberry," and information on the menu or label can include country of origin (Ethiopia, Costa Rica, Honduras, Indonesia)—sometimes specific plantation of origin—as well as methods of processing and coffee varieties. Local roaster websites offer educational information: portraits and minibiographies of growers, details about harvesting and roasting of the coffee beans, and more information than you might want to know about the different ways to make coffee (AeroPress, Chemex, French press, moka, Melitta, and more). Then there are the coffee tastings, or "cuppings" in the vernacular; barista competitions; and earnest espresso makers who let you know they make the Italian version of a macchiato, not what Starbucks invented. Much of this effort strives mightily to construct coffee consumption as a "local" good, even though that's impractical, if not impossible, in the United States (except in Hawaii, of course). It's also resulted in a much more informed (if not highly caffeinated) public and a large number of spaces for people to gather for social stimulation: "Do you want to have a cup of coffee?"

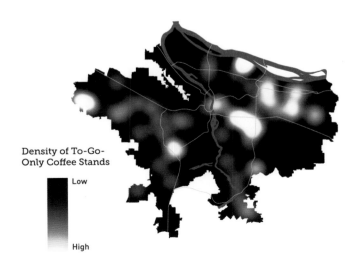

Density of To-Go-Only Coffee Stands

Low

High

ANYTHING YOU CAN DO, I CAN DO VEGAN

In Portland, there are a plethora of vegan subcultures and groups that deal with diet (raw vegans), corporate sabotage and activism (the Animal Liberation Front), and the environment (pop vegans). Veganism is also a spectrum: some people call themselves vegan while wearing leather jackets, and others use personal care products with honey in them. More strict vegans adhere to the "nothing with a face" rule and eschew both the dairy and meat industries.

As the map demonstrates, although vegan businesses are located throughout the city, there seems to be a discernible core in downtown and inner Southeast. Growth seems to be decidedly north and east. It's easy to be vegan in Portland; besides the plethora of vegan food options in restaurants, grocery stores, farmers' markets, and the fully vegan grocery called Food Fight!, there are cruelty-free options for everything from haircuts and tattoos to clothing and makeup. Social media and websites are updated constantly with new vegan restaurant and local product reviews, weekly events congregate vegans for drink meet-ups at bars, and there are even five-kilometer runs for animal rights. Local, artisan vegan products flourish as well: hand-screen-printed apparel with phrases like "vegan for the animals," cashew-based "cheese," and artwork reflecting vegan values can be found even in conventional grocery stores and local shops.

Environmental values and human rights are integral to Portland culture, exemplified by an emphasis on sustainability in everything from city planning to at-home recycling to locally made, sweatshop-free apparel to canvassers on street corners imploring residents to support the less fortunate. These values, too, inform veganism in Portland. Vegan culture here has incorporated these ideals by promoting the environmental benefits of eating lower on the food chain, supporting local vegan businesses, and advocating for handmade products over the mass-produced and imported. In this way, local vegans are making global changes, benefits of which conventional businesses and restaurants that cater to omnivores take note of. Being vegan is still a Portland stereotype, but with good reason: as vegan culture evolves, so does that of Portland. One informs the other, making veganism another part of what makes Portland, Portland.

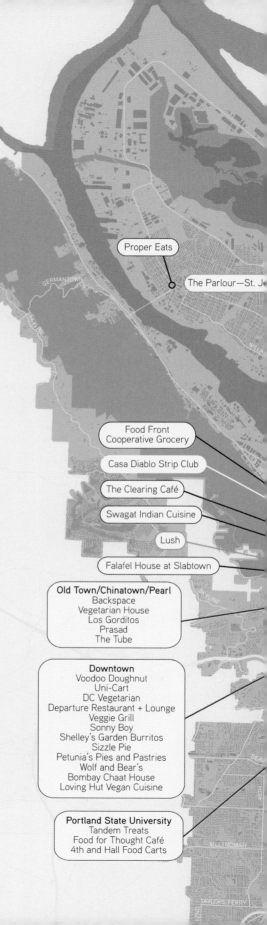

Proper Eats

The Parlour—St. J

Food Front Cooperative Grocery

Casa Diablo Strip Club

The Clearing Café

Swagat Indian Cuisine

Lush

Falafel House at Slabtown

Old Town/Chinatown/Pearl
Backspace
Vegetarian House
Los Gorditos
Prasad
The Tube

Downtown
Voodoo Doughnut
Uni-Cart
DC Vegetarian
Departure Restaurant + Lounge
Veggie Grill
Sonny Boy
Shelley's Garden Burritos
Sizzle Pie
Petunia's Pies and Pastries
Wolf and Bear's
Bombay Chaat House
Loving Hut Vegan Cuisine

Portland State University
Tandem Treats
Food for Thought Café
4th and Hall Food Carts

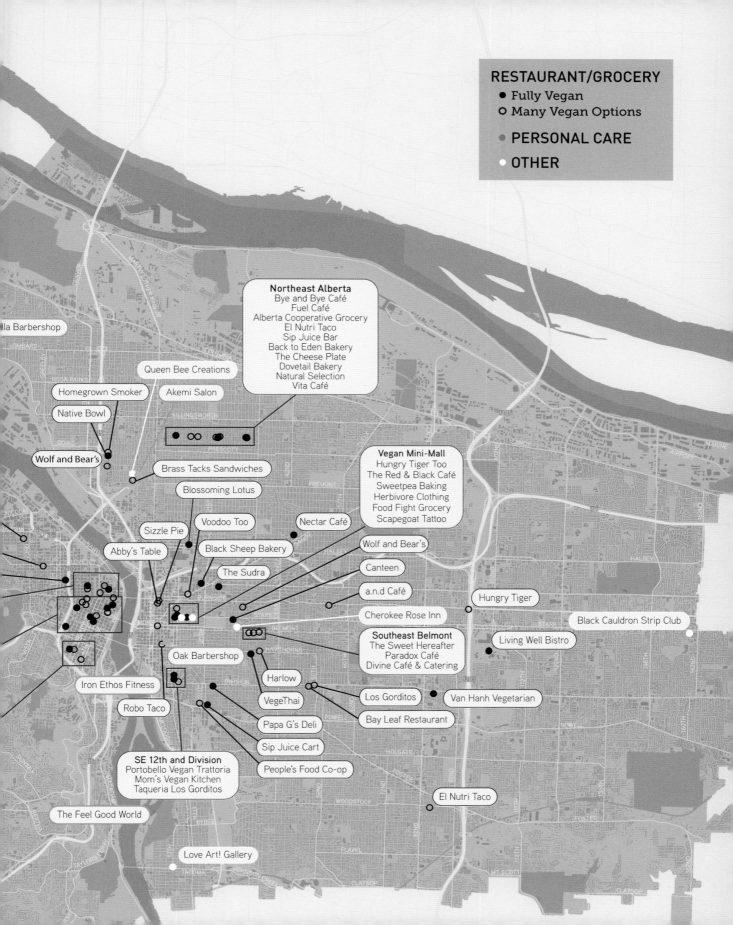

RESTAURANT/GROCERY
- ● Fully Vegan
- ○ Many Vegan Options

● PERSONAL CARE

○ OTHER

Northeast Alberta
Bye and Bye Café
Fuel Café
Alberta Cooperative Grocery
El Nutri Taco
Sip Juice Bar
Back to Eden Bakery
The Cheese Plate
Dovetail Bakery
Natural Selection
Vita Café

Vegan Mini-Mall
Hungry Tiger Too
The Red & Black Café
Sweetpea Baking
Herbivore Clothing
Food Fight Grocery
Scapegoat Tattoo

Southeast Belmont
The Sweet Hereafter
Paradox Café
Divine Café & Catering

SE 12th and Division
Portobello Vegan Trattoria
Mom's Vegan Kitchen
Taqueria Los Gorditos

la Barbershop
Queen Bee Creations
Homegrown Smoker
Akemi Salon
Native Bowl
Wolf and Bear's
Brass Tacks Sandwiches
Blossoming Lotus
Voodoo Too
Nectar Café
Sizzle Pie
Black Sheep Bakery
Wolf and Bear's
Abby's Table
The Sudra
Canteen
a.n.d Café
Hungry Tiger
Cherokee Rose Inn
Black Cauldron Strip Club
Living Well Bistro
Oak Barbershop
Harlow
VegeThai
Los Gorditos
Van Hanh Vegetarian
Iron Ethos Fitness
Robo Taco
Bay Leaf Restaurant
Papa G's Deli
Sip Juice Cart
People's Food Co-op
El Nutri Taco
The Feel Good World
Love Art! Gallery

FARM TO MARKET

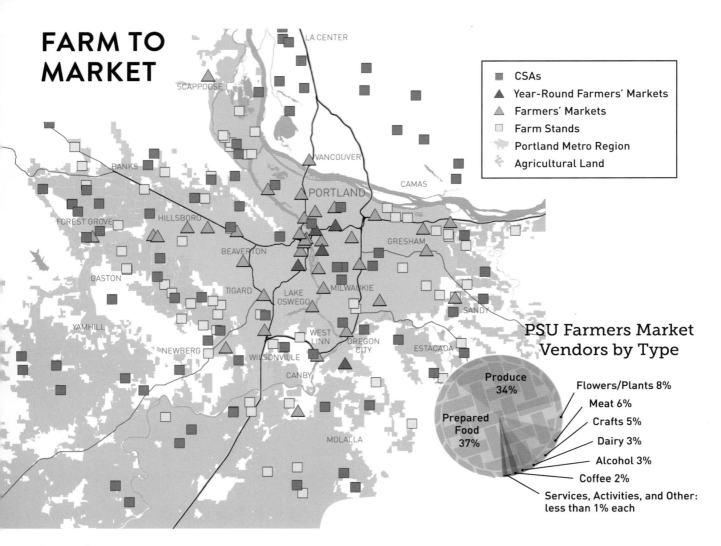

CSAs
Year-Round Farmers' Markets
Farmers' Markets
Farm Stands
Portland Metro Region
Agricultural Land

LA CENTER
SCAPPOOSE
BANKS
VANCOUVER
CAMAS
PORTLAND
FOREST GROVE
HILLSBORO
BEAVERTON
GRESHAM
GASTON
TIGARD
LAKE OSWEGO
MILWAUKIE
SANDY
YAMHILL
WEST LINN
OREGON CITY
ESTACADA
NEWBERG
WILSONVILLE
CANBY
MOLALLA

PSU Farmers Market Vendors by Type

Produce 34%
Flowers/Plants 8%
Meat 6%
Crafts 5%
Dairy 3%
Prepared Food 37%
Alcohol 3%
Coffee 2%
Services, Activities, and Other: less than 1% each

"Eat local" has become a mantra in certain cultural and economic circles, particularly for those who feel it satisfies a social or environmental mission. Many people in the United States strive to spend their food dollars on food produced within a not yet well-defined "local" area. While defining what constitutes local remains elusive—food produced within 50 miles of the market? 200 miles?—and the social and environmental benefits seem intuitive but aren't well-documented either, there's abundant evidence that this movement has changed the food-buying and food-consuming landscape in North America. Portland has enthusiastically embraced this idea. It's hard to go far in the city without seeing evidence: raised beds in parking strips planted with tomatoes, broccoli, beans, and the ever-popular kale; chicken coops in side yards; community gardens; and entire front yards devoted to vegetable gardens. One of the most visible aspects of a growing demand for ways to feel engaged with the local economy is the abundance of farmers' markets in and around the city. Portland

has them in nearly every neighborhood, every day of the week during the summer, and several operate on a year-round format. In some ways, farmers' markets have become an important part of the social, cultural, and economic fabric of the city.

Native American groups in the area have eaten locally and regionally for thousands of years. Early European settlers, who brought with them gardening and farming traditions, subsisted on their own efforts as well; eating local used to be the only option. Commercial agriculture has its origins in settlers growing wheat for export to the San Francisco Bay area and the California Gold Rush. Agriculture remains important in Oregon as well as overall in the Willamette Valley, and three of the Portland metropolitan area counties, Washington, Clackamas, and Yamhill, are in the top ten counties in terms of value of agricultural production. Most of the farms serving metro area farmers' markets are concentrated just outside the urban areas. This has helped keep an agricultural

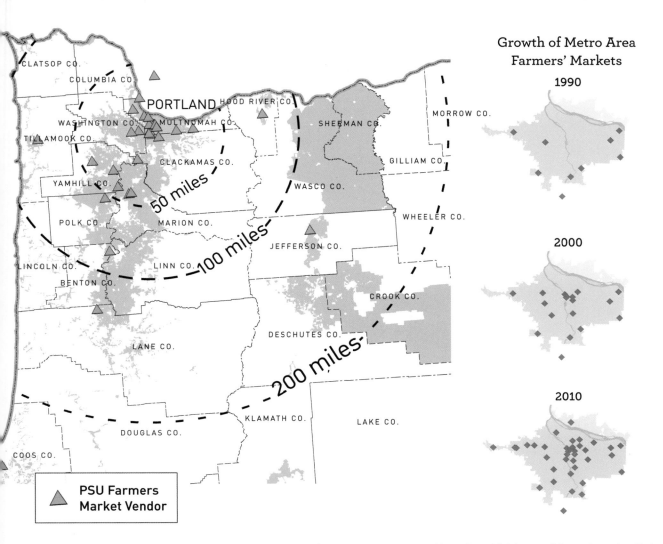

Growth of Metro Area Farmers' Markets

1990

2000

2010

△ PSU Farmers Market Vendor

landscape close to the city, facilitated, of course, by the state's land use planning laws, which established an Urban Growth Boundary.

While the notion of farmers' markets inevitably conjures up notions of farms, much of what's sold at markets is not fresh produce, and people often go to markets for reasons other than to purchase fresh food. They serve as a kind of urban agritainment—a city equivalent of the pumpkin patch or corn maze. Baked goods, prepared food, coffee, and crafts can occupy nearly 50 percent of the stands at a typical market. Individual markets regulate what percentage of each category of items can be sold; the Portland Farmers Market Association, which governs markets in Portland, doesn't allow craft sales, for example. Some markets clearly serve a neighborhood function and are small scale and low-key; the main Portland Farmers Market on the PSU campus can sometimes feel like a very hip county fair, with earnest thirty-somethings who've

recently moved here from Michigan or Wisconsin and well-dressed sixty-somethings who just stepped out of their high-priced condos to buy a fancy pastry and a bunch of flowers.

There's a lot to love about the dramatic increase in the number of farmers' markets in Portland and nationwide: they support local farms and help preserve an agricultural landscape around the city; they're bringing a much-needed younger generation into farming; they help people know and understand more about plants and the amazing diversity of food available to us; and they encourage people to cook. One hopes they can also serve as a bridge between the cultural values and economic realities of a time when "eating local" was the only option and our present time, when patronizing farmers' markets sometimes seems the special province of urban cultural elites.

THE FOOD CHAIN: DINING OUT

Portland's foodie reputation rests in many ways on its restaurant scene. A close look at the geography of Portland's restaurants reveals some interesting patterns, some of which seem congruent to Portland's foodie culture and some of which seem quite to the contrary.

Portland has the highest density of restaurants in the metropolitan area, a statistic that will shock no one. Many of these are one-of-a-kind restaurants or local chains. However, not all these eateries are Portland originals. There are many national and regional chains, but there's a curious division in the density of fast food restaurants (think McDonald's) compared to chain casual-dining restaurants (think Applebee's).

Contrary to the conventional foodie image of the city, Portland has the highest density of fast food restaurants in the region. Over 25 percent of these locations are Subways. The second most dominant fast food chain, McDonald's, makes up about 8 percent of the city's fast food eateries. Fast food establishments in Portland are most densely concentrated in downtown and the Lloyd District, with another pocket of density around Eighty-Second Avenue. The map below reveals few fast food deserts within Portland's city limits. The cities of Beaverton, Tigard, and Wilsonville—west of Portland—as well as Gresham to the east also reveal significant densities of fast food restaurants.

What Portland comparatively lacks is chain casual-dining destinations. Those restaurants cluster almost exclusively around the mall downtown, the Lloyd Center mall, and the Mall 205 area. Chain casual-dining establishments are more widespread outside Portland. Perhaps playing to type within the category of casual dining, some of the only restaurants that Portland has a greater percentage of than the overall metro region are breakfast places: Denny's, IHOP, Shari's, and Elmer's.

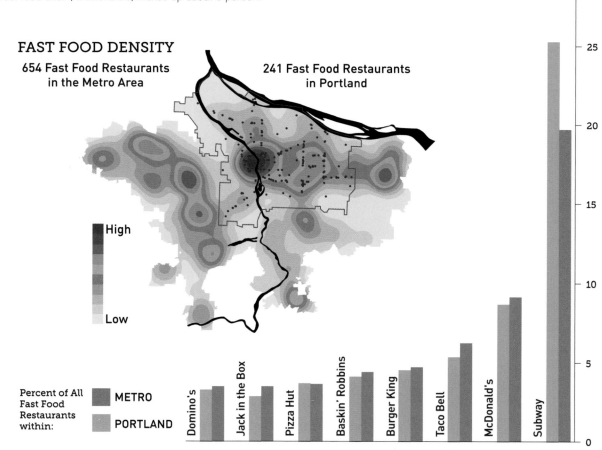

FAST FOOD DENSITY

654 Fast Food Restaurants in the Metro Area

241 Fast Food Restaurants in Portland

High

Low

Percent of All Fast Food Restaurants within:

METRO

PORTLAND

Domino's · Jack in the Box · Pizza Hut · Baskin' Robbins · Burger King · Taco Bell · McDonald's · Subway

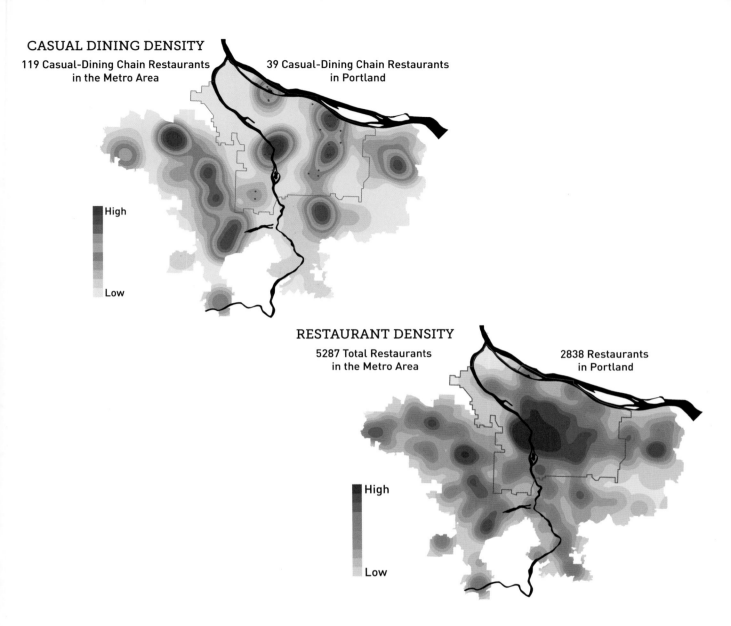

CASUAL DINING DENSITY

119 Casual-Dining Chain Restaurants in the Metro Area

39 Casual-Dining Chain Restaurants in Portland

High

Low

RESTAURANT DENSITY

5287 Total Restaurants in the Metro Area

2838 Restaurants in Portland

High

Low

RESTAURANTS PER CITY

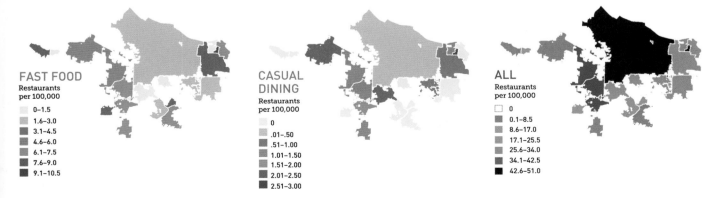

FAST FOOD
Restaurants
per 100,000

- 0–1.5
- 1.6–3.0
- 3.1–4.5
- 4.6–6.0
- 6.1–7.5
- 7.6–9.0
- 9.1–10.5

CASUAL DINING
Restaurants
per 100,000

- 0
- .01–.50
- .51–1.00
- 1.01–1.50
- 1.51–2.00
- 2.01–2.50
- 2.51–3.00

ALL
Restaurants
per 100,000

- 0
- 0.1–8.5
- 8.6–17.0
- 17.1–25.5
- 25.6–34.0
- 34.1–42.5
- 42.6–51.0

FOOD MIRAGES

Conventionally defined food deserts are rare in Portland. Grocery stores are well-distributed throughout the city, but not all grocery stores are created equal. The same basket of goods can range from less than $100 to over $200 depending on the store. Store price levels are clustered, with higher prices in the urban core and lower prices along the periphery. A food mirage describes a neighborhood served by only medium or high-cost stores, while low-cost stores are miles away. Such areas are tantamount to food deserts for low-income residents. A family in poverty might be within walking distance of a high-cost grocery store, but must travel miles farther to access healthy food at affordable prices. In a food mirage, good food is close at hand but economically out of reach. Hunger and food insecurity are rooted in income inequality. Increasing healthy food access for low-income households would require a shift toward a more equitable income distribution or a reduction in the cost of fresh produce. Efforts to improve food access on behalf of low-income households should not neglect ability to pay.

A food mirage is measured as the distance one must travel past the nearest grocery store to reach the nearest low-cost store. Most of the city is a food mirage for low-income households by this measure.

PRICE CHECK

What is affordable food? It depends on income. This study looks at healthy food affordability for low-income households (below 130 percent of poverty). Low-cost stores have prices that keep a healthy food budget within 30 percent of monthly income for low-income households. A high-cost store has prices 140 percent above the typical low-cost store.

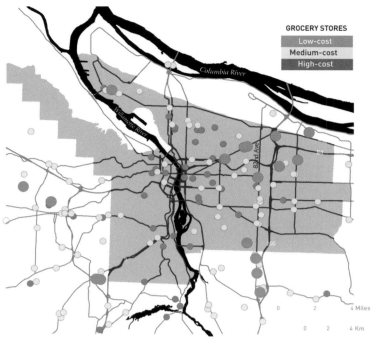

GROCERY STORES
- Low-cost
- Medium-cost
- High-cost

Columbia River

Willamette River

82nd Ave

0   2   4 Miles

0   2   4 Km

FOOD AND INCOME

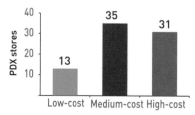

	WESTSIDE	EASTSIDE	
		West of 82nd	East of 82nd
SNAP (food stamp) usage	6%	13%	20%
Highest poverty rate by census tract	52.1%	35.1%	35.4%
Average household income	$70,000	$53,000	$43,000
Nearest grocery store (miles)	0.9	0.5	1.0
Food mirage distance (miles)	3.5	1.6	1.1

What makes a store affordable? Mainly the cost of fresh produce.

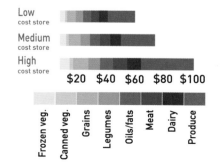

Low cost store

Medium cost store

High cost store

$20 $40 $60 $80 $100

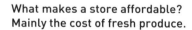

Frozen veg. | Canned veg. | Grains | Legumes | Oils/fats | Meat | Dairy | Produce

Are low-cost stores plentiful? Not in the city.

PDX stores

40
30
20
10

13 — Low-cost
35 — Medium-cost
31 — High-cost

Households experiencing severe poverty must travel the farthest to find affordable food.

Are food mirages linked to gentrification? Statistically, yes. Gentrifying eastside neighborhoods tend to have higher food mirage distances, although some diversifying areas are also food mirages. Gentrification pushes low-income households from close-in areas where grocery stores are plentiful but unaffordable to farther-out areas where prices are lower, but grocery stores are few and far between.

Are food mirages linked to poverty? Statistically, no. The west side of Portland is generally more affluent, although the deepest poverty is found downtown. On the eastside, households in poverty are spatially dispersed, dwelling in a variety of food environments. Eighty-three percent of households in poverty live more than one mile from a low-cost grocery store.

Distance to nearest low-cost grocery store:
PDX AVERAGE 2.5 miles

Distance to nearest grocery store:
PDX AVERAGE 0.7 miles

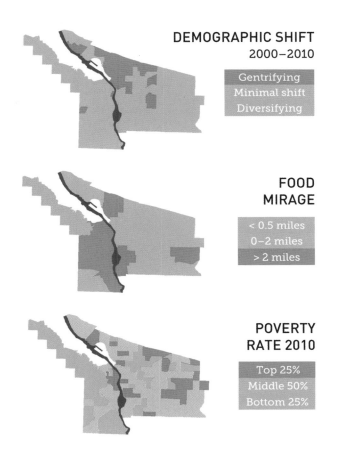

DEMOGRAPHIC SHIFT
2000–2010

- Gentrifying
- Minimal shift
- Diversifying

FOOD MIRAGE

- < 0.5 miles
- 0–2 miles
- > 2 miles

POVERTY RATE 2010

- Top 25%
- Middle 50%
- Bottom 25%

Food mirage distance:
PDX AVERAGE 1.8 miles

Distance by census tract:

< ½ mile	½–1 mile	> 1 mile

VII. POPULAR CULTURE

Popular culture is the everyday ways of life practiced by everyday people. Groups of people who engage in similar ways of life can form subcultures, which are attached to particular places. Music provides obvious examples—New Orleans is known for jazz, Detroit for soul, and Nashville for country. Not so much known for any one thing, Portland is a haven for many different, often quirky and peculiar subcultures. This is what gave birth to and makes meaningful the "Keep Portland Weird" slogan. That there are so many subcultures in Portland speaks to the wide variety of interests and ways of life of the people who live and spend time here. For those not interested in the intricacies of city hall politics, popular subcultures provide people with a different way of organizing and understanding the city.

This abundance of subcultures seems to be a big reason why many people move here despite the well-publicized dearth of jobs. People tend to move here because they think it'll be a nice place to live, not because it has lots of employment opportunities. Whatever it is you like to do, chances are that a large group of people are already doing it here. And chances are they're doing that thing obsessively. Tall bikes, roller derby, kickball, dodgeball, home spirit distillation, yarn bombing, Ultimate Frisbee, African drumming, Balkan/Eastern European folk music, dragon boating, competitive Scrabble—in Portland, there's a full-on established scene for each. Like many places on the West Coast, in Portland people tend to define themselves more by what they do for fun than by what they do for a living. And as a result, they often take what they do for fun very seriously. Subcultures provide people with a different way of relating to the city.

Portland also has a reputation for being tolerant of these many subcultures. This doesn't mean such tolerance is necessarily the case. However, if you're tempted to roll your eyes at another unicycle jousting tournament, chances are someone else is wondering why you care so much about artisan sauerkraut. Isn't that just cabbage, a food of last resort?

In this chapter, we tap into some of these subcultures for another set of perspectives about Portland.

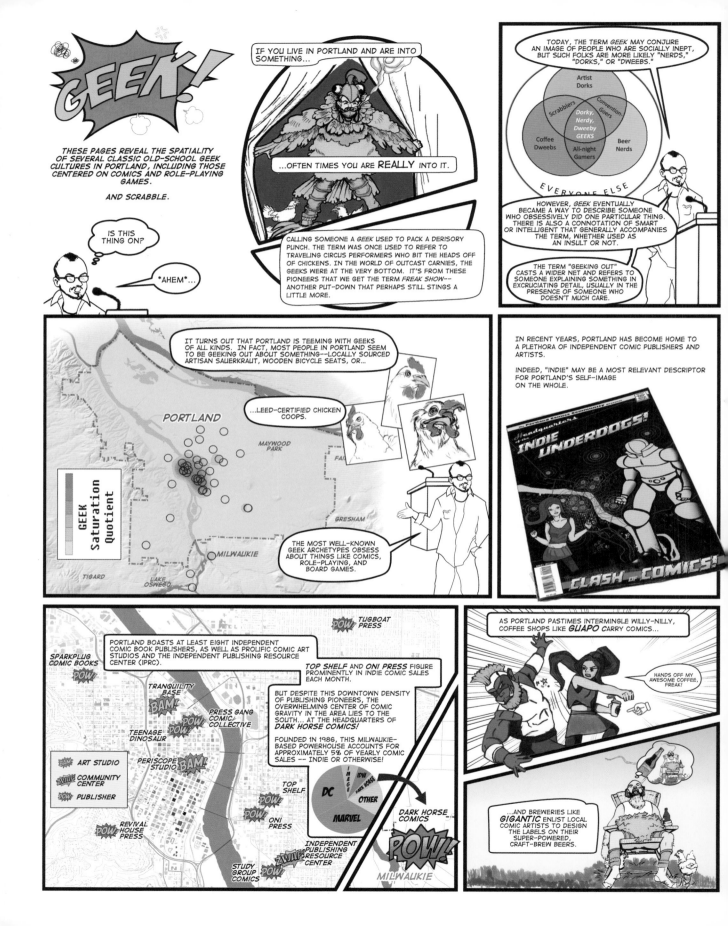

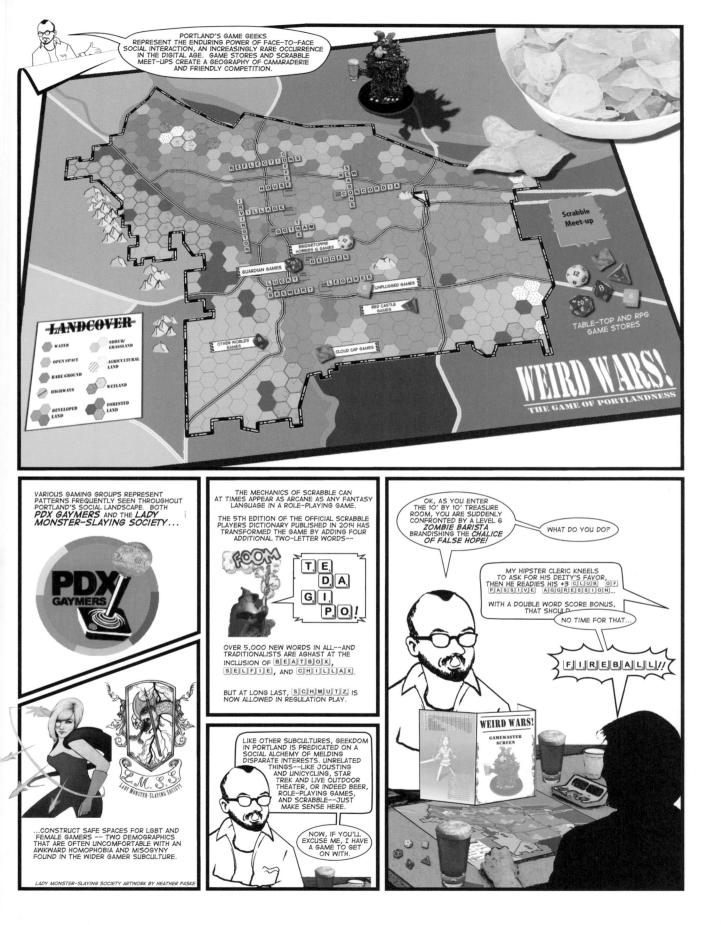

CORRIDORS OF CREATION

DOWNTOWN
● 1987

Art galleries appeared here in the mid-1980s, before the Pearl District nickname was even adopted. First Thursday, the monthly gallery walk in the neighborhood, began in 1986 when galleries were among the only retail businesses in an area dominated by warehouses and light industry. First Thursday attracted thousands of people to the neighborhood before the city and private developers began investing in the neighborhood. The Pacific Northwest College of Art and the advertising agency Wieden+Kennedy, located in the neighborhood, helped to set the scene. The number of galleries grew as light-rail construction made the area more palatable to many art aficionados. Later, restaurants and bars came to the area, which further established it as a destination. Now, however, many of these galleries are gone or have relocated—including all the galleries depicted on the map below near Southwest First and Second Avenues.

Alberta Arts District

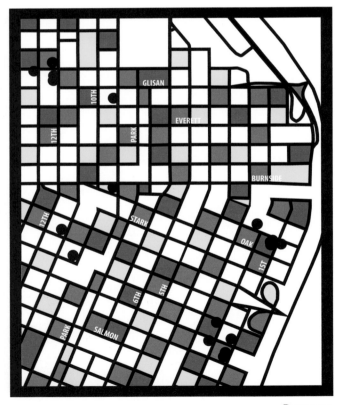

Downtown

THE ALBERTA ARTS DISTRICT
● Present

In the late 1990s and early 2000s, as the Pearl became increasingly upscale, another grassroots art walk arose in Northeast Portland: Last Thursday on Alberta Street. This, too, was an area that had been targeted for redevelopment and revitalization. In the 1980s and 1990s, Northeast Alberta was a case study in urban disinvestment: empty storefronts and houses, gang violence, and poor infrastructure. Community groups and the city worked together to create a redevelopment plan, part of which was the Alberta Streetscape Plan (2000), which included mural and public art in its vision for the street. Cheap rents attracted artists and galleries, and in 1997, a few of them opened their doors for the first Last Thursday. By 2009 the city was shutting down a stretch of the street to car traffic in order to accommodate the thousands of people, street performers, and vendors that flock to the event.

NORTHWEST ART GALLERIES
● Present

Another set of galleries arose in Old Town, another area continuing to undergo the urban renewal that began in the 1990s. The neighborhood had the cachet of being close to but not actually being the Pearl, whose sketchy edge has long been replaced by astronomical rents. One of the two original galleries in the Pearl, Butters Gallery, migrated to Old Town in 2000. However, by the mid-2000s many of the Old Town galleries closed or moved to other parts of the city because of escalating rents. The anchor for the art scene there is the Everett Street Lofts, three buildings that host forty-seven live-work art spaces and sixteen storefront studios. In 1989 a private developer bought the property and created the artist lofts. In 1998 the owner eschewed a higher profit by selling the building at market value to the artist-led national organization Artspace, which operates a network of thirty-five affordable arts live-work spaces in thirteen states. This allows artists to live and work downtown, shielded from the now skyrocketing rents in the neighborhood. A contingency of living in the Everett Street Lofts is participating in nine of the twelve annual First Thursdays.

DO IT YOURSELF

Portland is often associated with the DIY (do it yourself) movement. DIY means many different things. To some it's a life philosophy, and to others it's an aesthetic associated with the punk scene of the 1970s. DIY even relates to the Arts and Crafts movement in late nineteenth-century England. The industrial revolution brought a division of labor that mechanized production and catalyzed a decline in traditional approaches to making things. Value began to be placed on managing production and the use of machines rather than on skilled production. This movement advocated a return to individual craftsmanship and traditional preindustrial techniques in defiance of industrialization and its dehumanizing effects.

This movement diffused to North America, where it became known as craftsman style in the United States. The use of "style" in place of "movement" aptly captures the shift away from the socialist values that formed part of the Arts and Crafts movement in favor of focusing on the associated aesthetics. Also at this time, most pretenses of recapturing the modes of a preindustrial time were abandoned. In the United States the craftsman style developed primarily as an architectural approach.

During the first half of the twentieth century in the United States, the idea of "doing it yourself" was less a premeditated philosophy than it was stark reality. The affluent middle class that's associated with the United States today arose largely after World War II. People made do with what they had. After the war many people in the United States experienced an unprecedented growth in purchasing power. Buying something factory-made instead of making it yourself became a sign of both individual and national progress.

It didn't take long for some people to critique the increasing dependence on mass-produced consumer goods—a reaction similar in many ways, to the one that gave birth to the Arts and Crafts movement a hundred years earlier. This critique manifested itself in many ways, including DIY, which became a discernible contemporary movement in the 1970s, driven in part by environmentalism.

Today many of the subcultures associated with DIY—handcrafts, zines, and urban homesteading—are also associated with Portland. There's a vein of rejecting mass-produced consumer goods running through these subcultures as well. In tying the Arts and Crafts movement to DIY, this map highlights significant locations in the Portland handcraft scene.

The Naked Sheep Knit Shop

Dublin Bay Knitting Co.

Rose City Textiles

Floral Design Institute

Beet Gallery

Pacific Northwest College of Art

Pearl Fiber Arts

Museum of Contemporary Craft

Portland Saturday Market

Oregon College of Art and Craft

Knit Purl

The Playful Needle

Josephine's Dry Goods

Crafty Wonderland

Button Emporium & Ribbonry

Let It Bead

Handley Jewelry Supply

Angelika's Yarn Store

Northwest Wools

Multnomah Arts Cer

Opulent Fil

CRAFT STORES
- Education
- Studio or shop space
- Knitting or sewing supplies
- Jewelry-making supplies
- Crafts for sale

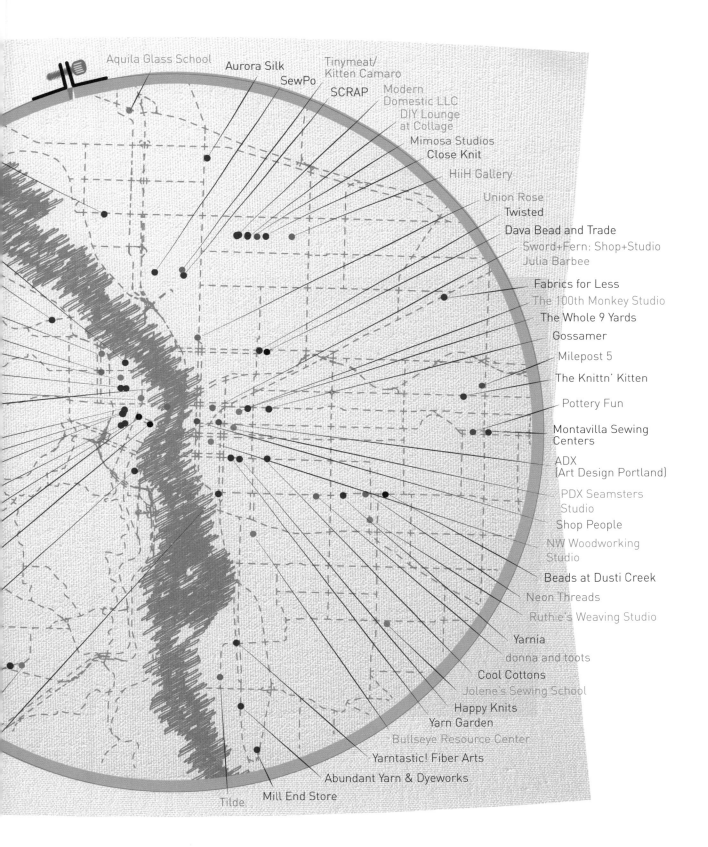

Aquila Glass School
Aurora Silk
SewPo
Tinymeat/
Kitten Camaro
SCRAP
Modern
Domestic LLC
DIY Lounge
at Collage
Mimosa Studios
Close Knit
HiiH Gallery
Union Rose
Twisted
Dava Bead and Trade
Sword+Fern: Shop+Studio
Julia Barbee
Fabrics for Less
The 100th Monkey Studio
The Whole 9 Yards
Gossamer
Milepost 5
The Knittn' Kitten
Pottery Fun
Montavilla Sewing
Centers
ADX
(Art Design Portland)
PDX Seamsters
Studio
Shop People
NW Woodworking
Studio
Beads at Dusti Creek
Neon Threads
Ruthie's Weaving Studio
Yarnia
donna and toots
Cool Cottons
Jolene's Sewing School
Happy Knits
Yarn Garden
Bullseye Resource Center
Yarntastic! Fiber Arts
Abundant Yarn & Dyeworks
Tilde
Mill End Store

RIDES, FESTS, AND PALOOZAS

THE ORIGINS OF OUR CELEBRATIONS

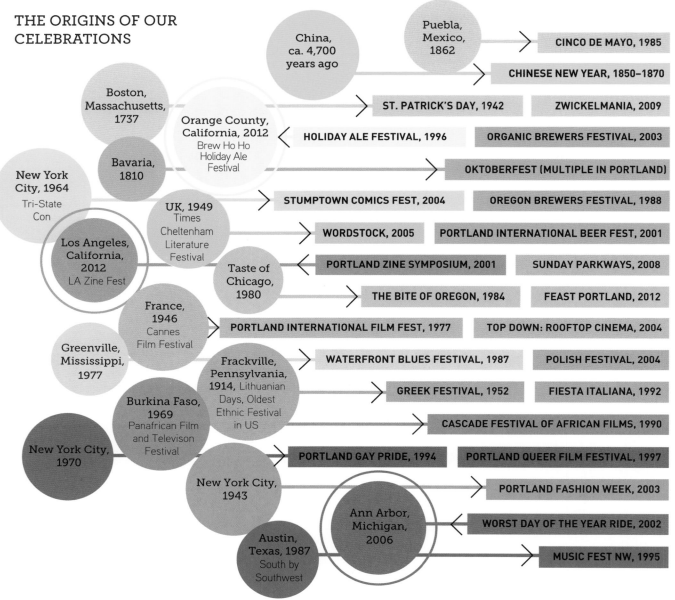

China, ca. 4,700 years ago

Puebla, Mexico, 1862 → **CINCO DE MAYO, 1985**

→ **CHINESE NEW YEAR, 1850–1870**

Boston, Massachusetts, 1737 → **ST. PATRICK'S DAY, 1942**   **ZWICKELMANIA, 2009**

Orange County, California, 2012
Brew Ho Ho Holiday Ale Festival ← **HOLIDAY ALE FESTIVAL, 1996**   **ORGANIC BREWERS FESTIVAL, 2003**

Bavaria, 1810 → **OKTOBERFEST (MULTIPLE IN PORTLAND)**

New York City, 1964
Tri-State Con

UK, 1949
Times Cheltenham Literature Festival → **STUMPTOWN COMICS FEST, 2004**   **OREGON BREWERS FESTIVAL, 1988**

→ **WORDSTOCK, 2005**   **PORTLAND INTERNATIONAL BEER FEST, 2001**

Los Angeles, California, 2012
LA Zine Fest

Taste of Chicago, 1980 ← **PORTLAND ZINE SYMPOSIUM, 2001**   **SUNDAY PARKWAYS, 2008**

→ **THE BITE OF OREGON, 1984**   **FEAST PORTLAND, 2012**

France, 1946
Cannes Film Festival → **PORTLAND INTERNATIONAL FILM FEST, 1977**   **TOP DOWN: ROOFTOP CINEMA, 2004**

Greenville, Mississippi, 1977

Frackville, Pennsylvania, 1914, Lithuanian Days, Oldest Ethnic Festival in US → **WATERFRONT BLUES FESTIVAL, 1987**   **POLISH FESTIVAL, 2004**

→ **GREEK FESTIVAL, 1952**   **FIESTA ITALIANA, 1992**

Burkina Faso, 1969
Panafrican Film and Televison Festival → **CASCADE FESTIVAL OF AFRICAN FILMS, 1990**

New York City, 1970 → **PORTLAND GAY PRIDE, 1994**   **PORTLAND QUEER FILM FESTIVAL, 1997**

New York City, 1943 → **PORTLAND FASHION WEEK, 2003**

Ann Arbor, Michigan, 2006 ← **WORST DAY OF THE YEAR RIDE, 2002**

Austin, Texas, 1987
South by Southwest → **MUSIC FEST NW, 1995**

Portland loves an excuse to party. No matter the season and no matter the weather, there seem to be ample opportunities to costume up, run with a mob, eat to excess, and get drunk (not necessarily in that order). Although most of these celebrations originated someplace else, Portland sure has embraced them all. The naked bike ride, for example, drew over 9,000 riders in 2014. Collectively, this array of parties contributes to the Keep Portland Weird philosophy.

Holidays and festivals provide opportunities for cultures and sub-cultures to be celebrated in very conscious and intentional ways and to display what makes different groups unique. Many of these events are standard fare in places throughout the country—ethnic holidays, music festivals, and road races. Portland has enthusiastically put a local spin on most of them and created many others of its own. The worst-day-of-the-year ride seems to have originated

PORTLAND MARATHON, 1972 ← Ancient Greece, ca. 2,500 years ago

PORTLAND HIGHLAND GAMES, 1952 ← Scotland, 11th century

PORTLAND ROSE FESTIVAL, 1907 ← Pasadena, California, 1890 — Tournament of Roses Parade

St. Paul, Minnesota, 2004 — Paint the Pavement

VILLAGE BUILDING CONVERGENCE, 2001 →

FERTILE GROUND, 2009 **SANTACON, 1996** ← San Francisco, California, 1994

CHRISTMAS SHIP PARADE, 1954 **ZOOLIGHTS, 1988** ← Indianapolis, Indiana, 1967

CATHEDRAL PARK JAZZ FESTIVAL, 1979 **PORTLAND JAZZ FESTIVAL, 2004** ← Newport, Rhode Island, 1954

Stockholm, Sweden, 1970s — Critical Mass Rides

PORTLAND RIDE OF SILENCE, 2006 **PEDALPALOOZA, 2002** ← Newbury, New Hampshire, 1934

BRIDGE PEDAL, 1996 **CRAFTY WONDERLAND, 2006** ←

FILMED BY BIKE, 2003 **WORLD NAKED BIKE RIDE, 2004** ← Seattle, Washington, 1998 — Became worldwide in 2004

Edinburgh, Scotland, 1947 — Fringe Festival

ART IN THE PEARL, 1997 **TIME-BASED ART FESTIVAL, 2003** ←

PDX POP NOW, 2004 → Brooklyn, NYC, 2009 — Northside Festival

PDX ADULT SOAPBOX DERBY, 1997 ← Dayton, Ohio, 1933 — Moved to Akron, Ohio, in 1935

PDX BRIDGE FESTIVAL, 2010 **HEMPSTALK, 2005** ← Amsterdam, The Netherlands, 1987 — Cannabis Cup

URBAN IDITAROD, 2001 ← Anchorage to Nome, Alaska, 1967 — Iditarod

DOGGIE DASH, 1988 → Santa Barbara, California, 2010 — Trails-n-Tails

in Portland. Although the ride is held in mid-February, for most years any day from October to May would do just as well. Portland also spawned the Holiday Ale Festival, the Village Building Convergence, the Portland Zine Symposium, Doggie Dash, and PDX Pop Now.

Perhaps the most established and traditional celebration is the Rose Festival—there's a parade, a dragon boat race, and a Rose Festival queen, and it all overlaps with Fleet Week. The Rose festival seems particularly popular with the bridge and tunnel crowd but a complete mystery to newcomers. And admittedly, it does seem a little odd to have so many beer festivals and celebrations in Portland, considering every day is Oktoberfest here.

TYPECASTING

THE CITY IN FILM

If you're going to shoot a film in Portland, be sure to warp the geography of the city to amuse the locals. Take advantage of the rain and cloudy skies, which create a fabulously gloomy atmosphere. If that's not dramatic enough for you, go ahead and fabricate some thunder and lightning plus a heavy downpour, even though those are rarities here. When recruiting extras, draw on Portland's large population of punks and homeless, or at least dress your extras up to look like them. It's required that you include at least one bridge, preferably multiple bridges, and if you can close one down for filming, all the better. But we are also a bunch of tree huggers around here, and your story should emphasize connections to the natural world, which is only minutes away in movie time, no matter where you live.

Wendy and Lucy (2008)
Portland's film persona: Down-and-Out Small Town

In this film Portland plays a much smaller, bleaker, down-on-its-luck Oregon town, although it maintains its real-life street names, bus lines, and other distinguishing features. Filmed mostly along North Lombard with cameos from Salem and Hillsboro, the film is populated by people who are barely scraping by. The wrong side of the railroad tracks is never too far away. Like a great actor, Portland is very convincing in this role. Or is it really not that much of a stretch: Is Portland playing its true self, and are the downtown tourist shots of other films the manufactured image?

The Hunted (2003)
Portland's film persona: The Urban Wilderness

The first view of Oregon is the wilderness of Silver Falls State Park, where elk run freely through lush greenery and waterfalls. Portland itself is always shown gray, damp, and chilly. The main character, an expert tracker, points out that the city is a wilderness too. Downtown streets are as crowded with pedestrians as the streets of Manhattan. Homeless folks and punks abound. After a bewildering, geographically incorrect, climactic chase scene, the bad guy scales the seemingly miles-long Hawthorne Bridge—with its nonexistent light-rail train—and dives into the Willamette River. He's then, oddly enough, conveyed "upstream" to Ross Island and Willamette Falls in Oregon City, then back to the natural wilderness, played by the Olympic Peninsula's Elwha River.

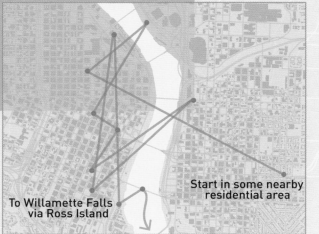

To Willamette Falls via Ross Island

Start in some nearby residential area

Feast of Love (2007)
Portland's film persona: Fecundity and Coffee

The Portland of this film is populated by intellectuals, small-business people, and free spirits who hang out at coffeehouses, ride bikes, and think deep thoughts in tree-filled parks and campuses. All these activities seem to alleviate the pain of heartbreak in its many guises. Overall, this is a pretty and hospitable Portland where it rains way too hard, but only when love goes cold. Geography warp alert! Reed College and PSU are all the same college campus (what a concept), which includes the former PGE Park and is very close to the Fresh Pot on North Mississippi Avenue.

Drugstore Cowboy (1989)
Portland's film persona: Postindustrial Ennui

The film was made in 1989 but takes place in 1971. Portland is dirty, gray, and decrepit. Residence hotels, highway underpasses, and mean streets serve as the playground for a crew of idle dope-fiends making ends meet, many of whom get hurt along the way. Most of the locations used in the film, such as the warehouses and train yard of the Pearl District, have since been turned into condos or high-end businesses, or have been demolished, making this movie required viewing for those who lament what's happened to the Pearl. Director Gus Van Sant's eye for Portland's grungy, deteriorating underbelly is also evident in other movies he's filmed here, such as *My Own Private Idaho* and *Paranoid Park*.

Free Willy (1993)
Portland's film persona: The Best of Cascadia

Portland, along with Astoria and the Puget Sound, plays a magical Cascadian city with everything you could want: the Pacific Coast; the Willamette and Columbia Rivers; a fish market; ferries; an aquarium (for orcas, on a river); a wise, stoic Native American; Nike product placement; and plenty of bridges, tall trees, and big mountains. We meet our hero spare-changing in Pioneer Courthouse Square with his gang of absurdly young and dirt-covered street kids. However, this is a sunny Portland, where a troubled, young street urchin can find redemption with the help of the power of nature and a bunch of good-hearted, working-class folks. Many viewers from Portland will wish the coast was as close as a short drive over the West Hills.

Gone (2012)
Portland's film persona: The Gloomy Beauty

Whatever the merits of the film itself (isolated and paranoid escapee from a serial killer hunts down her tormenter to save her kidnapped sister), the look of the city is stunning . . . at least to a citizen of Cascadia. Shot in the low light of the wet season, Portland is always in a state of just-finished showers with diffused sunlight, puddles on the streets, and raindrops on windows. Aerial shots of the city at twilight create an atmosphere suggestive of an outpost of civilization in the isolated far north. Forest Park is made to seem much bigger and wilder than the reality, with the scenery alternating between magical, as the serial killer says, and ominous, as the viewer feels. Even the industrial shots of the Central Eastside feel big-city sophisticated, rather than grungy, and the neighborhood residential shots—such as those in Ladd's Addition—are disarmingly pretty. Cameos by W. C. Winks Hardware store as itself and the US Custom House posing as police headquarters are nice touches. Many bridges are metaphorically crossed, none more so than St. Johns. But you will think twice about a solo walk in the wild north end of Forest Park.

TOUCHING DOWN: MIGRATION AND ALLEGIANCE

Where Portlanders drafted from across the US go to support their teams

There's an old saw native Portlanders tell (constantly) about how "they never meet any native Portlanders in Portland anymore." These observations stem mainly from the fact that Portland continues to attract a steady stream of people who might or might not realize that two defining characteristics of Portland are nine months of rain and a brutal job market. These people bring hopes and dreams. They bring skills and talents. They also bring deep attachments and connections to the places they left behind. One measure of this is ritually evident on weekends in sports bars. On display in high definition are national contests of college and professional sports, which quickly reveal where peoples' true allegiances to place lie.

Mapped here are sports bars (those with many TV screens) affiliated with supporters of various NFL teams (not including the Seahawks because there are so many Seattle migrants). The Green Bay Packers is the team best represented in Portland, with four bars (at least) dedicated to cheeseheads. Is anyone surprised?

San Francisco 49ers

Buffalo Bills

Cleveland Browns

Kansas City Chiefs

New York Jets

New Orleans Saints

Oakland Raiders

Green Bay Packers

Chicago Bears

Pittsburgh Steelers

Minnesota Vikings

Detroit Lions

Denver Broncos

New England Patriots

✗ Marks NFL bars with no team affiliation and many large screens

Tom's Pizza & Sports Bar

Saraveza

N GREELEY

NE

I-405

On Deck

NW LOVEJOY

Blitz Pearl

Yu

Kingston Bar & Grill

The Cheerful Bullpen

Cheerful Tortoise

SW MACADAM

I-5

The Clubhouse

Joll'

Jack's Taproom

SW BEAVERTON HILLSDALE HWY

Corb

Jimmy's Bar & Grill

SW CAPITOL HWY

The Ship

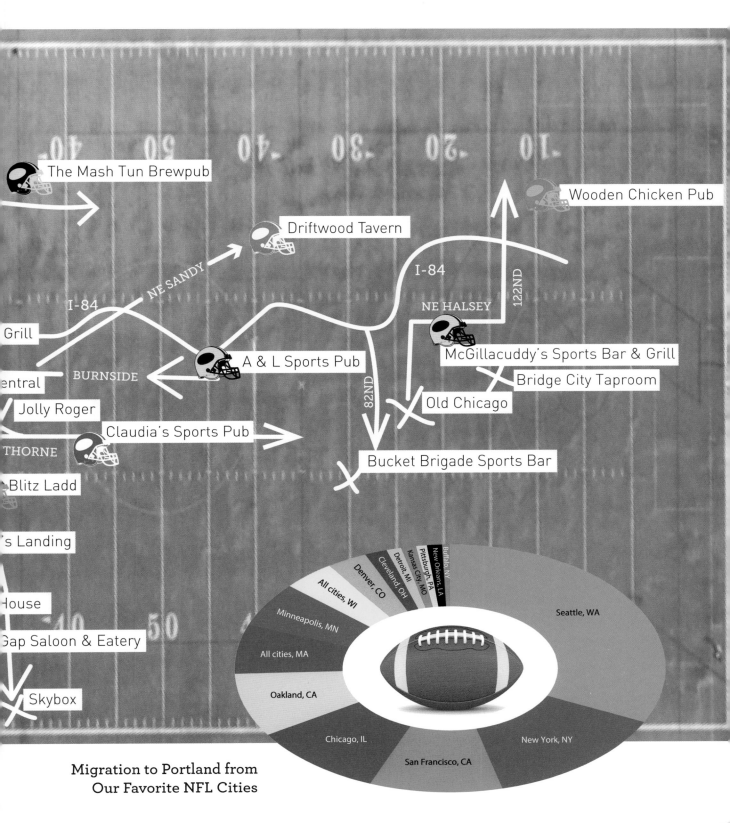

The Mash Tun Brewpub

Wooden Chicken Pub

Driftwood Tavern

NE SANDY

I-84

I-84

NE HALSEY

122ND

Grill

A & L Sports Pub

McGillacuddy's Sports Bar & Grill

BURNSIDE

Bridge City Taproom

entral

Jolly Roger

82ND

Old Chicago

Claudia's Sports Pub

THORNE

Blitz Ladd

Bucket Brigade Sports Bar

's Landing

House

Buffalo, NY

New Orleans, LA

Pittsburgh, PA

Kansas City, MO

Detroit, MI

Cleveland, OH

Denver, CO

All cities, WI

Minneapolis, MN

Seattle, WA

All cities, MA

Gap Saloon & Eatery

Oakland, CA

Skybox

Chicago, IL

New York, NY

San Francisco, CA

Migration to Portland from
Our Favorite NFL Cities

ODE TO THE WORKING MUSICIAN

For the quantitatively inclined, this data from a poll of local performers provides views of the working musician—and the work musicians take on to help cover the bills.

For the literary set, we've translated these statistics into three poems: a haiku, a sonnet, and a limerick.

Last night's reverb careening in my mind,
I walk through the rain to catch the next bus,
Duck beneath the nearest awning I find,
Tear in the fabric I have to adjust.
Callouses on all of my fingers,
Except one that throbs with a blister,
The taste of beer and smoke thickly still lingers,
Lyrics I wrote now seem a tongue twister.
Rhythm of the rain becomes a new beat,
Sounds of passing cars strangely melodic,
Involuntarily tapping my feet,
Early city morning misty hypnotic.
Slowly I go through my weekly transition,
Into the office, still a musician.

13%

25%

N/A, Ur
Retired

DISTANCE BETWEEN WORK AND LAST GIG

16%	51%	18%	15%	<1%
<1	1-5	5-10	>10	>100

Miles

broken guitar strings
a river of shattered chords
strobe light vertigo

How much money
do Portland
musicians make
playing music?

There once was a bassist from Mount Tabor
Who wielded her ax like a saber
By night it's the Schnitz
And a free case of Schlitz
But by day she rocks manual labor

- ▪ Aerophone: wind (saxophone, trumpet, accordion)
- ▪ Chordophone: strings (guitar, bass, ukulele)
- ▪ Electrophone: electronic (keyboards)
- ▪ Idiophone: vibration (percussion)
- ▪ Membranophone: vibrating membrane (drums)
- ▪ Vox: Voice

$10K–$100K

$0

39%

14%

22%

25%

$1–$1K

$1K–$10K

Gig Income

What kinds of day jobs do Portland musicians have?

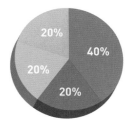

Administrative:
clerk, messenger,
admin

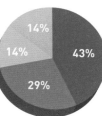

Education:
school teacher,
music teacher

Craft: electrician,
carpenter,
manufacturing

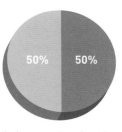

Laborer: stagehand,
warehouse,
maintenance

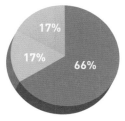

Service: food service,
event staff, barista,
barback

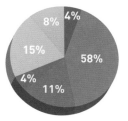

Professional Service:
musician, designer, engineer,
health services, editor, writer,
and one hired gun

Which instruments earn the most?

Employment Income vs. Gig Income

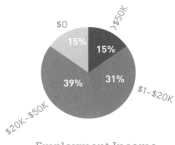

72% Male

28% Female

What instruments
do Portland
musicians play?

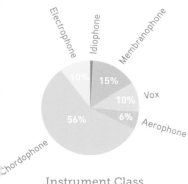

Instrument Class

What day jobs
do Portland
musicians work?

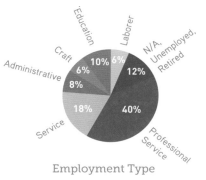

Employment Type

How much
do Portland musicians
earn from their day jobs?

Employment Income

SOCCER CITY, USA

The geography of season ticket holders for the Timbers and Thorns follow very similar patterns. Perhaps the most remarkable thing about the distribution of season ticket holders for both teams in Soccer City, USA, is the wide and relatively even spread throughout the area. In this way, soccer ties the city and region together like few other things do.

The maps on these pages illustrate the distribution of Timbers and Thorns 2014 season ticket holders for noncommercial locations. We decided to exclude commercial locations to account for the large numbers of season tickets held by businesses located downtown and to compensate for that bias. We feel the data displayed here gives a better visual representation of the distribution of where season ticket holders live.

For both the Timbers and the Thorns, there are high densities of season ticket holders in Northwest Portland, most concentrated

in the areas near the stadium, as well as North Portland, inner Northeast, inner Southeast, and Sellwood. There are also relatively high densities in areas west of the city, particularly Beaverton and Hillsboro. In the case of both teams, there's a marked decline in season ticket holder density in areas east of Highway 205 and lower densities in eastside suburbs than those west of the city.

Patterns of Timbers and Thorns season ticket holder densities outside the Portland area are also remarkably similar. Both enjoy significant support in Salem, which extends to Eugene, Bend, and Medford.

Season ticket holderdom spreads north as well, as the Thorns seem to have solid support in southern Washington. There are Timbers and Thorns season ticket holders throughout the Seattle area with a sizeable stack of Timbers season tickets sent to Seattle addresses every year—most no doubt ex-patriate Portlanders living in self-imposed exile.

Timbers Season Ticket Holders
Heights are proportional to the number of season ticket holders

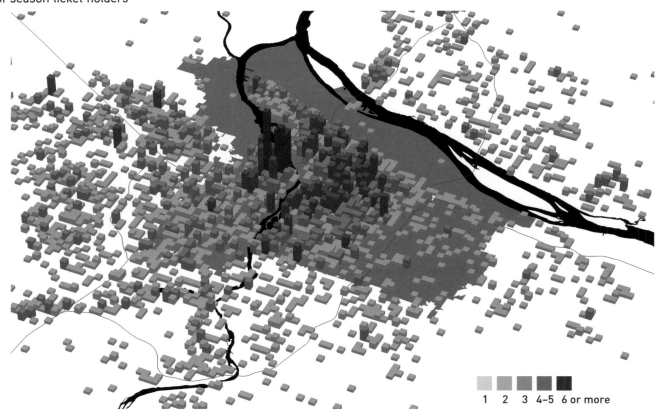

1 2 3 4–5 6 or more

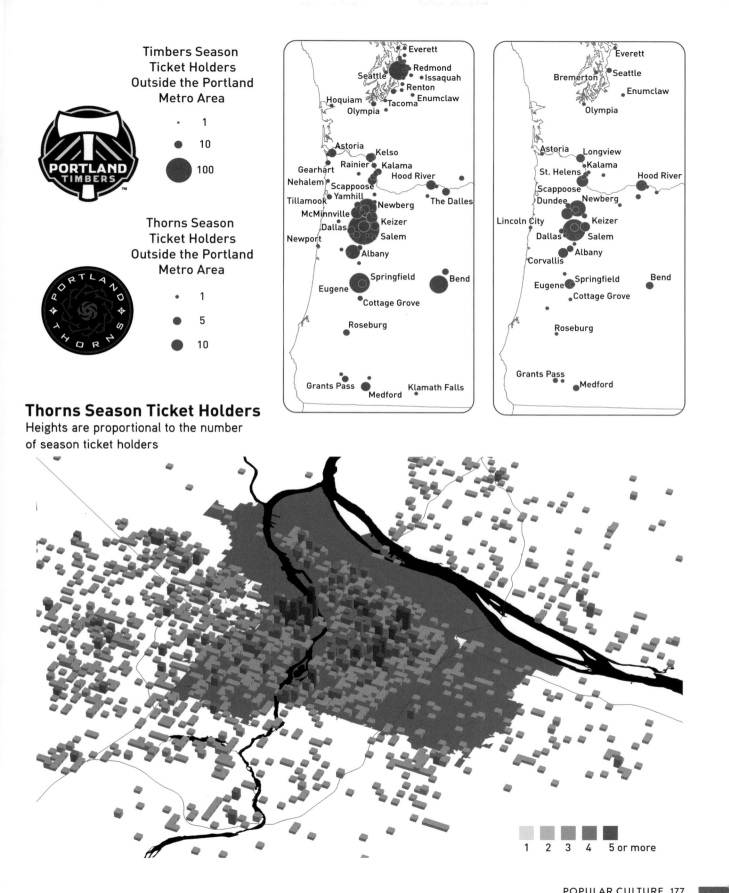

Timbers Season
Ticket Holders
Outside the Portland
Metro Area

· 1
● 10
⬤ 100

Thorns Season
Ticket Holders
Outside the Portland
Metro Area

· 1
● 5
⬤ 10

Thorns Season Ticket Holders

Heights are proportional to the number
of season ticket holders

1 2 3 4 5 or more

THE GEOGRAPHY OF LOUD

PORTLAND TIMBERS VS. SEATTLE SOUNDERS

These maps chronicle decibel readings taken at five different parts of Providence Park during a high-scoring and adrenaline-charged match between the Portland Timbers and the Seattle Sounders on April 5, 2014.

Our team of researchers positioned themselves in five distinct locations with sound meters and took decibel readings before the game and for every minute of regulation and injury time. We then compiled the data and mapped it by using 102 small maps of the stadium to give an overall visual picture of how the volume of the supporters varied throughout the fixture from area to area.

The upper right-hand part of the stadium diagram depicts readings taken in section 107, the core of the Timbers Army supporters group, where the loudest peaks were recorded. The upper left-hand section is in the southwest corner of the south deck, close to the traveling support for the Sounders.

The maps represent the geography and rhythm of sound that rises and falls throughout the match. The quietest moment recorded in the stadium was during the singing of the national anthem—supporters do sing along but not with a volume that compares to the din made throughout the game.

The noise in the stadium swelled when the Timbers took a shot on goal or were awarded a free kick. Free kicks given to Seattle tended to have the opposite effect. The Timbers goals—the loudest moments of the game—are easy to pick out, as dark red dominates nearly the entire stadium. The stadium quieted when Seattle scored two late goals, but picked up again as the end of the game neared and Portland threatened to score. The fast-paced contest finished in a 4–4 tie.

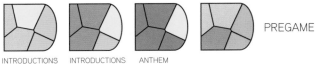

PREGAME

INTRODUCTIONS PDX   INTRODUCTIONS SEA   ANTHEM

FIRST HALF BY MINUTE

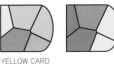

1st minute   SEA GOAL   PDX FREE KICK

16th minute

31st minute   YELLOW CARD   SEA FREE KICK

ADDITIONAL TIME

45 + 1

SECOND HALF BY MINUTE

46th minute   PDX SHOT   INJURY   YELLOW CARD

61st minute   PDX SHOT   PDX SHOT

76th minute   PDX SAVE

90 + 1   PDX SHOT   INJURY   PDX SHOT

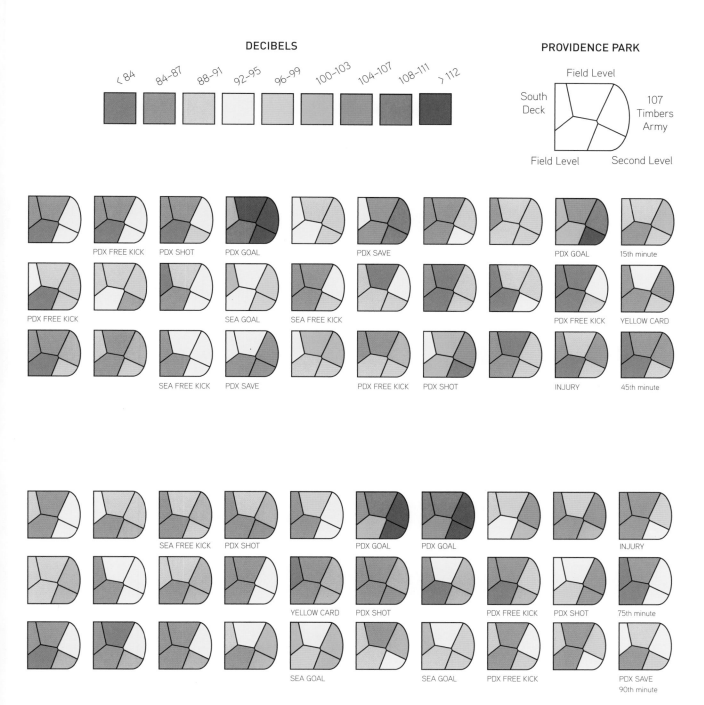

DECIBELS

<84 84–87 88–91 92–95 96–99 100–103 104–107 108–111 >112

PROVIDENCE PARK

Field Level

South Deck

107 Timbers Army

Field Level   Second Level

PDX FREE KICK   PDX SHOT   PDX GOAL   PDX SAVE   PDX GOAL   15th minute

PDX FREE KICK   SEA GOAL   SEA FREE KICK   PDX FREE KICK   YELLOW CARD

SEA FREE KICK   PDX SAVE   PDX FREE KICK   PDX SHOT   INJURY   45th minute

SEA FREE KICK   PDX SHOT   PDX GOAL   PDX GOAL   INJURY

YELLOW CARD   PDX SHOT   PDX FREE KICK   PDX SHOT   75th minute

SEA GOAL   SEA GOAL   PDX FREE KICK   PDX SAVE
90th minute

ADDITIONAL TIME

SOCCER CULTURE IN PORTLAND

Portland calls itself Soccer City, USA. People from other places probably wonder why this is. Why does this smallish city on the West Coast get to be Soccer City?

The moniker Soccer City, USA, originated in 1975, the inaugural season of the Portland Timbers in the North American Soccer League (NASL). The Timbers reached the championship game that season, buoyed by the zealous and devoted relationship between supporters and the players. Although the team lost that game, the enthusiasm of the supporters was unabated. Thus, the origin of the nickname is rooted in the passion of the fans and the full dedication of the players. Soccer City is a place where sporting success is measured in daily commitment.

The stadium itself holds a rich history. Providence Park, as it's been called since April 2014, has been the site of an athletic field since 1893. The field was built into the natural amphitheater formed by nearby Tanner Creek. Constructed by the Multnomah Athletic Club (MAC), the field and a small grandstand replaced a large collection of community gardens tended to by Chinese immigrants. Multnomah Stadium was built on the site in 1926. The city of Portland purchased the stadium from the MAC in 1966, renaming it Civic Stadium. The NASL held the 1977 championship match there, which proved to be the last competitive game of the Brazilian legend Pelé.

Tifo display by the Rose City Riveters, August 2014

In 1978, the Timbers signed defender Clive Charles, from Cardiff City in Wales, who became a fan favorite. After his playing career, Charles settled in the Portland area to coach high school and, in 1986, the University of Portland (UP) men's team. Three years later he was also hired to coach UP's women's team, which he led to a national championship in 2002. Charles, already a Portland soccer legend, died of cancer the following year at the age of fifty-one. In many ways, Charles's legacy and dedication to soccer in Portland cemented the reputation of Soccer City, USA, and bridges the past with the present.

In 1981 the Timbers stopped competing in the NASL, which itself folded in 1984. However, the Timbers were resurrected in 2001 to compete in the United Soccer League. Attendance was sparse at first but grew each year. In 2007, home matches on average drew over 6,800 spectators. Encouraged by the increasing support, the club joined Major League Soccer in 2011. In 2013, the Portland Thorns were established, joining the newly formed National Women's Soccer League. The Thorns won the league championship that inaugural year. On that team and scoring in the final was Christine Sinclair, who scored the winning goal for the University of Portland in their 2002 championship.

Yet history isn't the reason the name sticks; it's because of what happens today. Perhaps the best window for appreciating Portland as Soccer City, USA, is through the regional rivalry with Seattle. The most anticipated games for supporters of the Timbers and Thorns are the Seattle Sounders and the Seattle Reign, respectively. Attending each of these marquee match-ups gives some texture to soccer culture in Portland, as the experiences are at once similar and distinct.

A couple hours before a Thorns vs. Reign match, supporters decked out almost exclusively in red begin to head toward the stadium and line up. The gates open an hour before the game, by which time hundreds are lined up, mostly for entry to the general admission section in the north end of the stadium where the primary supporter group, the Rose City Riveters, amass.

For hours before the Timbers vs. Sounders game, thousands clad in green await entry. For the general admission section associated with the supporter group The Timbers Army, the gates open two hours early; thirty minutes later the stadium is open to all ticketholders. Members of the Emerald City Supporters, the primary

Tifo display by the Timbers Army, August 2014

supporter group associated with the Sounders, are allowed in as a group through the media gate at the southwest end of the stadium. The seating arrangement minimizes contact with members of the Timbers Army. Even before the Timbers Army and Emerald City Supporters have found their seats on opposite ends of the stadium, the chanting begins. The cacophony can be heard for blocks.

The demographics of the crowds at both Timbers and Thorns games are similar with some notable exceptions. One would expect some similarities—nearly a third of season ticket holders have season tickets to both the teams. As the maps of season ticket holders suggest, support for both is widespread, and people who attend games come from all over the city and region. There are many families at both matches, but noticeably more at the Thorns matches. There seem to be larger numbers of young children and senior citizens at Thorns matches. By contrast, a certain twenty- to thirty-something demographic that dominates the Timbers crowd seems to be largely absent at the Thorns game.

As match-time approaches and the national anthem is sung, both Timbers and Thorns supporters wave scarves, burnish more City of Portland and Cascadia flags than Old Glory, and finish scream-ing the line "Home of the . . ." with either "Thorns" or "Timbers" inserted at the end. In games such as these against Seattle, there are often tifos (visual displays created by supporters) revealed after the anthem, which usually take the form of large banners that laud the virtues of the home club and often malign the visitors.

The tifos from the Thorns vs. Reign match on August 17, 2014, and the Timbers vs. Sounders match on August 24, 2014, are depicted on this page and the previous one and suggest different modes of team support. The Rose City Riveters flew a banner with a Picasso quote that translates to "All that you can imagine is real." The Thorns needed to win this, the final game of the season, to advance to the playoffs. And they did.

The Timbers Army created a display with multiple elements, ulti-mately revealing Dorothy of The Wizard of Oz holding the gasoline can she just used to torch Seattle and standing in front of banners that indicate "There's no place like home." The Timbers lost the important (always important) but not decisive game 4–2.

Most amazing, perhaps, about these games is that the home reaction to both teams, one victorious and one roundly defeated, were nearly the same: raw support, chants, and adoration from the frenzied crowd. The teams take a lap around the stadium to acknowledge the supporters as they are, in turn, applauded by that support. In Portland, this happens win or lose—supporters of every age, of every background, from every part of the metro region stand and affirm not only the Timbers and the Thorns but the city itself. Portland supporters have a passion that transcends results. This is why Portland continues to be Soccer City, USA.

AUTHORS' NOTE

This atlas is a collaboration that includes the cartographic, textual, graphic, and photographic contributions of over forty people with the input and involvement of over a hundred others. David Banis and Hunter Shobe worked on the conceptualization and design of every page, and managed the production of the content. David edited the maps and Hunter edited the text. Joan Lundell designed the look and graphic standard of the book. The design of the maps belongs to the cartographers.

ACKNOWLEDGMENTS

David and Hunter would like to thank the project's lead cartographers, Corinna Kimball-Brown, Randy Morris, Jon Franczyk, Dan Coe, and Kirk McEwen, who each brought vital creative energy to the project at the times it was most needed. The quality of their work is the reason this book exists. Corinna, for the massive contributions in every possible realm—cartography, writing, photography, graphics, design, and research. This project could not have happened without her. Randy, for his vision, his risks, and his incredible effort at the end to help finalize production of the content. Joan Lundell, for her immediate understanding of our vision and her ability to translate that through design. Margo Pecha, for taking on the task of copyediting. The Fall 2011 Maps and Society class, the Summer 2012 Cultural Atlas Production class, and the Fall 2012 Maps and Society class at Portland State University for their brainstorming, research, ideas, and energy. The Spring 2012 and Spring 2013 Local Landscapes classes at Portland Community College and their instructor, Department Chair of Geography Christina Friedle, for giving us new ideas, new perspectives, and renewed energy for the project. Abbey Gaterud, for her advice, counsel, and encouragement, without which we would have been completely lost. Martha Works and Rebecca McLain, for their comments and suggestions on drafts of the book. Chris Wilson, Mike Golub, the Portland Timbers, and the Portland Thorns for their generous assistance and enthusiastic participation. The Department of Geography at Portland State University for supporting cartography on this project. Portland State University for The Faculty Enhancement Grant that helped to support our work during 2013 to 2014. Gary Luke and the entire team at Sasquatch Books, for taking on this book.

CREDITS AND KEY DATA SOURCES

OVERVIEW MAPS

Putting Our House in Order
CARTOGRAPHY: Jon Franczyk
TEXT: Hunter Shobe
THANKS TO: Corinna Kimball-Brown, Jon Franczyk, Kirk McEwen, Dan Coe, Melissa Katz-Moye, and Daron McCaulley for brainstorming room ideas

Neighborhood Color Palettes
CARTOGRAPHY: Dan Coe
TEXT: David Banis
THANKS TO: Torrey Vosk

PDX Tube
CARTOGRAPHY: Jon Franczyk
THANKS TO: Henrich Biorn

INTRODUCTION

Portland: A Cascadian City
CARTOGRAPHY: Jon Franczyk
TEXT: Hunter Shobe
KEY DATA SOURCES:
Baretich, Alexander. "Cascadian Flag ('the Doug') image." Wikimedia Commons. 2006. http://commons.wikimedia.org/wiki/File:Flag_of_Cascadia.svg.
Baretich, Alexander. "Symbolism of the Cascadian Flag." Portland Occupier. 2012. http://www.portlandoccupier.org.
Callenbach, Ernest. *Ecotopia: The Notebooks and Reports of William Weston.* Berkeley, CA: Banyan Tree Books, 1975.
Cascadian Independence Project. http://www.recollectionbooks.com/Cascadia.
Cascadia Now!. http://www.cascadianow.org.
Garreau, Joel. *The Nine Nations of North America.* Boston, MA: Houghton Mifflin, 1981.
McCloskey, David. *Cascadia: A Great Land on the Northeast Pacific Rim.* Seattle, WA: Cascadia Institute, 1988.
McKee, Bates. *Cascadia: The Geologic Evolution of the Pacific Northwest.* New York, NY: McGraw-Hill Book Company, 1972.
Pacific NorthWest Economic Region. http://www.pnwer.org.
Patail, Martin. "Cascadia Rising: Break Out the Fireworks for the Northwest's Independent State of Mind." *Portland Monthly Magazine,* 2012.
Resnick, Philip. "Secular Utopias Versus Religious Credos—One Cascadia or More?" In *Cascadia: The Elusive Utopia, Exploring the Spirit of the Northwest,* edited by Douglas Todd. Vancouver, BC: Ronsdale Press, 2008.
Schell, Paul, and John Hamer. "Cascadia: The New Binationalism of Western Canada and the U.S. Pacific Northwest." In *Identities in North America: The Search for Community,* edited by Robert L. Earle and John Wirth. Stanford, CA: Standford University Press, 1995.
Sightline Institute. http://www.sightline.org.
Sparke, Matthew. "Excavating the Future in Cascadia: Geoeconomics and the imagined geographies of a cross-border region." *BC Studies,* no. 127 (2000): 5–44.

Portlandness
CARTOGRAPHY: David Banis and Nicole Palmer
TEXT: David Banis
RESEARCH: David Banis and Sonia Singh
KEY DATA SOURCES:
"American Community Survey." US Census Bureau. http://www.census.gov/acs/www.
Clackamas County Elections Division. http://www.clackamas.us/elections.
Food Carts Portland. http://www.foodcartsportland.com.
Green Power Oregon. http://www.greenpoweroregon.com.
Multnomah County Elections Division. http://www.multco.us/elections.
Oregon Brewers Guild. http://oregoncraftbeer.org/guild/.
Oregon Craft Beer. http://oregoncraftbeer.org.
Washington County Elections Division. http://www.co.washington.or.us/elections.

Portland vs. Portland
CARTOGRAPHY: Randy Morris
TEXT: Annie Scriven and Hunter Shobe
RESEARCH: Randy Morris
THANKS TO: M. Nasir Shir, GISP, GIS Manager, IT, city of Portland, Maine
KEY DATA SOURCES:
American Fact Finder. http://www.factfinder.census.gov/faces/nav/jsf/pages/index.xhtml.
Portland, Maine, Building Footprints and Tax Lot Data. City of Portland, Maine.
US Census Bureau. http://www.census.gov.
US Climate Data. http://www.usclimatedata.com.

URBAN LANDSCAPES

Bridgetown
CARTOGRAPHY AND PHOTOGRAPHY: Dan Coe
TEXT: David Banis
KEY DATA SOURCES:
Oregon Department of Transportation. http://www.oregon.gov/odot/pages/index.aspx.
Portland Bridges. http://www.portlandbridges.com.

Under the Bridges
CARTOGRAPHY AND PHOTOGRAPHY: Dan Coe
TEXT: David Banis and Hunter Shobe

Where the Sidewalk Ends
CARTOGRAPHY: Kirk McEwen
TEXT: Elizabeth Specht and Hunter Shobe
PHOTOGRAPHY: David Banis and Hunter Shobe
RESEARCH: Summer 2012 Cultural Atlas Production class

Portland Cement
CARTOGRAPHY: Corinna Kimball-Brown
TEXT: David Banis and Hunter Shobe
KEY DATA SOURCES:
Civic Apps for Greater Portland. http://www.civicapps.org.
Portland Bureau of Transportation.
    http://www.portlandoregon.gov/transportation/32360.

Your Attention Please
CARTOGRAPHY: David Banis and Corinna Kimball-Brown
TEXT: Hunter Shobe
RESEARCH: Summer 2012 Cultural Atlas Production class

Stop! Writing on Stop Signs
CARTOGRAPHY AND PHOTOGRAPHY: Dan Coe
TEXT: Hunter Shobe and Dan Coe

Manufactured Spaces
CARTOGRAPHY: David Banis and Corinna Kimball-Brown
TEXT: Tiffany Conklin, Allison Jones, and David Banis
PHOTOGRAPHY: Tiffany Conklin (Pouring Paint wheatpaste), Anton Legoo
    (Inside of Taylor Electric), and Hunter Shobe (Outside of
    Taylor Electric)
KEY DATA SOURCES:
Central Eastside Industrial Council. http://www.ceic.cc/.
"Chapter 14B.80 Graffiti Nuisance Property." Office of the City Auditor.
    http://www.portlandonline.com/auditor/?c=28580/.
City of Portland. 2014. http://www.portlandoregon.gov/.
Conklin, Tiffany. "Street Art, Ideology and Public Space." Master's
    thesis, Portland State University, 2012.
Jones, Allison. "Industrial Decline in an Industrial Sanctuary: Portland's
    Central Eastside Industrial District, 1981-2014." Master's thesis,
    Portland State University.

Naked City
CARTOGRAPHY: Jon Franczyk, David Banis, and Randy Morris
TEXT: Wayne Coffey and Sean Wilson
GRAPHICS: Jon Franczyk and David Banis
RESEARCH: Wayne Coffey, Sean Wilson, and David Banis
PHOTOGRAPHY: Hunter Shobe

KEY DATA SOURCE:
Coffey, Wayne. "Myths and Measures: The Cultural Performance of
    Portland's Strip Club Identity." Master's thesis, Portland State
    University, 2012.

THE ONCE AND FUTURE CITY

Township and Change
CARTOGRAPHY: Dan Coe
TEXT: Corinna Kimball-Brown
KEY DATA SOURCES:
Bureau of Planning and Sustainability.
    http://www.portlandoregon.gov/bps.
"East Portland Historical Overview and Historic Preservation Study."
    Bureau of Planning and Sustainability, City of Portland. 2009.
    http://portlandoregon.gov/bps/article/214638.
The Oregon History Project, Oregon Historical Society.
    http://www.ohs.org/education/oregonhistory/.
US Census Bureau. http://www.census.gov/.

The Streets Speak the Language of the Past
CARTOGRAPHY: Corinna Kimball-Brown and David Banis
RESEARCH: Hunter Shobe and Corinna Kimball-Brown
TEXT: Hunter Shobe and Corinna Kimball-Brown
KEY DATA SOURCE:
Snyder, Eugene E. *Portland Names and Neighborhoods: Their Historic
    Origins.* Portland, OR: Binford & Mort, 1979.

Ethnic Imprints
CARTOGRAPHY AND TEXT: Corinna Kimball-Brown
PHOTOGRAPHY: "Aerial I405 Freeway construction and South
    Auditorium Urban Renewal Area." City of Portland Archives, Portland,
    OR, A2004-002.3582; "N Killingsworth looking east from Albina."
    City of Portland Archives, Portland, OR, A2004-002.2127
KEY DATA SOURCES:
Abbott, Carl. *Portland in Three Centuries: The Place and the People.*
    Corvallis, OR: Oregon State University Press, 2011.
"Foreign Born Population." US Census Bureau.
    http://www.census.gov/topics/populations/foreign-born.html.
Olsen, Polina. *The Immigrants' Children: Jewish and Italian Memories of
    Old South Portland.* Portland, OR: Smart Talk Publications, 2006.
Toll, William. "The Self-Promotional Metropolis: The Italian and Russian
    Jewish Settlements," The Oregon History Project. 2003.
    http://www.ohs.org/education/oregonhistory/narratives/subtopic.
    cfm?subtopic_ID=203.

Historic Chinatown
CARTOGRAPHY, TEXT, RESEARCH, AND PHOTOGRAPHY:
    Corinna Kimball-Brown
PHOTOGRAPHY: "Chinese Gardens and Houses in Tanner Creek Gulch."
    City of Portland Archives, Portland, OR, A2004-002.2544

KEY DATA SOURCES:

"Foreign Born Population." US Census Bureau. http://www.census.gov/topics/population/foreign-born.html.

"Historic GIS Data: Portland's People & Places." Teaching American History PDX. http://www.upa.pdx.edu/IMS/currentprojects/TAHv3/PDX_Places_GIS.html.

Wong, Marie Rose. *Sweet Cakes, Long Journey: The Chinatowns of Portland, Oregon.* Seattle, WA: University of Washington Press, 2004.

Modern Chinatown

CARTOGRAPHY, TEXT, AND RESEARCH: Corinna Kimball-Brown
PHOTOGRAPHY: Corinna Kimball-Brown and David Banis (Chinatown Gate)
KEY DATA SOURCE:

"Foreign Born Population." US Census Bureau. http://www.census.gov/topics/population/foreign-born.html.

Expo to Infill

CARTOGRAPHY: Daron McCaulley, Jackson Voelkel, and David Banis
TEXT: Rachel Berger
PHOTOGRAPHY: "View from Grand Staircase." Portland City Archives, Portland, OR, A2004-2307; map recreated from "Official Ground Plan of the Lewis and Clark Centennial Exposition." City of Portland Archives, Portland, OR
KEY DATA SOURCES:

Dibling, Karin, Julie Kay Martin, Meghan Stone Olson, and Gayle Webb. "Guild's Lake Industrial District: The Process of Change over Time." *Oregon Historical Society Quarterly* 1, no. 107 (2006): 88–105.

"Guild's Lake Industrial Sanctuary Plan." *The Oregon Encyclopedia.* Portland Bureau of Planning, City of Portland, 2001.

The Oregon History Project. Oregon Historical Society. http://www.ohs.org/education/oregonhistory/.

Tucker, Kathy. "Guilds Lake, 1904." Oregon History Project. 2002. http://www.ohs.org/education/oregonhistory/historical_records/dspDocument.cfm?doc_ID=EB3F7D8D-B88B-500C-A78F-6A488918A5F7.

From Isle to Peninsula

CARTOGRAPHY: Daron McCaulley and Jackson Voelkel
TEXT: Stephen Marotta
PHOTOGRAPHY: "Aerial of Swan Island Municipal Airport." City of Portland Archives, Portland, OR, A2005-005.1407.3; "USS Schenectady." Portland City Archives, Portland, OR, A204-002.2176; contemporary photo by David Banis
KEY DATA SOURCES:

"Kaiser & Oregon Shipyards." Oregon History Project. http://www.ohs.org/education/oregonhistory/historical_records/dspDocument.cfm?doc_ID=00088A33-E7AE-1E91-891B80B0527200A7.

"McCarthy Park Expedition." Cyclotram. http://www.cyclotram.blogspot.com/.

Profita, Cassandra. "A Guide to the Portland Harbor Superfund Site." Oregon Public Broadcasting. September 19, 2013. http://www.opb.org/news/blog/ecotrope/a-guide-to-the-portland-harbor-superfund-site/.

"Record Breakers." Oregon Shipbuilders Corporation. http://www.armed-guard.com/recbr1.html.

Willingham, William F. "Swan Island." *Oregon Encyclopedia.* http://www.oregonencyclopedia.org/articles/swan_island/#.VUpqRqYfjA4.

The City That Never Was

CARTOGRAPHY AND TEXT: Corinna Kimball-Brown and David Banis
THANKS TO: Dirk Kinsey
KEY DATA SOURCES:

Abbott, Carl. *Portland in Three Centuries: The Place and the People.* Corvallis, OR: Oregon State University, 2011.

Bennett, Edward. *Greater Portland Plan.* 1912.

"Central City Plan." Bureau of Planning, City of Portland, Oregon. 1988.

"Comprehensive Development Plan." City of Portland Archives, Portland, OR. 1966.

"Olmsted's Plan of Parks and Boulevards." City of Portland Archives, Portland, OR. 1903.

"Olympic Bid Proposal." City of Portland Archives, Portland, OR.

"Streetcar System Concept Plan." City of Portland Archives, Portland, OR. 2009.

"Urban Design Assessment: Central Portland Plan." Bureau of Planning, City of Portland, Oregon. 2008.

Haunted

CARTOGRAPHY: Melissa Katz-Moye and Randy Morris
TEXT: Hunter Shobe
PHOTOGRAPHY: Dan Coe
THANKS TO: Pam Rooney

Maywood Park

CARTOGRAPHY: Randy Morris
TEXT AND PHOTOGRAPHY: Sean Wilson
THANKS TO: the City of Maywood Park
KEY DATA SOURCES:

City of Maywood Park. http://cityofmaywoodpark.com.

Bureau of Planning. City of Portland. https://www.portlandoregon.gov/bps/.

East Portland Review, November 2007.

"Maywood Park citizens get involved." *Mid-County Memo* 21, no. 9 (2006).

US Census Bureau. http://www.census.gov/.

WILDNESS

Stumptown

CARTOGRAPHY: Randy Morris
TEXT: David Banis and Randy Morris
PHOTOGRAPHY: "Front Ave Looking South from Alder." City of Portland Archives, Portland, OR, A2004-002.2096; photograph of Naito Parkway by Randy Morris

KEY DATA SOURCES:
American Forests. https://www.americanforests.org.
Ryerson, Mike, Norm Gholston, and Tracy J. Prince.
    Portland's Slabtown. 2013.
"Urban Canopy Report." Portland Parks and Recreation. 2012.
"Portland Tree Canopy Interactive Map." *The Oregonian*.
    http://projects.oregonlive.com/maps/portland-trees/.

Scattered Showers and Sunbreaks
CARTOGRAPHY AND GRAPHICS: Corinna Kimball-Brown
TEXT: Corinna Kimball-Brown and David Banis
KEY DATA SOURCES:
Current Results. http://www.currentresults.com/Weather/.
Prism Climate Group. Oregon State University.
    http://www.prism.oregonstate.edu.
Science Facts. http://www.science-facts.com.

Lost Waters and Phantom Streams
CARTOGRAPHY AND PHOTOGRAPHY: Randy Morris
TEXT: Randy Morris and David Banis
PHOTOGRAPHY: "Vista Bridge." Wikimedia Commons. 2012.
    http://commons.wikimedia.org/wiki/Category:Vista_Bridge.
KEY DATA SOURCES:
ES Glover's Birdseye View of Portland Oregon.
    Library of Congress. 1879.
Prince, Tracy J. *Portland's Goose Hollow*. Charleston, SC:
    Arcadia Pub., 2011.
"Tanner Creek Water Quality Characterization." City of Portland. June
    2011 (BES). https://www.portlandoregon.gov/bes/article/354686.

The City Chicken and the Country Coyote
CARTOGRAPHY: Corinna Kimball-Brown
TEXT: Corinna Kimball-Brown and Hunter Shobe
PHOTOGRAPHY: Traci Friedl (coyote) and Riho Katagiri (lost chicken sign)
KEY DATA SOURCES:
Growing Gardens. http://growing-gardens.org.
PSU Urban Coyote Project. http://urbancoyoteproject.weebly.com.

Plight of the Honeybee
CARTOGRAPHY: Randy Morris
TEXT, PHOTOGRAPHY, AND RESEARCH: Jenai Fitzpatrick
KEY DATA SOURCE:
Dewey Caron, Jenai Fitzpatrick, Andrew Miller, and Tim Wessles.
    "Portland Urban Beekeepers (PUB) 2014 Bee Survey."
    March 28, 2014.

Oaks Bottom
CARTOGRAPHY: Corinna Kimball-Brown
TEXT AND PHOTOGRAPHY: Mike Houck
KEY DATA SOURCE:
"Suggested plan for the development of Sellwwod—Oaks Aqua Park and
    Transportation Musuem [Oaks Bottom]—Parks and Recreation."
    City of Portland Archives, Portland, OR, M/3462 12/31/1958.

Rodents of Unusual Size
CARTOGRAPHY AND TEXT: Corinna Kimball-Brown
GRAPHICS: Kezia Rasmussen and Laura DeVito
KEY DATA SOURCES:
"August Sale of Furs Begins Tomorrow." *The Oregonian*, July 26, 1936.
"Business Briefs: Nutria Said Risky." *The Oregonian*, June 3, 1957.
"Furry Colonists Arrive by Water." *The Oregonian*, August 11, 1931.
Kuhn, Lee W. and Paul E. Peloquin. *Oregon's Nutria Problem*.
    Proceedings of the 6th Vertebrate Pest Conference. 1974.
Sheffels, Trevor and Mark Sytsma. "Report on Nutria Management and
    Research in the Pacific Northwest." *Center for Lakes and Reservoirs
    Publications*, no. 24 (2007).
Sheffels, Trevor, Mark Sytsma, and Jacoby Carter. "An Overview of
    Nutria, with Special Reference to the Pacific Northwest." Presented
    at Nutria Management in the Northwest Workshop. USGS
    Nonindigenous Aquatic Species Program. March 28, 2013.

Heterotopia: The Columbia Slough
CARTOGRAPHY AND TEXT: Randy Morris
PHOTOGRAPHY: Mark Gamba
KEY DATA SOURCES:
*Columbia Slough Sediment Study: Lower Slough between River Mile 5.9
    and 8.7*. State of Oregon DEQ. January 2012 update.
Hetherington, Kevin. *The Badlands of Modernity: Heterotopia and Social
    Ordering*. 1997.
Olmsted, John Charles and Frederick Law Olmsted Jr. "Report of the
    Park Board." *Report of the Olmsted Brothers, Landscape Architects*.
    City of Portland. Portland, OR. 1903.
Stroud, Ellen. "Troubled Waters in Ecotopia: Environmental Racism in
    Portland, Oregon." *Radical History Review*, no. 74 (1999): 65–95.

VIEWS OF THE CITY

Imagined Population Densities
CARTOGRAPHY AND RESEARCH: Corinna Kimball-Brown
TEXT: Hunter Shobe and Corinna Kimball-Brown
KEY DATA SOURCE:
Demographia World Urban Areas, 9th Annual Edition. March 2013.
"2013 Population Estimates." US Census Bureau.
    http://www.census.gov/popest/.

Islands of Diversity
CARTOGRAPHY: Jon Franczyk
TEXT: David Banis and Hunter Shobe
KEY DATA SOURCE:
"2010." US Census Bureau. http://www.census.gov.

Psychogeography
CARTOGRAPHY: David Banis
TEXT: Christina Friedle and Hunter Shobe
MENTAL MAP COMPILATION: Karin Waller and David Banis

Street Emotion

CARTOGRAPHY: Christina Friedle
TEXT: Christina Friedle and Hunter Shobe
RESEARCH: Ratnanjali Adhar, Sam Johnson, and Anita Parco

Sounds of the City

CARTOGRAPHY: Zuriel Rasmussen and David Banis
TEXT: Zuriel Rasmussen

City of Noses

CARTOGRAPHY: Corinna Kimball-Brown
TEXT: Corinna Kimball-Brown and Hunter Shobe
THANKS TO: Dan Coe, Jon Franczyk, Tony Hair, Melissa Katz-Moye, Daron McCaulley, and Kirk McEwen for brainstorming

Third-Graders Illustrate the City

CARTOGRAPHY: Nicole Penoncello and David Banis
TEXT: Nicole Penoncello
THANKS TO: the third-grade art students at Jason Lee Elementary School (2013 to 2014)

Tales from Outside the Doughnut Hole

CARTOGRAPHY: Randy Morris and David Banis
TEXT: Hunter Shobe
PHOTOGRAPHY: Dan Coe
THANKS TO: Voodoo Doughnuts

Cully

CARTOGRAPHY AND TEXT: Joseph Bard
KEY DATA SOURCES:
Detailed profile of Cully neighborhood in Portland, OR, 97213, 97218. http://www.usa.com.
"Not in Cully: Anti-Displacement Strategies for the Cully Neighborhood." A report prepared for Living Cully: A Cully Ecodistrict.

Foster-Powell

CARTOGRAPHY: Randy Morris and David Banis
TEXT: Stephen Marotta and Rachel Berger
KEY DATA SOURCES:
Foster-Powell: A Neighborhood Blog. http://fosterpowellpdx.com.
Foster-Powell Neighborhood Association. http://fosterpowell.com.

Multnomah Village

CARTOGRAPHY: Randy Morris and David Banis
TEXT: Christina Friedle

Parkrose

CARTOGRAPHY: Randy Morris and David Banis
TEXT: Stephen Marotta
KEY DATA SOURCES:
Main Street Parkrose Redevelopment Plan.
Parkrose Business Association. http://parkrosebusiness.org.
Parkrose Neighborhood Association. http://parkrose.eastportland.org.
Plan PDX.

South Waterfront

CARTOGRAPHY: Randy Morris and David Banis
TEXT: Stephen Marotta
KEY DATA SOURCE:
Culverwell, Wendy. "South Waterfront: The Failure that Wasn't." *Portland Business Journal*, August 16, 2013.

SOCIAL RELATIONS

Mission Invisible

CARTOGRAPHY AND GRAPHICS: Kirk McEwen
TEXT AND PHOTOGRAPHY: Hunter Shobe
RESEARCH: Summer 2012 Cultural Atlas Production class

Green Paradise

CARTOGRAPHY: Corinna Kimball-Brown
TEXT: Stephen Marotta and Corinna Kimball-Brown
GRAPHICS: Nicole Penoncello
PHOTOGRAPHY: David Banis (ecoroofs, LEED plaque) and Corinna Kimball-Brown (bioswale)
KEY DATA SOURCES:
Green Streets Dataset, Community Gardens Program. Parks and Recreation, City of Portland.
"LEED-certified commercial buildings in Oregon." *Sustainable Business Oregon*, November 4, 2012.
"Oregon Non-profit Organizations." State of Oregon. http://www.oregon.gov/Pages/index.aspx.
"Portland Ecoroof Program." City of Portland Environmental Services. https://www.portlandoregon.gov/bes/44422.
"Portland Harbor Superfund Site." Environmental Protection Agency. http://yosemite.epa.gov/r10/cleanup.nsf/sites/ptldharbor.
"Sustainable Stormwater Management." City of Portland Environmental Services. https://www.portlandoregon.gov/bes/34598.

Risk-Oblivious Youth

CARTOGRAPHY, TEXT, AND PHOTOGRAPHY: Corinna Kimball-Brown
RESEARCH: Erin Aliperti, Dwayne Hedstrom, Kick Nyte, Diego Ponce, Erik Trexel, and Corinna Kimball-Brown

The Invisibility of Homelessness

CARTOGRAPHY AND GRAPHICS: Kirk McEwen
TEXT: Stephen Przybylinski and David Banis
PHOTOGRAPHY: Stephen Przybylinski

KEY DATA SOURCES:
2013 Point-In-Time Count of Homelessness in
Portland/Multnomah County, Oregon.
Przybylinski, Stephen. *The Right to Dream: Assessing the Spatiality of
a Homeless Rest Site in Portland, Oregon.* Master's thesis, Portland
State University, 2015.

The Red line . . . and the Bottom line
CARTOGRAPHY, TEXT, AND GRAPHICS: Corinna Kimball-Brown
RESEARCH: Corinna Kimball-Brown and Neil Loehlein
PHOTOGRAPHY: "Guilds Lake Courts housing units." City of Portland
Archives, Portland, OR, A2001-025.265; "Aerial photo of Vanport."
City of Portland Archives, Portland, OR, A2001-025.626; photos of
"hipsterville" graffiti and "Red Line District" sign by Hunter Shobe
KEY DATA SOURCES:
"The Albina Community Plan." Bureau of Planning. Portland, OR. 1993.
https://www.portlandoregon.gov/bps/article/58586.
"Gentrification and Displacement Study Overview." Bureau of Planning
and Sustainability. City of Portland. Portland, OR. 2013.
Gibson, Karen J. "Bleeding Albina: A History of Community
Disinvestment, 1940 to 2000." *Transforming Anthropology* 15,
no. 1, 3–25.
"The History of Portland's African-American Community (1805 to the
Present)." Bureau of Planning. Portland, OR. 1993.
https://www.portlandoregon.gov/bps/article/91454.
"Interstate Corridor Urban Renewal Plan." Portland Development Com-
mission. August 2000. http://www.pdc.us/Libraries/Interstate_
Corridor/Interstate_URA_plan_pdf.sflb.ashx.
Loving, Lisa. "The North Williams Avenue That Was." *The Skanner*,
August 9, 2011.
TAHPDX: Teaching American History Project. Portland State University
and the University of Portland.
US Census Bureau. 2010. http://www.census.gov/2010census/.

Pouring Art into the Streets
CARTOGRAPHY: Laura DeVito
TEXT: Corinna Kimball-Brown
PHOTOGRAPHY: Dan Coe (intersection murals) and Laura DeVito
(children painting)
KEY DATA SOURCES:
Fink, Jordan. Personal communication with Corinna Kimball-Brown.
May 22, 2013.
Village Building Convergence. City Repair. 2012.
http://www.cityrepair.org.

FOOD AND DRINK

Any Given Sunday
CARTOGRAPHY: Corinna Kimball-Brown
TEXT: Hunter Shobe; wait times were collected by phone on
November 3, 2013.
THANKS TO: Gwyneth Manser

KEY DATA SOURCE:
Stuff White People Like. http://stuffwhitepeoplelike.com.

Food Cart-o-Grams
CARTOGRAPHY AND GRAPHICS: Randy Morris
TEXT: Hunter Shobe
RESEACH: David Banis, Robert Kalai Miller, Gabriel Rousseau,
and Jackson Voelkel
KEY DATA SOURCES:
Food Carts Portland. http://www.foodcartsportland.com.
Google. https://www.google.com.
Yelp. http://www.yelp.com.

A Paler Shade of Ale
CARTOGRAPHY: Jon Franczyk and David Banis
TEXT: Hunter Shobe
GRAPHICS: Jon Franczyk
THANKS TO: Thomas Jackson
KEY DATA SOURCES:
Brewers Association. https://www.brewersassociation.org.
Oregon Brewers Guild. http://oregoncraftbeer.org/guild/.
Oregon Craft Beer. http://oregoncraftbeer.org.

Small Half-Caff Skinny Extra-Hot Caramel Cappuccino with Extra Foam in a Large Cup
CARTOGRAPHY: Jackson Voelkel
TEXT: Martha Works
RESEARCH: David Banis
KEY DATA SOURCES:
Google. https://www.google.com.
Peets. http://www.peets.com.
Starbucks. http://www.starbucks.com.
Yelp. http://www.yelp.com.

Anything You Can Do, I Can Do Vegan
CARTOGRAPHY: Corinna Kimball-Brown
TEXT: Rachel Berger
RESEARCH: Rachel Berger and Corinna Kimball-Brown
KEY DATA SOURCES:
Food Fight! Grocery. http://www.foodfightgrocery.com/pdxguide/.
PDX Vegan Guide

Farm to Market
CARTOGRAPHY: Randy Morris and Corinna Kimball-Brown
GRAPHICS: Corinna Kimball-Brown
TEXT: Martha Works
RESEARCH: Melanie Miller
KEY DATA SOURCES:
"Farmers Markets." *Edible Portland.*
Local Harvest. http://www.localharvest.org.
Manage My Market. https://managemymarket.com.
Portland Farmers Market. http://www.portlandfarmersmarket.org.

The Food Chain: Dining out

CARTOGRAPHY, GRAPHICS, AND RESEARCH: Jackson Voelkel

TEXT: Hunter Shobe

KEY DATA SOURCES:

Clackamas County Health Department.
http://www.clackamas.us/publichealth/.

Multnomah County Health Department. https://multco.us/health.

Washington County Health Department.
http://www.co.washington.or.us/HHS/.

Food Mirages

CARTOGRAPHY, TEXT, AND GRAPHICS: Betsy Breyer

KEY DATA SOURCES:

Breyer, Betsy and Adriana Voss-Andreae. "Food Mirages: Geographic
and Economic Barriers to Healthful Food Access in Portland,
Oregon." *Health and Place*, no. 24 (2013): 131–39.

POPULAR CULTURE

Geek!

CARTOGRAPHY AND GRAPHICS: Randy Morris

TEXT: Hunter Shobe and Randy Morris

GRAPHICS: Jessica Sullivan, Chauncey Morris, and Randy Morris

THANKS TO: the Lady Monster-slaying Society and Heather Paske,
for allowing us to use their logo; to the PDX Gaymers and Mathew
Gauvin, for allowing us to use their logo; and to Belinda Beller and
Jason Carlough

Corridors of Creation

CARTOGRAPHY: David Banis, Corinna Kimball-Brown, and Laura DeVito

RESEARCH: David Banis

TEXT: David Banis, Corinna Kimball-Brown, and Hunter Shobe

RESEARCH: Gary Miller and David Banis

THANKS TO: Amy Chen

KEY DATA SOURCES:

"Alberta Street History." Alberta Main Street.
http://albertamainst.org/about-2/history/.

Giegerich, Andy. "Pearl's First Thursday Fetes 25 Years." *Portland
Business Journal*, September 2, 2011.

First Thursday Portland. http://www.firstthursdayportland.com.

Johnson, Barry. "Pearls of Art Warehouse District Become Home to
Art Galleries Studios." *The Oregonian*, September 25, 1987.

Last Thursday on Alberta. http://www.lastthursdayonalberta.com.

Do It Yourself

CARTOGRAPHY AND RESEARCH: Meara Butler and Corinna Kimball-Brown

TEXT: Hunter Shobe

KEY DATA SOURCE:

Gilleland, Diane. "Mapping the Crafty." Crafty Pod.
http://www.craftypod.com/categories/web-crafty?page=1.

Rides, Fests, and Paloozas

GRAPHICS: Dan Coe

RESEARCH: Alyx Lesko, David Banis, and Hunter Shobe

Typecasting

CARTOGRAPHY, TEXT, AND RESEARCH: David Banis and
Corinna Kimball-Brown

GRAPHICS: Corinna Kimball-Brown

RESEARCH: Summer 2012 Cultural Atlas Production class

KEY DATA SOURCES:

Drugstore Cowboy. Gus Van Sant. 1989. Film.

Feast of Love. Robert Benton. 2007. Film.

Free Willy. Simon Wincer. 1993. Film.

Gone. Heitor Dhalia. 2012. Film.

The Hunted. William Friedkin. 2003. Film.

Wendy and Lucy. Kelly Reichardt. 2008. Film.

Touching Down: Migration and Allegiance

CARTOGRAPHY: Corinna Kimball-Brown

TEXT: Hunter Shobe

RESEARCH: Laurel Willi and David Banis

PHOTOGRAPHY: "Football." Pixabay

KEY DATA SOURCE:

"American Migration [Interactive Map]." Forbes. http://www.forbes.com/
special-report/2011/migration.html.

Ode to the Working Musician

CARTOGRAPHY, RESEARCH, AND GRAPHICS: Melissa Katz-Moye

TEXT AND POEMS: Hunter Shobe

Soccer City, USA

CARTOGRAPHY: David Banis

TEXT: Hunter Shobe

PHOTOGRAPHY: Courtesy of the Portland Timbers/Thorns and
Major League Soccer

RESEARCH: Chris Wilson

SOUND DATA RESEARCH: Corinna Kimball-Brown, Dan Coe, Daron
McCaulley, Jon Franczyk, David Banis, and Hunter Shobe

THANKS TO: Mike Golub and Chris Wilson

KEY DATA SOURCE:

Timbers/Thorns Season Ticket holder information provided by the
Portland Timbers and Portland Thorns

ABOUT THE AUTHORS

DAVID BANIS has managed the Center for Spatial Analysis and Research in the Department of Geography at Portland State University since 2006. He teaches courses on cartography and geographic information systems. His work explores the diverse ways that cartographers can tell stories with maps, with a focus on public participatory mapping.

HUNTER SHOBE is a cultural geographer and an associate professor in the Department of Geography at Portland State University. He holds a PhD in geography from the University of Oregon. His research explores the cultural and political dimensions of how people connect to and create meaning in different places.

Printed in China

Published by Sasquatch Books

19 18 17 16 15   9 8 7 6 5 4 3 2 1

Editor: Gary Luke
Production editors: Em Gale, Emma Reh
Cover design: Joyce Hwang
Cover map: Jon Franczyk
Interior design: Joan Lundell
Copyeditor: Margo Pecha
Proofreader: Janice Lee

Library of Congress Cataloging-in-Publication Data is available.

ISBN: 978-1-63217-000-2   **33614056454357**

Sasquatch Books
1904 Third Avenue, Suite 710
Seattle, WA 98101
(206) 467-4300
www.sasquatchbooks.com
custserv@sasquatchbooks.com